THE VOICE,
THE WORD,
THE BOOKS

THE VOICE, THE WORD, THE BOOKS

❧❦❧

The Sacred Scripture of the Jews, Christians, and Muslims

F. E. Peters

PRINCETON UNIVERSITY PRESS   Princeton and Oxford

Published by Princeton University Press,
41 William Street,
Princeton, New Jersey 08540

Library of Congress Cataloging-in-Publication Data
Peters, F. E. (Francis E.)
The voice, the Word, the books : the sacred scripture of the Jews,
Christians, and Muslims / F. E. Peters.
p. cm.
Includes index.
ISBN-13: 978-0-691-13112-2 (hardcover : alk. paper)
ISBN-10: 0-691-13112-0 (hardcover : alk. paper)
1. Monotheism—Comparative studies.
2. Judaism—Sacred books.
3. Christianity—Sacred books.
4. Islam—Sacred books.   I. Title.
BL221.P395 2007
208'.2—dc22   2006036912

This book has been composed in Minion Pro

Printed on acid-free paper. ∞

pup.princeton.edu

Printed in the United States of America

1 3 5 7 9 10 8 6 4 2

For
María Rosa Menocal

Contents

☙⟨6⟩☙

THE VOICE,
THE WORD,
THE BOOKS

Introduction

The Voice from Sinai

༺༺༻༻

Jews, Christians, and Muslims, when ranged side by side, are more notable perhaps for their often violent differences than for their shared heritage as "Children of Abraham." But they do agree on one enormously consequential point, and it is precisely that concurrence that makes them so contentious. It is that the Creator God has spoken directly to His Creation, and more, that those to whom He spoke have remembered His words, have recorded and preserved them, and have, over the long centuries—now looking reproachfully at one another—striven to fulfill the divine will expressed therein. God's speech was in some large sense intended for all of humankind, but it was directed in the first instance to a privileged audience, themselves. And they, and they alone, have heard, faithfully preserved, and equally faithfully observed the Word of God.

This book is about the antecedents and consequences of the claims of the Jews, Christians, and Muslims to be in possession of the Word of God. It does not, of course, decide whether it was really God speaking, or whether God *can* speak, or indeed, whether there is a God to begin with. Rather, it investigates the extremely complex process of identifying and hearkening to that voice thought to have been first heard authoritatively from Sinai; of proclaiming those words believed to have been sent down from on high; and then of recording, collecting, and arranging them; and finally of preserving and transmitting them for the benefit of succeeding generations of believers.

The long history of monotheism begins with what was understood to be a communication of God—who already had a history—with an Bronze Age patriarch called Abraham. Their conversation had to do with a "covenant," an agreement dictated by the Creator and assented to by Abraham. That covenant promised God's favor to Abraham and his descendants, and it is here that the monotheists part company and begin to tell their own stories in their own Scriptures. Each group, whether we call it a tribe or a church or a community, identifies itself, and itself alone, with those favored descendants of Abraham, either by birthright (the Jews), or by transference from the firstborn (the Christians), or by an act of supersession (the Muslims). The fearsome implications of that difference have been played out over many centuries and continue to trouble the monotheists (and their nonbelieving neighbors) even today. Yet what concerns us here is not the inheritance of God's Promise but another issue.

The monotheists agree that before Abraham, Adam had heard the speech of God, as did Noah, with promises and warnings to each. But then, the commonly received story goes, the register changed. With Moses, a distant descendant of Abraham, God chose not a principal but a messenger, someone commissioned to carry the divine words, and the divine commands and prohibitions, to an increasingly specific audience, and more, to write them down.

On this the monotheists all agree. That agreement goes a little further: all recognize that there were other designated messengers—the preferred term is "prophet"—after Moses, though who and how many are the subject of fierce contention among the three. The Jews reckoned that the God-speech had ended with the last of their prophets, Daniel, while the Muslims maintained that revelation continued well past the point where the Jews ended it—certainly as far as Jesus, whom the Quran regards as a prophet, and preeminently, and finally, to Muhammad, who is characterized as the "Seal of the Prophets" (Quran 33:40), and so the end of revelation.

Abraham stands at the beginning of a long process; at its end are now three books or, rather more precisely, three collections of books or pieces. An impartial observer, if such ever existed, might call them edited books, which makes believers uneasy since the term "edited" calls attention, undue attention, it would seem, to the fact that if all these words had a Divine Author, they also had some very human editors whose errant thumbprints are all over Scripture. That issue will be addressed in detail, but in the meantime let us simply note that the Sacred Books called the Bible, the New Testament, and the Quran are all collections of pieces dating from the "sundry times and divers places" Paul referred to in the opening of the Letter to the Hebrews, times that stretched over many centuries with the Bible, and over some decades in the cases of the New Testament and the Quran.

The books, then, that are called Scripture are complex, and so too is their history. That history was first written by believers who had what may be called the "workshop product" before them, God's Words inscribed on paper or papyrus or parchment, written in an unmistakably human hand; the stories of how this came to be, when and where—less often how, which seems to bother us more than it did them. How God came to speak to humankind was sometimes told in the Scripture itself—the Bible is particularly helpful in this regard—but just as often in stories circulating orally just outside the Scriptural orbit. We can collect and unpack these stories and compose some relatively coherent account of revelation as the believers understood it. That is a modestly circumscribed goal, "as the believers understood it," because the secular historian, with limited tools and a deliberately limited imagination, cannot, or perhaps need not, understand revelation at all.

There is no such easy escape from the rest of the process. The historian does have the tools, and the obligation, to attempt to explain the passage of the now safely "alleged" Words of God from the prophet who heard, or thought he heard, them to his earliest followers who recorded them in memory or symbol or script and then to the somewhat later followers who copied them and tidied them up into the form we have today. How? When? Why? These are all legitimate questions for the historian and the answers forthcoming in the pages that follow. But the answers are tentative, not out of inhibition or delicacy but because of the thinness of the evidence—the witnesses to these matters were far less interested in those questions of how and when and why than are we, and, perhaps more consequentially, because those same witnesses had, and their spiritual descendants continue to have, their own issues of inhibition and delicacy regarding Scripture, their own Scripture. The custodians of the Words of God, whether Jews or Christians or Muslims, are most reluctant to stand and deliver on the historians' favorite topic, the Works of Man. To rule man into Scripture is, in that precise degree, to rule God out.

We do our best here to overcome their inhibitions and to elicit from these generally reluctant witnesses an answer to the historian's questions. But first, some clarifications. This account begins, in the best Scriptural manner, in the beginning, on Sinai, in a manner of speaking. But it ends, somewhat later than the Scripture itself but much earlier than a *Compleat Historie of Scripture*, at the age of printing. The reason is that, though this is a work of history, it is not a history of Scripture. It is rather what the Arabs would call a "Book of Beginnings." Printing fixed Scripture, albeit mechanically, in a way that it had never been fixed before. And even though the history of Scripture translation was merely hitting its stride, and the history of Scriptural textual criticism was just beginning, the long and broad evolutionary phase of Scripture from word to fixed text was effectively complete. So this account ends there, with Gutenberg in Mainz and Luther and Cranach the Elder in Wittenberg, with Cardinal Jiménez de Cisneros on one side of the divide, in Alcalá, and Desiderius Erasmus on the other, in Rotterdam.

This is, then, a book about both process and things. It is about the revelation, proclamation, and publication of God's speech, but it is also about divine Words and tantalizing books both divine and human; it is about how the commands and instructions first heard in Eden or Sinai or on the shores of Galilee or in a cave near Mecca finally came to rest in script, and occasionally in pictures, produced in a masorete's workshop in Iraq or in a committee room in a mud brick house in Medina, in an artist's atelier in France or, somewhat later, in a print shop in Germany.

↪⃝↩

The reader will perhaps also notice that when I use the term "Bible," I am referring exclusively to the Jewish Bible, what the Jews call Tanak and what the Christians call the Old Testament. Even though it is a widespread Christian custom to include their New Testament in the term "Bible," I do not: I refer to the Jewish Scripture as the Bible and the Christian Scripture as the New Testament. The Old Testament, which is the Christian, and somewhat different, version of the Jewish Scripture, I call exactly that, the Old Testament. And since all three communities use a different religious calendar—and here I confess to some unwonted delicacy—I reduce all dates to CE, the "Common Era," and BCE, "Before the Common Era."

Chapter 1

Sacred Words, Sacred Book

ᔑ(6ᔑᐤ

Before embarking on the perilous how and when of the Holy Writ of the three monotheistic communities, it is useful to review the contents of each. The Christians do read—indeed they *must* read—the Jewish Scripture they call the Old Testament, but Jews and Muslims do not—in fact, need not and perhaps must not—reciprocate: both regard the New Testament from a distance, and Jews and Christians have even less of an idea of what is in the Quran.

To begin, the faith of the Jews, Christians, and Muslims, the identity of each as a community, and their shared hope for salvation are all inextricably tied to a book; they are indeed preeminently "People of the Book," as the Muslims call them. But not the same book, nor, in fact, the same books, since the Jews and Christians at least have in their possession not a single Sacred Book but a collection of the same, which they refer to collectively as The Writing or, more commonly in English, Scripture.

Scripture for the Jews, here called the Bible, is quintessentially "Instruction" (*torah*), which becomes, in its "published" form, a "Recitation" (*miqra*). For Muslims, the Quran is, from the outset and self-professedly, likewise a "Recitation" (*qur'an*), and then, also by self-designation, a "Remembrance" (*dhikr*). In both terms the thrust is toward the integration of God's Word in the mind and heart of the believer. The Christians' New Testament/Covenant, in contrast, is by its title both assertive and argumentative, while its core documents, the four Gospels, are markedly different from both the Torah and the Quran. They are each called the "Good News" (*euangelion*), and their kerygmatic purpose was already clear well before they became the documents of faith. "Go, then, to all nations and make them my disciples," says Jesus at the end of Matthew's Gospel. "Baptize them . . . and teach them to observe all I have commanded you" (28:19–20), which is precisely what Paul and the others did, proclaiming the "Good News" before it became either a text or a book (Acts 8:35; 11:20; 1 Cor. 1:17, etc.).

The earliest chapters or suras of the Quran, not the first chapters in our copies of that Book but rather what are thought to be Muhammad's earliest revelations recorded in it, are even more manifestly preaching than the Gospels: the Gospels proclaim a message embedded in a life; the Quran straightforwardly announces the message itself; it *is* the Message Itself. The Torah professes to explain how all this came about, when and why this people then called the Israelites and now the Jews came to believe that there was one God and how that God rewarded them for their beliefs by singling them out for His special favor and His special reward. In the Bible's account, the radical assertion of monotheism, that "There is but One God," is taught early on to the Israelites, even before they were known as Israelites and were simply identified as Hebrews or "wanderers," one undistinguished family of nomads among many such in the Middle East of the Bronze Age.

God's special favor, all its claimants agree, was mediated through a compact or covenant made between the Creator God and one of His creatures. That creature was, again they all concur, one Abram or Abraham, a minor tribal shaykh who had migrated from Mesopotamia across the Fertile Crescent and settled in the land of Canaan, the wedge of territory caught between Syria and Egypt and later called Palestine. This Abraham was, somewhat inexplicably in the Bible—the Quran (21:51–71) claims to know more about it—an early (the earliest?) worshiper of the One True God, and it was to him the deity had promised His hopefully eternal favor, to Abraham, that is, and to his descendants.

The worshipers of that One True God are one in affirming that He spoke to Abraham and that that conversation was recollected and recorded: its record constitutes the foundation document of what they call the Covenant and of monotheism itself. And, they further agree, God continued for a time to speak to His favored creatures, always and necessarily the same One True God, but in the end, it was to different worshipers. These privileged conversations—"revelations," as they are almost invariably described—all proceeded from a single divine source, it is agreed, but they were also occasional in their occurrence—Paul's "sundry times and divers places"—and as such they were directed to different human agents, the various "prophets" and "messengers" who served as the mediums of revelation.

It is to the recollected and recorded utterances and writings, the Scripture, that issued from those various privileged mediums that we now turn. What we possess, however, are the words not as they came forth from God's mouth, nor even from the prophets' mouths or inspired pens, but in a redacted book form, or rather, in the collections of writings that the monotheists call their Scripture. There is a great deal to say about how they became such, but we begin by inspecting their present contents, a surface worn smooth by public and private repetition and polished to near perfection by centuries of careful and controlled exegesis.

"Thus Spake Yahweh": What Is the Bible?

It is easier to describe the Bible than to discover its original name. The expression "in the books," where "books" is a rendering of the plural of *sefer*, is used in reference to earlier revelations in the Hebrew text of the Biblical book called Daniel. The oldest Greek version of the Bible, the one used by both Jews and Christians, translates it as *biblia*, "books," and that same word occurs in a similar Scriptural context in the non-Biblical books of Maccabees. The New Testament refers to Jewish Scripture exactly as such, *hai graphai*, "the Writings," but among the Greek-speaking Christians and Jews *biblia* eventually won out and the Jewish Scripture came to be called the Bible by Jews and Christians alike.

Formally the Bible begins "in the beginning," the very beginning, with the story of Creation—the first book is called Genesis—and its opening chapters (1–3) provide the common template for the Jewish, Christian, and Muslim understanding of the creation of the universe and of the primal couple, Adam and Eve, the garden or paradise (a loanword from Persian) in which they were placed, and their sin and consequent expulsion. Jews and Christians read the same text—the Bible is Bible for both—and the story is not repeated but retold in the Quran, though in bits and pieces, not as a consecutive narrative. Each group puts different emphases in the story—the Christians' explosive explanation of the fall of Adam and Eve into the Original Sin of humankind is probably the best-known example—and each has later added details, like the parallel fall from grace of another set of God's creatures, the angels, and the rise to prominence of one of them, Satan, all of which go unmentioned in Genesis itself.

The literary critic looking at Genesis recognizes in its narrative of Creation a myth, a transcendental account that is neither history nor science. Myths are not "true" in themselves; rather, they reflect truths. The Jews who told the creation story, and the Christians and Muslims who repeated and enriched it, knew no such distinction. Scripture was not only "true," each and every word of it; it was also *inerrant*, incapable of being false. All three communities have been more than able to treat Genesis as "myth," to unpack from it the moral and spiritual "truths" found within the narrative. But they have also treated it as what we would call "science." Once exposed to the ancient rationalist tradition in its most invasive Hellenic form, Jews, Christians, and Muslims all made strenuous and obviously well-intentioned efforts to reconcile what their scientific cosmology instructed them about the Creation and the present form of the universe and what their Scripture asserted on the same subject.

That process of reconciliation and assimilation began in Jewish circles in Alexandria in the third century BCE. It continued down to the days of Galileo and Copernicus, when a radical change in the scientific model of the universe left the Jews, and more particularly the Christians, who were far more committed to harmonizing Genesis with contemporary science, with a grave—and still unresolved—problem. The Jews generally preferred a more mystical reading of the text, and there is a rich store of Jewish esoterica called "The Work of Creation" and clearly labeled with a warning against general consumption. Christians, from the *hexaemeron* or "Six Days" literature of the Christian Fathers down to the summas of Albert the Great and Thomas Aquinas, had possessed themselves of a prodigiously wrought model of the universe. But after the scientific revolutions of the sixteenth and nineteenth centuries, it was a universe that no longer worked, and a scientific interpretation of Genesis that no longer convinced.

Galileo and Copernicus arrived late in Islam, but Muslims were less affected by the paradigm shift when it did arrive since they had been far less ardent to in linking Scriptural creation to science. And since the Quran adverted to Creation rather than describing or explaining it, there was abundant space within which Muslim commentators could and did construct their explanations of how the world began. What lingers, however, in Muslim no less than in Christian and Jewish minds, is the absolute conviction of the "truthfulness" of Scripture, and nowhere has that truth gaunt-let been more daringly cast down than in the first three chapters of the book of Genesis.

Genesis 4–11 tells the story of humankind from Adam's own children down to Abraham, who dominate the narrative thereafter. The task is not an easy one. Genesis 6:1–5, for example, is constrained to have the "sons of God" mingle with the "daughters of man" to produce a very mixed breed of "giants" (*nephilim*) to confound believers forever after. Even more puzzling is the somewhat later information that "the Lord," that is, the Creator God of Genesis who had begun to be worshiped by humans in the generation of Adam's grandchildren (4:26), now "repented that He had made humankind" (6:6), and resolved to destroy it, all, that is, save Noah and his family and two breeding specimens of all animal life. There follows the story of the building of Noah's ark and of the flood that destroys the rest of the human race (6:14–7:19).

After the waters recede, Noah builds an altar and offers animal sacrifice on it. God is pleased with the odor of the burnt offerings and pledges not to destroy humankind again. More, the Lord makes a covenant with Noah and his descendants (9:1–17), the prototype of the later one with Abraham and his. Circumcision will be the sign of Abraham's covenant, but the symbol of Noah's is God's "bow in the clouds," the divine weapon hung up and harmless. By the terms of the new covenant Noah and his heirs are given permission to eat the flesh of all animals—humans were apparently vegetarian up to this point—except they were not to eat flesh with its own blood still in it.

Genesis next hurries through the generations of Noah's descendants (9:18–11:32), pausing only to tell the engaging tale of the builders of the "tower of Babylonia," the ill-advised architectural project that caused the Lord to turn his human creation into confused polyglots (11:1–9) and would lead, many centuries later, to the ticklish problem of how to bring God's Word to babblers who no longer speak God's Sacred Tongue.

The story of Abraham that follows (12:1–25:11) unfolds episodically but in circumstantial detail. The family of sheepherding nomads was originally from Mesopotamia ("Ur of the Chaldees") but had chosen to migrate to the land of Canaan. It had reached as far as Harran, in what is now southern Turkey, when Abraham's father died, and it was there that God spoke—we are not told why—almost abruptly, but grandly and with an emphatic optimism, to the seventy-five-year-old Abraham, now the family shaykh: "I will make you a great nation . . . and in you all nations will be blessed" (12:3–4). This is a promise perhaps and not yet a covenant, but the terms of a blessing and a land are repeated and expanded and refined in the following chapters of Genesis and other details added to it.

The family history of Abraham continues to unfold through Genesis, with secondary speaking roles assigned to Lot, Abraham's nephew, and to his own wife, Sarah. There is an encounter with a strange personage who appears to be an unrelated worshiper of the Lord, Melchizedek, king of Salem and "priest of the Most High," to whom Abraham gives a tithe (14:18–20). The aged and childless Abraham has doubts, however, about the many offspring and the spacious lands that have been promised him, and this provokes a great oracular confirmation and a very formal encounter with the Divine Will (15:1–20). "That day the Lord made a covenant with Abram," Genesis says, and the land of the promise is grandiosely described as "this land from the river of Egypt to the Great River, the river Euphrates" (15:18).

In chapter 16 of Genesis a solution to the heir problem comes not from the Lord but from Abraham's wife, Sarah, who suggests that he father a child on her Egyptian slave girl Hagar. Abraham is agreeable and a son, Ishmael, is born to them. This does not please Sarah, or at least Hagar does not, and there is an uneasy peace in Abraham's tents. The Covenant meanwhile grows more formal: Abraham is commanded, as a "sign of the Covenant," to have himself, all the male members of his family, and even his male slaves circumcised (17). The Lord later recalls that Sarah had laughed when they had been promised a son. "No, I didn't," she says. "Yes, you did," the Lord insists (18:1–15). The Lord is right, of course, and for all her laughter the elderly Sarah becomes pregnant by the even more elderly Abraham. A son is born, Isaac, and the vengeful Sarah has her way: Hagar and Ishmael are cast forth from the camp to what would have been certain death in the wilderness had not God intervened (21:1–20). The Lord confirms that the promise will descend through the line of Isaac, but Abraham is consoled by the Lord regarding Ishmael: he, the firstborn, will also father a great nation.

The final piece in the great Abrahamic mosaic is the Lord's unexpected and heart-chilling command to Abraham to "take your son, your only son Isaac, whom you love," to a mountaintop and to make of him a burnt sacrifice to God (22:2). It is a test, we are told, of Abraham's obedience, which he passes in quite extraordinary fashion. He is ready to plunge the knife into the heart of his only son when God restrains him, and then rewards him: "By My own Self I swear it because you have done this and have not withheld your son, your only son, I shall bless you abundantly and make your descendants as numerous as the stars in the sky or the grains of sand on the seashore. Your descendants will possess the cities of their enemies. All nations on earth will wish to be blessed as your descendants are blessed, because you have been obedient to Me" (22:16–18).

Abraham's death occurs in Genesis 25:7, aged 175 years. He is buried by his sons—Ishmael reappears for the event—at Hebron, where his grave is still shown.

There is scarcely a detail in this extraordinary narrative, which accounts for only a small fraction of the Bible, that does not come into play in the long history of the Covenant as it was understood by Jews, Christians, and Muslims. Abraham's conversion to the worship of God is often described in the Quran (6:74–83; 21:51–72; 26:69–102, etc.). Abraham is the host in the Gospel's imagining of heaven (Luke 16:22). Ishmael is later construed as the ancestor of the great tribes of the Arabs, and indeed the Quran depicts Abraham and Ishmael building the original Kaʿba in Mecca (2:125). For Paul, Hagar and Sarah are "an allegory" (Gal. 4:24)—the slave and the free, the Jew and the Christian—and from Paul too comes the definitive Christian word on Abraham's willingness to sacrifice Isaac: it was an act of pure faith, and God "reckoned it to him as righteousness" (Rom. 4:3), the verse in which Luther found his own salvation and provided a point of departure for the Reformation.

Genesis follows the line of Abraham's descent through Isaac, with a recurring motif. Just as Abraham's firstborn, Ishmael, was replaced by Isaac, so Isaac's own firstborn, Esau, is replaced by a second son, Jacob (Gen. 27), who then becomes the focus of the narrative. The Covenant is reconfirmed for Jacob in a dream at Bethel—"This is none other than the house of God, and this is the gate of heaven" (28:10–22)—and he wrestles with God Himself, a match Jacob appears to win. In any event, his name is changed: henceforward he is called "Israel" (32:22–32); and, we can add, his sons will be known as "Israelites" and the land promised them as "Israel," at least down to the division of that land into an "Israel" and a "Judah," when the promise will pass to the latter.

With Jacob's sons Genesis passes from family chronicle to tribal history: his twelve sons are the progenitors of the Twelve Tribes who, at the beginning of the book of Joshua, will occupy the Land of the Promise. The transformation takes place in Egypt whither the twelve brethren have been drawn and where they first prosper and grow into a people and then fall into a wretched slavery (Gen. 37–Exod. 1). At the opening of the book called Exodus, the Israelites are sent their savior in the person of Moses, the Israelite with the Egyptian name raised in the Pharaoh's own household (2:1–10). Moses is called by God—who reveals to him His own name—from a flaming bush, is given marvelous powers, and is sent to the Pharaoh, first to persuade and then to threaten the ruler to release the Israelites from their bondage(3:1–6:28). "I have made you a God to Pharaoh," God declares to Moses. "I will lay my hand upon Egypt and bring my people, the Israelites, company by company, out of the land of Egypt by great acts of judgment" (7:1–4). The "great acts of judgment" are terrible plagues that strike the land, and they come to a climax in the divinely decreed death of every firstborn in Egypt, after which the Israelites are released (7:14–12:51).

After a miraculous crossing of the Red Sea, Moses and the Israelites set their uncertain course into the great wilderness of Sinai (14:1–15:22). They pause at a mountain in Sinai and Moses is summoned by the Lord to ascend there alone. At its summit he is given the Ten Commandments (20:1–17). They are inscribed on tablets of stone, "the two tablets of the Covenant . . . written on both sides, written on the front and on the back. The two tablets were the work of God and the writing was the writing of God inscribed on the tablets" (32:15–16). Moses is given much more than the Ten Commandments. He spends forty days and forty nights on the mountain and the account of God's instructions to Moses on Sinai fill chapters 25 to 31 of the book of Exodus. The Covenant is reaffirmed (34:10–27), then the Israelites construct the mobile tent-temple that God has prescribed for His worship and take up their trek once again, God now following as a cloud by day, as a pillar of fire by night (35:4–40:38).

The next three books of the Pentateuch double back on the narrative. We return to Sinai and God is once again communicating to Moses the increasingly small print of the Covenant. Leviticus lays out the laws that will govern the worship of God and sacrifice (1–8), including the establishment of a priesthood descended from Moses' brother Aaron (9). Noah had been prohibited no foods, but now clean and unclean food are distinguished for the Israelites (11), and the category of unclean is extended to women after childbirth (12) and conditions of the body (13–15). The special ritual of the Day of Atonement (*Yom ha-Kippur*) is prescribed (16). At some point here modern scholarship has discerned a shift in sensibilities from a priestly view of holiness, which is concerned with the sanctity of the priests and the sanctuary—now merely a tent-compound but eventually a permanent structure in Jerusalem—to another view, which stands behind the second half of Leviticus (17–26) and sees holiness as extending over the entirety of the Promised Land and all who dwell in it: there is now an emphasis on the holiness, sexual and social, of all the Israelites.

In the book called Numbers the journey resumes. The Israelites continue through the wilderness of Sinai (1:1–10:10). They pass eastward to the "wilderness of Paran," which they traverse. They cross the Wadi Arabah and enter into the Transjordan (10:11–22:1), where they finally turn northward to the plain of Moab on the eastern side of the Dead Sea (22:2–36:13). The title "Numbers" derives from the two military musters, the Bible's "Catalog of the Ships." The first opens the book (1:1–4:49) and the second punctuates it again at chapter 26. It is after the latter that Joshua is appointed Moses' successor (27:12–23).

Deuteronomy, literally the "Second Law" and the last book of the five-book (*pentateuches*) Torah, is now thought to be the same "book of the Law" discovered by the high priest Hilkiah in the Jerusalem Temple in the days of King Josiah (2 Kings 3:20–22). It does not confess itself as such, but it is the only book of the Pentateuch that explicitly identifies itself as Torah, as its preface makes clear: "In the land of Moab Moses undertook to explain the Law as follows" (1:5). Deuteronomy both adds to and, at least in theory, explains what Moses proclaimed from Sinai; it has been called the "interpretive key to the Torah," a high-concept midrash that is itself Torah, much in the same way that Paul's explanatory letters will be Writ for Christians. The book's influence is present and visible to such extent in all the books that follow, from Joshua to the second book of Kings, that some have thought, as we shall see, that they and Deuteronomy together formed the original nucleus of the Bible.

Deuteronomy's central section—"This is the law that Moses said before the Israelites"—which runs from the close of chapter 4 to the end of chapter 28, begins with Moses' solemn adjuration: "Hear, O Israel, the statutes and ordinances I am addressing to you today" (5:1). These "statutes and ordinances" follow from the beginning of chapter 5 to the end of chapter 11. The rules governing the Covenantal polity are then set out in some detail (12:1–26:15), including the offices to function in it (17:14–18:22) together with the various juridical principles to be observed (19:1–25:19), among them the protocols for holy war (20:1–20) and a section on the ratification of the Covenant and the sanctions against its transgression (26:16–28:68). There is another Covenant enacted in Moab (29–30), after which the historical narrative resumes and finally comes to an end with the death of Moses (34:5), "but no one knows his grave," we are warned.

This is the end of the Pentateuch, the Covenantal heart and soul of the Torah embedded in a narrative of the Israelites' trek across the Sinai after escape from Egypt and before their entry into the Land of Promise, the "Land for Israel" (*Eretz Israel*). The Israelites had been nomads up to this point, sometimes by design, sometimes by necessity, but by the end of Deuteronomy they are poised to enter the Canaanite territory where they will become eventually the settled population. Those events are narrated in the books of Joshua and Judges. The land is conquered and its inhabitants driven off or decimated. Israelites organize themselves in some type of tribal federation around shrine centers. God's favor and presence still dwells among them, now localized above the "Ark of the Covenant," a richly decorated chest built to divine specifications (Exod. 25:10–22) and containing the Ten Commandments. The Ark is carried across Sinai and then moved from shrine to shrine in the land of Canaan until it is eventually deposited in Jerusalem.

The Greek translation of the Bible from the third century BCE joined the following books, the two books of Samuel and two called Kings, into a single volume called "Concerning the Kingdoms," though in fact it is more about kings than kingdoms. The kings in question come into the narrative after the governance of tribal leaders called "Judges" is deemed inadequate, and the last of them, a charismatic prophet named Samuel (1 Sam. 3:20–4:1), is reluctantly prevailed upon by Israel's elders to anoint a king for them (8–10).

The struggle for Canaan comes down to the Israelites' attempt to dislodge the Philistines from the coastal plain. Saul is heroic in this regard, but incapable of fulfilling the Lord's most dire command: to eradicate the enemy Amalekites, "men and women, children and babes in arms, herds and flocks, camels and donkeys" (1 Sam. 15:3). Saul kills them all but spares some of the flocks, "to sacrifice to the Lord," he claims. God is angry at the disobedience and resolves, despite Samuel's objection, to deprive Saul of his kingship (15:10–35). In his stead, a young Israelite, David, son of Jesse of Bethlehem and Saul's armor-bearer, whom Saul first loves and then, as David's renown as a warrior grows, despises and hates (16:1–31:13), is anointed second king of Israel (2 Sam. 1).

The second book of Samuel and the first eleven chapters of the first book of Kings are accounts of the reigns of the two greatest, David and Solomon, taken, as we are told, from the "annals of Solomon" (1 Kings 11:41) or the "annals of the kings of Israel" (14:9) or "of Judah" (14:29). The narrative is filled with vividly human detail—the "annals of the kings" must have had a distinct taste for royal gossip and intrigue. David, aged thirty, is anointed king at Hebron (2 Sam. 5:1–5), but he does not long reign there. It is David's idea to capture the Jebusite city of Jerusalem in the north of Judah and move his capital there (5:6–16). And to establish his religious authority, the king soon arranges to bring the Ark of the Covenant from its latest shrine lodging into his new capital, where it is housed in a tent, still a nomad among the now increasingly sedentary Israelites (6:1–19), as the Lord himself complains (7:1–3).

David is ordered by God to build a more permanent temple (7:4–17), and embedded in the command is another highly consequential promise, a divine quid pro quo: "He (David) shall build a house for My Name," God says, "and I will establish the throne of his kingdom forever" (7:13). For as long as Israel will have a king, he will be of the house of David, and for as long as Israel awaits a king, he too will be descended from David. We hear no more of this temple project in Samuel, but at the very end of 2 Samuel, David purchases from its Jebusite owner a threshing floor on which to build "an altar to the Lord" (24:18–25). The parallel account in chapter 22 of the first book of Chronicles is more forthcoming, however: this was to be the site of the projected temple and David was actually making preparations to build it when he died.

The Jerusalem temple becomes the work of David's son, Solomon, and is recognized as his forever thereafter: Solomon the wise man (1 Kings 4:28–34) and Solomon the builder are the Israelite king's characterizations for centuries thereafter, not only among Jews but among Christians and Muslims as well. No physical trace remains of Solomon's temple—but its construction, its furnishings, and its dedication are all described in great detail in the first book of Kings (5–8). There are other, equally grandiose buildings, including a palace called "the Forest of Lebanon" and a separate building for his wives, many of whom, including their principal ornament, the Pharaoh's daughter, are foreigners (11:1–8). And like many of his successors, Solomon's wisdom does not extend to women: he succumbs to the religio-political needs or whims of his ladies and houses and honors their gods, which inevitably provokes his own God and results in a divided kingdom (11:9–13).

All these books, from Joshua down through the second book of Kings, belong to a Biblical category the rabbis called "Prophets" (*Nebi'im*). Other books in the same category, Isaiah and Jeremiah, for example, do sound genuinely prophetic to our ears, whereas the books just passed in review we would more generally categorize as history. Our intuitive view is supported by a further distinction among the *Nebi'im*, that between the "Former Prophets" (Joshua, Judges, the two books each of Samuel and Kings) and the "Latter Prophets" (Isaiah, Jeremiah, Ezekiel, and the twelve books of the "Minor Prophets," so denominated by reason of their reduced length, not their lesser importance).

There are prophets and Prophets in the Bible. The first are the various men and women called "prophet" (*nabi*) or "seer" (*hozeh*) who come and go in the Biblical text, individually and in groups. What links them is their common claim to have received a communication from God addressed either to individuals, often the ruler, or to all of Israel. There are false prophets as well, like Zedekiah of 1 Kings 22:11–25 or the 450 prophets of Baal in 1 Kings 18. The tradition of prophets continues on into Christianity (Acts 5:22; 1 Cor. 12:28); indeed, some of his contemporaries thought Jesus himself might be "one of the prophets" (Matt. 16:14). And the office of prophet is, of course, the foundation stone on which the entire edifice of Islam rests.

One such prophetic individual, Samuel, has Biblical books named after him, but apparently because they are largely (though by no means exclusively) *about* him rather than constituting a message *from* or *by* him. But there are other books, the (Latter) Prophets properly so-called, that are precisely such: the messages delivered by Isaiah, by Jeremiah, by Ezekiel, and in the twelve named books collected under the already mentioned rubric of the "Minor Prophets" (Hosea, Joel, Amos, Obadiah, Jonah, Micah, Nahum, Habakkuk, Zephaniah, Haggai, Zechariah, and Malachi).

What has been called the "Golden Age of Israelite prophecy" begins in the eighth century BCE with Amos and Hosea and continues into the aftermath of the Babylonian exile. It is constituted of the prophets memorialized by Biblical books, and their message is broad and varied, though there is a notable emphasis on social justice, on the sins of Israel, on the catastrophic events to follow on that sinfulness, and on the reconciliation that will eventually occur. The Bible's prophetic oracles are ridden with doom and at the same time suffused with gleams of hope. They are cautionary, moral, and forward-looking, predictive in the narrow sense of the word "prophecy," and it is precisely for this latter sense that the Christians later scanned their pages. While many Jews of Second Temple times continued to read the Prophets for clues to the future and found it easy to substitute the Romans for the Prophets' Babylonian scourges of Israel, the Christians looked forward to something else. They saw in the Prophets' hopes the glimmering outlines of the New Covenant of their own messianic aspirations.

The Hebrew Bible (but not the Christian Old Testament) ends with a confessed miscellany of songs, sayings, and stories both folk and romantic lumped generally under the rubric "Writings" (*Ketubim*). It contains the books called Psalms, Proverbs, Job, Song of Songs, Ruth, Lamentations, Ecclesiastes, Esther, the late visionary prophet Daniel, the history book of Ezra-Nehemiah that tells of the return from Exile, and two books of Chronicles that resume the narratives in Kings. They were the latest to be composed and the last to be included in the body of the Jewish Scripture.

"Then the Lord Said": What Is the New Testament?

Although the nomenclature of the Jewish Scripture is somewhat varied— Bible, Torah, and the acronym Tanak are all in use—there is no such uncertainty about what the Christians eventually came to regard as their own Scripture and on a par with the Bible of the Jews. The writings the Christians esteem as Scripture are called collectively the New Testament, a name that is both assertive and argumentative. It hearkens back to Jeremiah's prophecy that there would one day be a "new covenant" (Jer. 31:31) and to Jesus' own use of that same expression—"This cup is the new covenant sealed by my blood (1 Cor. 11:25)—to describe the approaching sacrifice of his own life.

Thus the New Testament is at the same time an idea and a collection of documents. The texts included in it are all in Greek now, not in the classical Biblical Hebrew or the then current Jewish Aramaic. They were brought together by the early Christians who thought they both described (as in the Gospels) and explained (as in Paul's letters) how the events of Jesus' life, both the happenings and his teachings, were the means by which God had indeed initiated the "new covenant/ testament" promised by the Prophets.

The lead documents of the Christians' Scripture are called the "Good News" (*euangelion*). That word was in fairly wide circulation in Jewish circles in Jesus' day in Greek and in Aramaic, the latter an echo of an equally familiar Biblical Hebrew term. "Good news" was used of announcements, the messages of both prophets and heralds, and in the royal and secular realm as well as in a religious context. It fit perfectly both the preaching of John the Baptist as a messianic herald, Jesus' own message regarding the Kingdom, and the later pronouncements about him.

But at the head of each of these four initial texts of the New Testament, the expression "Good News" or Gospel represents a descriptive title, each followed by a qualification: ". . . according to. . . ." This is a new literary genre, this Gospel, though the form is familiar. The matter is obviously biographical, of the type Greek-speaking contemporaries called a *Bios* or "Life" and shot through with the ancients' penchant for a moralizing and even hagiographical treatment of its subject. In its original form, before it was recorded and published as a book, what the Judean Jews called a "Good News" was more simply and generally a *kerygma*, preaching or pronouncement on the part of Jesus' followers. We can readily detect its traces in the accounts in the Acts of the Apostles (2:14–36 is an early example) that follow the Gospels as well as between and under the lines of Paul's letters (1 Cor. 1:17; 2 Cor. 1:12, etc.) that explain the Good News even before there was a written Gospel.

There are four textual versions of the Good News in the New Testament, each with an ascribed author: the Gospel "according to" Matthew, Mark, Luke, and John, in the traditional Church order. Each account professes to unfold the life, teachings, and death of Jesus of Nazareth, and though they agree in many regards, they also display remarkable differences on the events of Jesus' life and what he is reported to have said in public and private. Most noticeable is how John's Gospel stands apart from the other three, and in perhaps irreducible ways. John describes many events the others ignore and excludes others they describe in detail. John's chronology is also different, both overall for Jesus' life and even more consequentially in the detailed chronology of his last days. Finally, John's Jesus speaks not in the kind of aphorisms recorded in the other Gospels but in long discourses, and the discourses themselves are couched not in the simple, direct, and even homely idiom of the sage but in the transcendental language of the mystic and the theologian.

Matthew, Mark, and Luke cohere far more closely—they have been dubbed "synoptics" by reason of that cohesion—but even here there are differences. One which rises immediately off the page is that Mark, together with John, after his prologue, begins his account of Jesus' life at the point where the adult Jesus is baptized at the Jordan by another charismatic preacher, John, surnamed "the Baptizer." It was this latter who said that "God could raise up children of Abraham from these stones" (Matt. 3:9), apparently scoffing at the idea that one could inherit the promise of the Abrahamic Covenant simply by an accident of birth, and in the Gospels John is shown preaching a conversion ritual to his fellow Jews, perhaps to remind them that by their repentance they might become "born again Jews" or perhaps simply "true Jews."

This was Jesus' spiritual background, his and a number of his first followers'. The Gospels themselves are clearly puzzled that the Messiah was the disciple of another preacher, but the fact is evident, as is that Jesus too preached the imminent end of the world and that his circle, and perhaps Jesus himself (so John 4:1), used the baptism ritual on their own followers. John came to a violent end. He was arrested by Herod's son, Herod Antipas (ruler of Galilee 4 BCE–39 CE), and executed for personal reasons according to the Gospels, for political ones according to Josephus; possibly for both.

If we use the three Synoptic Gospels as our baseline, as the Christian tradition generally does, the New Testament's life of Jesus falls into three main acts or parts, with prologues and an appendix. The prologues vary. John begins his Gospel with a meditation on Jesus as the Word of God (1:1–18), Matthew with a genealogy of Jesus from Abraham upward (1:1–17). Luke postpones his genealogy, which proceeds from Adam upward to Jesus, to his third chapter (3:23–38), and instead opens his Gospel with a dedicatory preface to a patron (1:1–4). The first act of Jesus' life, then, consists of two quite different accounts of the events leading up to and surrounding Jesus' birth, or Nativity, in Bethlehem. They are found only in Matthew (1:18–2:23) and Luke (1:5–2:52, which ends with Jesus a twelve-year-old) and they have aroused considerable suspicion in modern critics, many of whom regard them as additions to the Gospel texts by a later generation of believers who wished to demonstrate that Jesus was, and was recognized as, the divinely sent Messiah from his birth and to establish that he was born in Bethlehem, the appropriately messianic "city of David."

The two central acts of the Gospels, as all four evangelists agree, are those that cover the two or three years of Jesus' ministry in Galilee stretching from his baptism by John down to the prediction of his own coming death (Mark 1:1–10:31 and parallels) and the somewhat less than two weeks in Jerusalem where he was arrested and executed (Mark 10:32–15:47). What the evangelists give us in the first part is a portrait of an itinerant teacher-preacher accompanied by his chosen followers, "the Twelve" (Matt. 10:1–11:1), and a somewhat wider circle of disciples, men and women, on whose alms he may have depended. Mark summed up Jesus' teaching, which he calls "the good news of God," in two simple sentences: "The time has arrived; the kingdom of God is upon you. Repent and believe in the good news" (1:14–15). It is the announcement of an event—the appointed eschatological "moment" was at hand—and a call to repentance (*metanoia*), a life change. It was essentially the same message being preached by the John who had initiated Jesus and some of Jesus' disciples into his own eschatological movement.

Jesus spent his brief ministry preaching and teaching, chiefly in synagogues but also in open-air venues. The teaching was accompanied by miracles, cures of all kinds of illnesses (Matt. 4–25), and exorcisms (Matt. 8:28–34; 11:4–6) and was just as often associated with an act of faith on the part of the subject. There were even resuscitations of the dead (Matt. 9:18–26).

Jesus' instruction was often aphoristic, and his brief and pithy sayings resonated in the memory of his followers: "Do not store of treasures on earth" . . . "No one can serve two masters" . . . "Do not worry about tomorrow, for tomorrow will bring worries of its own" . . . "Do not judge so that you may not be judged." (There is a collection of such in Matthew 6–7.) More uniquely, his teachings took a particular form called the parable in English (Gk. *parabole*), a kind of curveball of a story, brief and homely in its detail, with a paradoxical snap at the end.

Jesus' teachings present their own paradox. If they were intended to be a warning about the imminent End-Time, Jesus' ethical instructions during his ministry show no particular urgency, and Paul, who certainly believed the End-Time was near at hand, simply ignores them. "Love God and love your neighbor" is described by Jesus as the great commandment of the Jewish law (Matt. 22:36–40), and it is a fair summary of his own teaching, though hardly a clarion eschatological call; nor are the so-called Beatitudes (Matt. 5:3–11), which are thought to represent the heart of his ethical instruction. But though he insisted he had not come to abolish the Law (Matt. 5:17–20), Jesus had no hesitation in altering its provisions on his own authority, albeit generally toward greater severity (5:21–48).

Jesus' teaching raises another issue that carries us into the second act of the Gospel story. This is the very detailed account—far more events and particulars of time and place are crammed into the day and a half before his death than in the narrative of the preceding three years—of Jesus' week or so in Jerusalem. It grows particularly detailed for the hours from late Thursday of that week to the afternoon of Friday, the Passover of what was likely the year 28 CE (Mark 11:1–15:47 and parallels). Like the observant Jew he obviously was, Jesus comes to Jerusalem to celebrate the feast of Passover. The visit is filled with the threat and foreboding of Jesus' eschatological vision and his prediction of his own death. There is a moment of triumph as well when his entry into the city is greeted with public acclamation. A brief and violent incident in the Temple precincts instigated by Jesus against those who did their (apparently legal) business there quickly follows.

The narrative has now reached the Thursday at whose sunset Passover begins. Jesus has made plans to celebrate his Passover meal inside the city, as the Law requires, but the supper turns out to be something else: a ritual meal at which he announces to the Twelve that the bread and the wine before them on the table are his body and his blood. "Take, and eat," he commands them. The Christians later remember and repeat the ceremony; they call it the "Thanksgiving" (Gk. *eucharistes*).

The meal over, Jesus and his followers go outside the city walls to pray in a garden called Gethsemane. There he is seized and arrested in the night, though no effort is made to detain any of the Twelve. He is immediately taken before the high priest for a hearing on a variety of charges including blasphemy. After a night in custody, he is taken on Friday morning, still under arrest, to the residence of Pontius Pilate, the Roman ruler of Judea, on the stated grounds that the Judeans had not the power to impose the death penalty. Pilate likewise judges him guilty, and Jesus, after being flogged, is marched outside the city walls to a hill called Golgotha and there he is crucified—the convicted is hung on a cross until he expires from either suffocation or shock—with two other men who appear to be political prisoners. At three o'clock Jesus breathes his last. His body is taken down from the cross by a few of his fearful followers and quickly buried in a tomb nearby.

The entire affair of Jesus' death, we are told in the Gospels, was a plot hatched and put into action by the Jewish Temple priesthood, or at least its leaders (Matt. 26:1–5 and parallels). What we do not fully understand is why this preacher of an idealistic and seemingly harmless message should have posed such a threat to them, and to the Romans, as to merit execution. Jews were not normally put to death for holding divergent views on their religion, nor were they handed over to the Romans for teaching a different ethic. Did that Temple incident presage some more serious threat to priestly control? Was it Jesus' Messiahship, his sometimes reluctant claim to be the savior of Israel—he famously told his followers not to reveal his identity (Mark 8:2)—whose political consequences might have endangered both Jewish and Roman authority? The Jesus of the Gospels is scrubbed clean of politics, but that time and that place were filled with political storm and stress, and with people who perished in it.

Jesus' death dispirited his followers, who seemed ill-prepared for the event despite the Gospels' frequent predictions of it. But they were buoyed up once again. Later described by Paul as the keystone of Christian belief, Jesus' resurrection occurred sometime during the Sabbath following his death. It is not described in the Gospels. Recounted in what appear to be appendices hastily, almost carelessly, tacked onto the account of his death (particularly Mark 16:1–11; John 21) is the testimony of witnesses, first to his empty tomb on Sunday morning (Matt. 28:1–18 and parallels), then to encounters with the risen Jesus himself—in the flesh, it has been made clear—and not simply resuscitated: he has risen in a new and almost, but not quite, unrecognizable embodiment (Luke 24:15–35; John 20:19–24).

Note: The Word Incarnate.

The opening of the Pauline Letter to the Hebrews states the anomaly of the Christian "revelation" in the clearest terms: "When in times past God spoke to our forefathers, he spoke in many and varied ways through the prophets. But in this the final age He has spoken to us in His son whom He has appointed heir of all things; and through him He created the universe." God spoke *in* Jesus. Jesus was, in short, the *Word* of God, though not recorded or committed to writing, but, astonishingly, as John's Gospel puts it, "the Word became flesh"(1:14).

There are Jewish antecedents to this, as with much else in Christianity. Wisdom was profoundly personified in Ben Sirah/Ecclesiasticus and then, boldly, "She has built an everlasting house among mortals" (1:15). Philo, the Diaspora Jew who lived just before Jesus but in the very different world of profoundly Hellenized Alexandria, had also experimented with God's eternal "Word," who—we are confronted by another personification—was an agent in Creation. The Jewish expressions never quite exceeded the bounds of metaphor perhaps, but the Christian "incarnation" certainly did, as both Jews and Christians were eventually aware. The issue is theologically important, but equally important here is that in a sense it relegates the Christian "Scripture" called the New Testament to a secondary status, a body of texts that are not so much the Revelation as *about* the revelation.

In the light of its urgent call to monotheism, it is not surprising that the Quran should flatly deny the Incarnation (19:35–36): Jesus was a prophet, it insists, like Moses before him and Muhammad after him (3:48–51), and so the Gospel is not *about* Jesus, as the Christians maintain, but a book of revelation given to him. More unexpected is the Quran's equally vehement denial, this to rebut local Jewish claims, that Jesus was crucified, or indeed, that he died at all (4:157). Rather, he ascended to God (3:55), whence, the Muslim tradition later affirmed, he will one day return to suffer the death that is the lot of all mortals.

Christians were convinced from the beginning that they knew who composed these Gospel accounts and when. Eusebius, writing in the 330s in his *Church History*, quotes Papias, whose works are otherwise lost and who was a bishop circa 130 CE, on the subject. According to this, our oldest authority, Mark was a follower of Peter, the earliest and the most important of the Twelve, and he wrote down Peter's recollections. According to the same source, Matthew, who was also one of the Twelve (Matt. 9:9), originally wrote his Gospel "in Hebrew," that is, his and Jesus' native Aramaic. Papias says nothing of Luke, who was, as we shall see, a companion of Paul and whom Christian tradition thought was a Gentile physician of Antioch who had been converted to Judaism. The "John" who wrote the Fourth Gospel was identified as "the disciple whom Jesus loved" (John 19:26; 21:20, 24) and one of the Twelve by Ireneus, the Christian bishop who was probably living in Ephesus around 198 CE and knew the bishop there, who had himself been a disciple of that John.

This then is what the Church thought: that the Gospels were written by eyewitnesses to Jesus' life or by men of the next generation who had access to such witnesses. Modern scholarship does not disagree, though it is not so sure about the identity of the individual authors and tends to look upon the production of the Gospels as a community, rather than an individual, creation. In any event, it places the composition of the Gospels sometime between 60 or 70 CE (Mark) and 100 CE (John), with Matthew and Luke in between, yet long enough after Mark for both of them to have used his Gospel since they repeat verbatim a good deal of it.

The Gospels are immediately followed in the New Testament by the equivalent of the Bible's historical books, the Acts of the Apostles, which was written by Luke as the sequel to his Gospel (Acts 1:1). It traces the growth of the Jesus movement beginning with Jesus' miraculous ascension into heaven (1:9), through the quite extraordinary infusion of strength and confidence into his immediate circle, the Twelve, on the Jewish feast of *Shabuoth* or "Weeks" (Gk. *Pentekostes*, "Fifty," that is, seven weeks after Passover, when Jesus had been put to death). The event (Acts 2) was recollected as the descent of the Holy Spirit upon the believers, the veritable birth day of the new community of those Jews, and soon of Gentiles as well, who believed Jesus was the promised Messiah and who soon came to be called "Christians" (11:26).

The narrative in Acts is rapid and direct and initially keeps its focus on the small but growing "assembly" (*ekklesia*) of Jesus' followers in Jerusalem, the marvels they accomplished, their trials at the hands of the Jewish authorities, and the internal strains suffered by the new movement. One was simply the extension of a fault line that ran through the Jewish community at large, that between Hellenized Jews, chiefly from the Diaspora outside Palestine, and the local Aramaic-speaking Jews (Acts 6), which came to a terrible climax in the execution of one of the Hellenized followers of Jesus, Stephen (Acts 7). It is here that Saul, a fire-breathing Pharisaic Jew from Tarsus, makes his dramatic entry into the narrative (7:58), which he soon dominates. Saul, renamed Paul, undergoes a miraculous conversion on the road to Damascus (9:3–7) and thereafter becomes an energetic spreader of the "Good News" of Jesus of Nazareth.

Paul, who had never seen Jesus in the flesh and who seems to have kept his distance from the Twelve in Jerusalem, not only claims their title of "apostle" but preaches the message of the risen Jesus across the dense network of Hellenized synagogues in Syria and Anatolia. There were interested and sympathetic Gentiles too in those synagogue congregations. The problem of how the Apostles should deal with them had already arisen in Palestine, and it was decided, on Peter's authority, that they might be proselytized (Acts 11). But the matter is not so simple, and when Paul is confronted with the same issue, he passes on to the larger question: Gentiles who became followers of Jesus did not by that fact have to become Jews, Paul rules; they did not have to be circumcised and did not have to observe Torah law (Acts 13–14). Paul is summoned to Jerusalem to explain this extraordinary decision to the rigidly observant James, "the brother of the Lord," and the Twelve (Acts 15). In the end he receives grudging approval, but grudging or not, the Christians came, perhaps unwittingly, to a fork in the road sometime around 49 CE, two decades after the death of Jesus, and they turned to the left.

From this point on, the focus of the Acts of the Apostles remains fixed on Paul. At one point Luke slips from "he" to "we" (16:11) and we assume that we now have an eyewitness account of Paul's missionary journeys across the eastern Mediterranean and his travails in Jerusalem, where he is arrested and tried by the Roman authorities (21:33–26:32) and eventually sent off on appeal to Rome (27:1). The narrative ends rather abruptly with Paul's arrival in Rome (28:31). According to the Christian tradition, Paul died there, together with Peter, perhaps in Nero's persecutions in the late 60s CE. This is rather odd since Luke is now thought to have been writing in the 80s or 90s and if so, he would certainly have known of his hero's death.

What follows then in the New Testament are the letters bearing the name of Paul, the Diaspora Jew who soon after Jesus' death was converted to the movement and whom we have already encountered in the Acts of the Apostles. They are by and about the same person, clearly, but the Paul of the letters is somewhat more feisty and argumentative, and caring of his charges, than the one portrayed in the Acts. In the letters we are given some brief autobiographical sketches, most substantially in Galatians 1:13–21, and a great many personal reactions. The letters were written in the 50s of the first century and so are the oldest documents included in the New Testament and the oldest datable testimony to Jesus over all. They do indeed testify to Jesus' divinely ordained mission of salvation, to his redemptive death, to his continued presence in the souls of individual Christians and in the new congregations of Christians around the Mediterranean. But Paul passes over in silence, or with only the most general kind of comment, the cures, healings, exorcisms, and broad menu of teachings that are featured so prominently in the Gospels.

The letters were written to assemblies or congregations (*ekklesiai*) to which Paul had originally carried the "Good News" or which he had later visited: Ephesus and other cities in Anatolia, the cities in the province of Galatia there, the cities of Philippi in Thrace, Salonica in Thessaly, and Corinth in Greece, and, last of all, the congregation in Rome. A few letters, those to Timothy and Titus, are addressed to individuals and offer counsel for the guidance of Christian congregations. Most of the letters were written in response to queries and problems that had arisen in these local "churches," issues of both belief and practice. The new followers were feeling their way in their interpretation of the faith, in matters of ritual like Baptism and Eucharist, moral dilemmas concerning the great sea of paganism that surrounded them, and, with particular urgency and difficulty, the issue of their relationship to Judaism, for some the faith of their fathers, for others the religious ideal that had drawn them as Gentiles into the synagogue in the first place.

Paul was more than a local missionary-preacher. He had both the authority and the will to address the problems of these local congregations, and his answers were circulated by their addressees to other churches. Later, when the New Testament was being formed, his letters were included right after the works of the four evangelists and so became the authorized standard of belief and practice for all of Christianity. This man, who had never seen or heard Jesus, became the most important Christian after the founder because those other early Christians—and all who followed them—were convinced that Paul's testimony to Jesus, however personal it might appear, was undoubtedly authentic.

From all we know, Paul was the leading figure in opening the communities of Jesus' followers, which were entirely composed of Jews, to the Gentiles, the non-Jews. As both a Jew and a Christian, Paul had to counsel the new Christians (and some of the old Jewish Christians) on how they should regard the Jews and Judaism. The subject comes up often but two letters, that to the Galatians and the later one to the Romans, provide an extensive meditation on the subject of Torah, the Law. Paul attacked the issue from a variety of angles. One of his more striking images is that of the Jewish Law as a tutor. Like a tutor, the Torah was useful, Paul maintained, for the guidance of a child, but the coming of Jesus and the establishment of the New Covenant made the Christian in effect an adult who could now proceed, in Christ, without benefit of nursemaid or pedagogue.

How did Jesus achieve this effect? It was, Paul argued, through his death. One of Paul's most profound and far-reaching insights into Jesus' work is the notion of redemption. The death of Jesus, the divinely appointed Messiah and the Son of God, paid an infinite ransom to buy back humankind from its slavery to sin. Adam, the original man, had led humankind into its servitude by his original sin in the Garden of Eden. Jesus, the second Adam, bought it back with his own voluntary death. That death, and the favor (Gk. *charis;* Lt. *gratia;* Eng. "grace") it won from God, is more than enough to save every human, present or future, who avails him or herself of it.

Paul's letters are followed by others attributed to early followers of Jesus: one by James, the "brother of the Lord"; two by Peter, the chief of the Apostles; three by a John, also identified as the Apostle; and one by a "Jude" who calls himself the "brother of James," which would make him a brother of Jesus as well, though few are now inclined to accept either identification. They are all brief, and though they were obviously accepted by the churches as authentic testimonies to the truth of Christianity, they share none of the weight or the fire of the Pauline epistles.

The Jews who were not convinced by proselytizers like Paul and others had strong arguments against the Messiahship of Jesus. There was, in the first instance, the ignominious execution suffered by Jesus, which was not one envisioned by most Jews who were expecting a Messiah. The Christians found prophetic texts, Isaiah 52:13–53:12, for example, to demonstrate that even a humiliating death had been predicted of God's Chosen One. But a more powerfully transparent counterargument was the fact that none of the signs and portents of the End-Time had occurred, the cataclysmic events and the cosmic upheaval that everyone, including Jesus' followers, and Jesus himself (Mark 13 and parallels), had expected. The day of Jesus' alleged resurrection dawned no differently from the day of his death.

To answer this objection, both to the Jews and to themselves, Jesus' followers soon began to affirm a Second Coming, a messianic "presence" (*parousia*) that would usher in the expected End-Time. And, thought Paul and many of the Christians, it would come soon. "Lord, come!" is a very early prayer in Christian Aramaic and it echoes the expectation found in Paul's letters to the believers at Thessalonica. "The Lord himself will descend from heaven. . . . Then we who are still alive shall join them, caught up in clouds to meet the Lord in the air" (1 Thess. 4:16–17). That did not occur in Paul's lifetime, of course, nor in the decades that followed. And if the hope receded in time, it did not in either vividness or urgency.

The last book of the New Testament, the Apocalypse or Revelation of John, whom the Christians eventually identified with that other John, the Apostle and, it was believed, the author of the Fourth Gospel, is a prophetic vision of the entire complex scenario of the Last Days, bound up, like many of its Jewish antecedents—Revelation has been called the most Jewish book in the New Testament—in a furiously opaque imagery that hints but never reveals, describes but never explains.

"Recite! in the Name of God": What Is the Quran?

The Quran, a book roughly the size of the New Testament, is no less than the other Scriptures, a collected work, though in a very different manner. The Jewish and Christian Scriptures bring together inspired books from different authors' hands; the Quran holds between its covers the formal public testimonies made by a single individual, Muhammad, over the twenty-two or twenty-three years of his ministry. These pronouncements or "recitations," which took place at different times and under differing circumstances, were eventually brought together, divided into 114 suras or chapters, and each was given, like the Biblical Psalms, some small prefatory matter. From the perspective of belief, what is in these suras are messages sent down by God for delivery to humankind by the Prophet Muhammad; what the historian can certify is that collected here are the utterances that emerged from Muhammad's mouth at Mecca and Medina in the first decades of the seventh century.

We assuredly do not have in the Quran everything Muhammad uttered on those occasions, as the Muslim tradition itself concedes: there are numerous testimonies that certain of Muhammad's companions, his contemporaries at Mecca or Medina, could recall verses, sometimes many verses, that did not end up in the final and official version of the Quran. But it is likewise true that everything that is now in the Quran likely proceeded from Muhammad's mouth and no others'. There is no indication that anyone else added a single line to the collection of texts that is called the Quran.

This is not to say there are no human fingerprints on our Quran. There are in the first place Muhammad's own, traces of his own editorial work in the text, and there are, more obviously, those of the anonymous editors who, we are told by Muslim tradition, collected the scattered records of Muhammad's revelations, added the headings now prefaced to each sura, and then arranged the suras in the order they now appear. Apart from an opening sura which is a prayer, that order appears to be, to the historians' considerable chagrin, roughly that of descending length. As all concede, it is certainly not the order in which the revelations were made public in Mecca or Medina, to which the Muslim adds, nor does it much matter. For the Quran, like the Bible and the New Testament, is totally and *simultaneously* true.

But it does matter for the historian. As we shall see, it is possible to discern, at least in its general outlines, the original chronological order of the suras. Muslims and non-Muslims alike have tried their hand at this exercise and with very similar results. But once the suras are reordered, even in the most approximate chronological terms, immediately a new problem arises. On the face of it, many, if not most, of the suras appear to be composites—rhyme and assonance schemes are broken off; there are syntactical anomalies and abrupt changes of style and subject; that is, pericopes from different times and settings have been stitched together to form a single and quite artificial sura unit. Whether Muhammad himself did this and the resultant sura thus possesses a deliberate auteur unity, as most Muslims and some non-Muslims believe, or whether the stitching came from a later hand, as a growing number of non-Muslims are persuaded, the result is the same: the discovery of the original setting and circumstances of the Quranic pericopes is a matter not merely of locating a sura in context, but often of trying to determine the setting of parts, and often indistinct parts, of a single sura.

Of the three sets of Scriptures, only the Quran enjoys a self-conferred canonicity. In verses 77–78 of sura 56, which is among the earliest revelations, it describes itself as "a clear recitation" in the form of a "written book," and then adds, with an unmistakable echo of the Jewish tradition of a sacramental Torah, "which none may touch except the purified." And it is, finally, a "revelation"—the Arabic, which does not have the unveiling figure of "revelation," uses the expression "sending down"—a sending down "from the Lord of all beings." Thus the Quran, this "recitation," anoints itself as both Revelation and Scripture.

The Quran's self-identification as a "Book" suggests a single comprehensive whole, something "between two covers" as the early Muslim tradition itself describes it. The Quran is surely that, but equally surely the Muslim Scripture is a collection. Indeed, its very layout directs the reader's attention to its composition. The text that lies before us is already divided into 114 distinct units, each with its own name and the descriptive heading "Mecca" or "Medina," the two places where the revelations were "sent down."

Though the book names itself—*al-Qur'an*, "The Recitation" and *al-Kitab*, "The Book" are two of the most common self-designations—and makes clear that the listener is in the presence of a divine revelation, the Muslim Scripture never explains itself much beyond the fact that it is "Arabic" and it is "clear" or "manifest." We are not told by a narrative, authorial, or other voice in the text the manner, means, or circumstances of its origin, nor whether the suras are compositional or editorial units, revelations, fragments of revelations, or sewn-up composites of a number of revelations. What it was in its original context, when and how and where the voice of God came to Muhammad in seventh-century Mecca and Medina, is left to speculation, that of the early Muslims in the first instance and of a long succession of scholars, Muslim and non-Muslim alike, in the sequel.

The Quran is not interested in merely human history; its focus is on

Sacred History, the "ways of God with man." In the Quran the *acta hominum* are inevitably *acta Dei*, stories told piecemeal from the past, generally the Biblical past, to make the point that God's will cannot be thwarted. It adverts seldom if ever to contemporary persons, places, or events, while there is in it considerable reflection on Abraham, Moses, and other figures of the Old and New Testaments. Some of the suras are kerygmatic, preaching intended to convince and convert a pagan audience. Others, the longer and later ones, are heavily didactic: instruction and guidance are given to those who are already "submitters" (*muslimun* < *islam*, "submission").

There are, however, some contemporary voices in the Quran as well, those of Muhammad's opponents, whether pagan, Jewish, or Christian. They are given voice, but anonymously, only to be refuted and condemned. We can never be quite sure who is speaking in the text, or why, much less when or where. It has been justly remarked that we cannot interpret the Quran unless we already have before us a chronological sketch of Muhammad's life. But Muhammad's Muslim biographers may have been doing precisely the reverse, attempting to imagine, or invent, the circumstances that would make sense of the Quran's pronouncements, denials, warnings, threats, parables, and stories. There is an entire branch of Arabic letters that is unabashedly devoted to just that. *Asbab al-nuzul* it is called, the "Occasions of Revelation," or, perhaps more accurately, if the authors actually had no independent information on Muhammad's life, "Imagining Revelation."

Somewhat later we shall ourselves attempt to imagine the manner of revelation; here we follow in the steps of the early Muslims and try to see the Quran in the context of the Prophet's own life, and in that way attempt to illuminate its contents. The ordinary Muslim does not need such context to understand or internalize the Quran, just as neither the Jew nor the Christian requires the services of the historian to grasp the truth of the Bible or the New Testament. But it is difficult for the common reader to take hold of the contents of this extraordinary book at first glance, and even after many glances, without imposing some organization on it.

Muslims have already done this, as has been remarked, first by attempting to determine the original sequence of the suras and then by extending them in that order across what had been handed down about the life of Muhammad. Their motive, at least of some, was not to understand the Quran but rather to understand one or other of its parts. The "some" in this instance were Islam's lawyers, the learned class or *ulama*, who were interested in the "occasion of revelation," the *Sitz im Leben* of the Biblical critic, of a verse or a number of connected verses for the light it might cast on the moral application or legal extension or restriction of its prescription.

The events of Muhammad's life were and are important to the Muslim for another reason. They do not constitute a sacred drama or come to climax in a redemptive act, as Jesus' life does for Christians. Nor are his life and times for Muslims the matrix out of which Islam emerged, as modern secular scholars generally read them. But Muhammad's life was, for all that, remembered by Muslims, in great and vivid detail, and it was soon inscribed in the collective memory of the community that venerates him as its Prophet. Muhammad was and is the primary moral exemplar of a Muslim life, and as such, not only the events of his life but also his preferences and aversions were worth preserving *ad perpetuam agentis memoriam.*

To turn, then, for the moment to Muhammad himself, we have two sets of documents that relate to him. The first is the Quran. Although Muslims regard it more as a testimony to God than to His Prophet, it nevertheless proceeded from Muhammad's mouth and was directed at Muhammad's audience, and so it is held by secular historians to be a fundamental and authentic source for both Muhammad and his environment. "The primary source for the biography of Muhammad is the Quran." So begins one of the first critical biographies of the Prophet in the modern era, and no evidence since discovered, or judgment subsequently rendered, has altered that fact.

The primary sources of information on the life of Jesus were and remain the four biographical tracts included by the early Christians in their New Testament as "Gospels," and though they offer the testimony of believers, the Gospels are verifiably of that time and place. We are not so fortunate with Muhammad. He was surrounded by eyewitnesses no less than Jesus, and not merely as a prophet but as the head of a seventh-century "state" in Western Arabia. But the works that preserved the earliest recollections of him are now lost. We have instead a heavily edited ninth-century version of an eighth-century biography composed in Baghdad by one Muhammad ibn Ishaq (d. 768) and two later parallel but independent accounts: a "Book of Campaigns" on the Prophet's military expeditions by al-Waqidi (d. 823) and another biography by the latter's student Ibn Sa'd (d. 843). Finally, there were in circulation thousands of free-floating fragments of information professing to be eyewitness reports of one or other of the Prophet's deeds or sayings.

The material on Muhammad is, then, extensive but relatively late, and refracted, like the Gospels, through the sensibilities of believers. If the evangelists saw Jesus through what they believed to be a miraculous and authenticating resurrection from the dead, Muhammad's biographers regarded their hero through the prism of a worldwide military and political vindication of his sacred calling and mission. The details of his life are many but often contradictory, and the free-floating pieces of information, the so-called *hadith* or "Prophetic reports," which not only undergird the structure of Islamic law but are the material out of which Ibn Ishaq, his lost predecessors, and his many successors constructed their own *Lives*, are overcast with the grave suspicion of wholesale forgery. Some hadith are doubtless true, some undeniably false, but few non-Muslim historians profess the ability to tell which is which. What is left to do, short of lapsing into silence, is to construct a plausible account out of at times highly implausible material.

Muhammad's life falls, like the Quran itself, into two phases. There is his relatively unsuccessful mission to his native shrine-town of Mecca from his "call" sometime about 610 CE down to his forced exile in 622, followed by his highly successful career at the oasis of Medina from 622 to his death in 632. Legend apart, we are ill-informed about Muhammad's earliest years. We know he was an orphan raised by relatives, and by the time he reached adulthood he was married and, through his wife Khadija, had some modest share in what was probably the equally modest commercial life of his hometown. Mecca possessed a central shrine to the widely worshiped deity named simply "the God" (Ar. *allah*) and whose presence, though not his effigy, was housed in a rude building called "the Cube" (*ka'ba*). In the sacred area around it had been collected a variety of cult objects of other deities, the gods and goddesses of the neighboring tribes who were now drawn to Mecca, where they could, under the protection of a sacred truce, worship and trade. The paramount tribe of Mecca, the Quraysh, controlled and profited from both the worship and the trade, and the not very well-connected Muhammad of the minor clan of the Banu Hashim took his own small share.

Then—the absence of reliable circumstance baffles the historian—the adult Muhammad experienced an epiphany, an experience of "the God"

Himself perhaps or, as was later more modestly believed, through the angel Gabriel, who began to entrust him with revelations. These were messages—the revelations were oral rather than visual—intended for the pagan polytheists of Mecca. After some initial misgivings and hesitation, Muhammad took to the public places of Mecca, likely in the shadow of the Ka'ba, and repeated the messages he had received. They were in a familiar cantillation style and his audience quickly identified his "recitation" as "poetry" and Muhammad himself as a "poet." The burden of the message is not unfamiliar to us. Give up the worship of false gods. The Creator God, the one who made the world and sustains it and us in it, will one day demand a reckoning of every mortal. For His friends there are the rewards of "the Garden"; for the sinners, the extraordinary pains of "Gehenna." God is, Muhammad never tires of repeating, "the Compassionate, the Merciful One," but He is also the God of a severe and unrelenting justice.

This is familiar ground since it is quite patently Biblical both in its underlying monotheistic thrust and in the circumstantial details in which it is framed: Gabriel, Eden, Gehenna. Oddly, it seems to have been familiar to the audience as well, even when Muhammad begins to unfold tales of the Biblical prophets. In the Quran's economy of revelation, Muhammad was but the last, the "seal," of a long line of prophets sent to humankind with counsels of salvation. Most of them were Biblical: Moses, David, Solomon—oddly neither Isaiah, Jeremiah, nor Ezekiel figure here—and Jesus too, and they have been ignored by mortals to their own fatal peril. These cautionary tales, allusions often rather than full-blown stories, appear to have been recognized and understood by Muhammad's audience even though they were not convinced by them.

Muhammad's message of radical monotheism and divine justice, the recognition of divine rights and human responsibilities that the Quran terms "submission" (*islam*), made few believers in Mecca. But the lords of the town did not simply ignore this undistinguished local God-crier; his calls to do away with the tutelary totems clustered around the Ka'ba threatened the fragile underpinnings of Meccan privilege and prosperity. He was troublesome and, they thought, possibly dangerous and would have to be removed. After twelve years of public preaching at Mecca, Muhammad was marked for assassination by the Quraysh.

He escaped, just barely. A call from the oasis of Medina—275 miles away over rough terrain—saved his life. Some of the Medinese had seen and heard Muhammad in Mecca and persuaded their fellows that this holy man might be the solution to the oasis' problem. That problem was social, not religious: a civil war was brewing between the two major tribal groups, each with its Jewish clients, that were crowded into the palm grove. Again, it was likely Muhammad's manner rather than his message that got him hailed to Medina, but once there, along with his followers from Mecca, he stayed resolutely on message. When his attention did turn elsewhere, in vengeance toward the Quraysh and in apparent surprise and then anger at the oasis' Jews who denied his prophetic claims and the authenticity of his message, it found quick validation in the Quran.

Shortly after his arrival in Medina, the oasis's new ratified ruler raided and sacked a Meccan caravan returning home from the north. The spoils were rich, rich enough to begin to turn Medinese heads away from civil strife to the new and profitable civic enterprise of raiding. The numbers of the Muslim raiders grew and so did the range of the raiding. The goal was no longer vengeance or booty, as it had been in that first instance, but the spread of "Islam": settlements were given the choice of "submission" or annihilation. Most chose submission; the Arabian towns do not appear to have been very bellicose societies, and "war" had little meaning outside the Bedouin's relatively bloodless jostlings and joustings on the steppe in the name of honor, camels, and womenfolk.

The annual raids deep into Arabia with Muhammad at their head were the grist of the later Muslim historians, but the Medinese suras of the Quran almost completely ignore them. Instead, they are concerned with matters internal to the new Muslim *umma*, the community of Muslims that was both a polity and a church, with Muhammad as the undisputed ruler of both. He appears to have been equally adept as statesman and prophet, but it is chiefly the voice of the latter that we hear in the Quran. It is, in a sense, a new voice, or rather, a familiar voice in a new register. Whereas the Meccan suras attempted, with their vivid imagery, highly wrought language, and powerful affective tone, to turn the listeners away from polytheism to the sole worship of the One True God, the long Medinese suras are more practical, more didactic, and more restrained: God is now speaking prose. The audience is also now Muslim; it requires not persuasion, but instruction and reinforcement.

What constitutes "Islam" in the public sphere is made much clearer in the Medina revelations. What was a dangerous and so a clandestine enterprise at Mecca was now the established (and unique) religion of Medina and of ever increasing numbers of Arabs in the peninsula. They had to be taught to pray in a new solemn mode prescribed by the Quran, to tithe alms to the community treasury, to fast, and to perform the *hajj*, the ritual pilgrimage to the newly "liberated" (630 CE) Mecca. The lives of the believers were shaped to new ends: a more modest, more generous morality was unfolded in the Medina suras of the Quran; questions were answered, doubts resolved.

References to the contemporary Jews grow darker and more truculent as the Quran progresses: little wonder since the Jews of Medina rejected both the Prophet and his message, a rejection Muhammad read as both religious infidelity and political treason. He was convinced that the Jews were plotting to hand over the oasis to the Quraysh. And out of this rejection the Quran also fashions a new understanding of the place of Islam in Sacred History. Both the Jews and the Christians—at Medina Muhammad had still not encountered many Christians—had been sent prophets, Moses to the first, Jesus to the second, each with a genuine Scripture, the *Tawrat* and the *Injil*. Out of this had emerged in each case a religious community, the Jews and the Christians, who in the end were unfaithful to God's message and had distorted the Scripture. Thus the call of Muhammad to prophethood and the "sending down" of the Quran. But Islam was not merely the third and last in a series of revelations; it was a return to the base, to the *original* community contract with Abraham. Islam was neither Judaism nor Christianity: as the "religion of Abraham" it was the pristine form of monotheism.

Muhammad died, aged sixty-two, in his own bed in Medina in 632, and with his death the revelations ceased and the Quran was closed forever. It was already, as its messenger understood even as he was delivering it, a Book in the sense of a Scripture. But it was not yet a book between covers. The task of making it such fell to his followers.

∂⟨⟩∂   *Note: The Heavenly Book.*

Of the three Scriptures, the New Testament is distinctly earthbound: its named authors may be "inspired" by the Holy Spirit and so guided into inerrancy, but their work products, the biographies, history, letters, and apocalypse of the New Testament, are patently literary issue and not Words from On High. It is quite otherwise with the Hebrew Bible and the Arabic Quran, both of which are associated with—the Quran on its own explicit testimony—a venerable Middle Eastern tradition of the "Heavenly Book."

The "Heavenly Book" may have had its remote origins in the widespread conviction that there is a Fate, a locus where human events are foreordained, and recorded, by divine fiat; and eventually, with the newly affirmed belief in human survival into an Afterlife, where each mortal's acts are recorded for later reward or punishment. The notion of a Book of Fate never quite disappears from the backstory of either the Bible or the Quran, and it can even be glimpsed in the complex imagery of the New Testament's book of Revelation, with its scrolls from which emerge the harbingers of future events (5:1 and ff.). But it is overcome by another, related concept, that of the heavenly prototype.

In the Bible, it is the Torah that is adorned with this notion of a heavenly antecedent. Although "heavenly tablets" with the Law inscribed on them are mentioned in the extra-Biblical Jubilees (3:10), the development of the idea is primarily rabbinic. "Wisdom" not only is personified but has an eternal preexistence when she makes her appearance in the Biblical books of Ben Sirah and Solomon, and the rabbis followed easily in the steps of their Hellenized predecessors like Aristobulus and Philo of Alexandria in equating that personified wisdom with the Torah. The Torah too existed in some heavenly form and in some eternal dimension before the creation of the universe—the proof text is Proverbs 8:22, which refers quite explicitly to "Wisdom"—and our copy is precisely that, a time-bound (and author-conditioned?) copy of an eternal and unchanging original. And the fevered imagery of the Christian Apocalypse also displays an "angel flying in mid-heaven with an eternal Gospel to proclaim to those on earth" (Rev. 14:6).

The Quran, which also knows a book of recorded deeds, a ledger kept by the angels (82:10–12, etc.), three times invokes the expression "Mother of the Book" (3:7; 13:39; 43:4). Its contexts prompt us to see it as the equivalent of a record of divine decrees, the same as the Quran's "Well-Guarded Tablet" (85:22), which is with God, but the Muslim understanding of the phrase quickly broadened to embrace the notion of the "Mother of the Book" as a heavenly prototype of our Quran, the one that was "sent down" piecemeal to Muhammad over the course of the last twenty-two years of his life.

Chapter 2

Book Shaping

The Making of a Canon

ᘓᑖᘒ

The Scriptures, we have now seen, are collections. To the nonbeliever they appear to be a collection of documents, and since at least the nineteenth century they have been treated exactly as such, no different from other literary remains of antiquity. But for the believers—and their "belief" is founded on this very point—what is called Scripture is a repository and record of God's special favor to humankind. God has left His signs throughout His creation, the believers hold, for all of humanity to behold; but the Scripture is more precisely directed to those in the first instance whom God has chosen, the special mortals elected as representatives of a Chosen People, but also for those who choose to heed, for those in Jesus' audience, or Muhammad's, "who have ears to hear."

God's favors are distributed across the pages of Scripture as both words of promise and deeds of fulfillment. Scripture is a collection of God's various sayings and messages, records of His direct communications with mortals like Abraham and Sarah, or later, Moses; or large swathes of pronouncements that can be found in the Biblical books like Leviticus and Numbers or parts of the Quran, or issuing from the mouth of the God-man Jesus; or messages mediated through prophets like Samuel or Nathan or Isaiah. But Scripture is not merely a record of what God said. From what has been preserved as Holy Writ there can be no doubt that the *acta Dei* were as important as the divine *dicta*. The actions, whether human or divine, that followed upon God's speech were as meaningful to the believers as the speech itself. History too, as it turned out, was regarded as a form of revelation, and it too was remembered, recorded, and preserved.

That is what Scripture tells us. But similar words and deeds fill up the books cherished by the believers. What makes some of them Scripture and some not? Who discerns the Word of God, and how? In short, what makes up the *canon of* Scripture? The word "canon" itself is not Scriptural but a term of art that enters into the monotheists' discourse from the outside, more specifically from the literary culture of the Hellenistic world of the third century BCE. The Greek word may have more ancient antecedents, but as it applies here, it means "measure" and was used to describe both the measuring instrument, the "ruler," and the thing measured, which in this instance are literary units, the books that make up both the Jewish Bible and the Christian New Testament. The Quran, in contrast, is not constituted of "books" but is rather a single work composed of literary units that are closer to what we understand by "chapters" and so the notion of a "canon" does not much apply.

Sacred Scripture was not the first body of writing to have its contents weighed and defined. Though the word "canon" was not used to describe it, the process of sorting and filtering literary works began in secular academic circles, more precisely in Alexandria, the city that was for the millennium between the third century BCE and the seventh CE the intellectual center of the eastern Mediterranean. Scholars working there under royal patronage had begun to assemble (and edit) what were to become, by that very act of criticism, the "classics" of Hellenism and the nucleus of the "Great Books" of Western civilization.

The Alexandrian academics who sifted through the Greek tragedians and the lyric poets were not principally interested in authenticity. Their criterion in selecting certain books, or rather, authors, for inclusion in the lists that were the product of their reflections was almost uniquely aesthetic. They were interested in textual authenticity, of course, and a number of them pioneered in preparing "critical" editions of the poets, one whose text had been "tested" and emended where necessary. But inclusion in the Alexandrians' canonical lists was largely a matter of taste: these were the authors who were thought to represent the best in nine literary categories from epic and lyric poetry, through drama, to history, philosophy, and rhetoric. The choice was authoritative from the outset; it was made by literary and scholarly eminences at Alexandria's *Museion,* the "birdcage of the Muses," as it was called, and, we may add, the habitat too of the professorial caretakers of those noisy songbirds.

Who wanted or needed such lists? There is always an audience for list makers of the "best-worst" variety, even among the Second Temple Jews, who enjoyed Ben Sirah's roll call of the "Makers of Jewish History" in his famous "Let us now praise famous men" (49:1–50:21). Discriminating lists of this type were useful to both the teachers and the taught in that Hellenistic society where the notion of "culture" was born and where Hellenic acculturation was the pathway to a better and brighter future, even for Jewish priests in Jerusalem who, according to Josephus, preferred to spend their time in the gymnasium rather than in the Temple.

The Greeks had no name for their selective lists of "Who's Who in the Ancient Literary World"—more comprehensive lists of library holdings and such; what we might call catalogs, they called *pinakes*—and they only came to be called "canons" in the eighteenth century as a direct borrowing from Christian usage. The word "canon" was already current in Christian circles in the second century to denote, as it did in Greek, a rule, but in the Christian instance it meant, more specifically, the "rule of faith," the norm of belief in a world that was very bothered by that question. By the fourth century, "canon" not only was being employed of Christian works that were thought to embody that "rule of faith," but was in widespread use in both the Greek and the Latin Churches to describe the Old and the New Testaments. But the word was never used by the Jews to describe their own Scripture until the beginning of the modern era.

Though canonization is related to standardization, it is a different process. Standardization has to do with stabilizing a given literary text, sacred or profane, either by producing one signed with the seal of an authority that makes it standard, as Uthman attempted to do with the Quran in the mid-seventh century and the Council of Trent mandated of the New Testament in the sixteenth, or else by producing a version of that text whose credentials are such that it drives all other versions out of circulation, like modern critical editions of the New Testament, or Luther's German version of the Bible. Canonization seeks to construct a category, to set borders and to assign items, in our context literary pieces, to places inside or outside those borders.

Both canonization and standardization have to do with written rather than oral texts. These latter, whose "publication" is invariably performative and which are, as a result, variable, are in a constant state of flux: oral performances are rarely identical from one occasion to the next. Thus, the first step in the standardization of a text is to write it down. Canonization too seems to have to do with written texts. The performance of a given piece, a mythic poem of origins or a battle saga, may in fact become *traditional* in a society where a consensus on the matter develops over a number of generations. Scriptural canonization is a far more aggressive procedure however. The inclusion of a literary piece within the Scriptural canon may be the outcome of a consensus of the learned or even of the entire community, but its protection is a function of community authority, as is the protection of the category of canon itself. The notion of "Scripture" must be shielded from contamination and confusion.

We have seen what is in Scripture; we now ask why precisely it is there. The answer is, on the face of it, a simple one: what is included in Scripture is there first of all because it is thought to come from God; and second, its remembrance, and, since it includes as many prescriptions as it does promises, its fulfillment, is essential to salvation, however that latter notion is understood by the community of believers. The problem, quite obviously, is in determining, in the presence of counterfeits, precisely which are the Words of God and, when it is a question of mediated speech from on high, who are God's authentic prophets and genuine spokesmen and who are the false. It is obviously to the advantage of many to claim to be speaking in God's name or on God's behalf, and the construction and population of a canon called Scripture is a determination of who actually was and who was not. We cannot always tell who was making that determination, or when, or on what grounds. The product of the judgment, the actual canon of Scripture, is our primary and best evidence; often we can only infer the process by which it was achieved.

From *Biblia* to Book: The Making of the Bible

Though "Bible" is the most commonly used name for the Jewish Scripture, there is another, almost as common appellation that is current among Jews and comes from a somewhat different semantic direction. This is the acronym *Tanak*, the name and the thing named both composed of the elements of *Torah* ("Law"), *Nebi'im* ("Prophets"), and *Ketubim* ("Writings"). Unlike the baldly descriptive "Bible," "Tanak" gives us a glimpse of what is within the Sacred Book. The name acknowledges, and other evidence confirms very early on, that the Bible was a collection, and not merely of three parts, as Tanak might seem to suggest, but of twenty-four quite distinct books, four of them (Samuel, Kings, Chronicles, and Ezra-Nehemiah) in two volumes.

Those twenty-four books by no means represent all the sacred writings of the Jews. The Bible itself is filled with references to other works that were known to the Biblical authors but were afterward lost or discarded for one reason or another. Most of them appear to be historical works, royal annals in the main, like the "Annals of Samuel" mentioned in the first book of Chronicles (29:29), or battle sagas like the "Book of the Wars of Yahweh" (Numbers 21:14), to name only two. In post-Exilic times the literary horizon broadened considerably, and from that era we hear of (but no longer possess) the intriguing "Book of the Daughters of Adam" and the no less than sixty books of the "Apocryphon of Lamech." And from the same era are preserved a great many works that were once regarded as sacred by some, or many, or all Jews, but were not in the end included in the Bible. They are valuable in that they enable us to at least surmise—we are not told the reasons—why they were not.

Of the books we do now possess that constitute the Bible, the first is (appropriately for the content) called Genesis, and it begins with the creation of the universe—at some point before Creation actually—and the last book in the Bible, Ezra-Nehemiah, describes the Israelites' return from their exile in Babylonia late in the sixth century BCE. But though Ezra-Nehemiah is the last book in the collection as it now stands, another book called Daniel, while professedly recounting portentous things that befell the Israelites during the Babylonian Exile, is actually obliquely referring to the discernibly latest datable events recorded in our Bible, those surrounding the reign of the Seleucid king Antiochus V Epiphanes (r. 175–163).

Who authored the books that comprised this Tanak, who composed them, when, and under what circumstances, is an obscure and perhaps irresolvable matter. Here we turn first to an apparently simpler question: once written, when and why were they put together in a single compendium, that is, into a collective work named "The Book" or "The Books," thought to be important to the identity of the community called, in that same collection, *Benei Israel* or Israelites?

One answer provided by the Jewish tradition first appears in a book called 4 Ezra, that is, the fourth of the series of books bearing that author's

name. Though the "original" Ezra, the priestly scribe who was an important figure in the Israelites' return from their Exile, lived and wrote his
Biblical book in the sixth century BCE, this work with his name on it was
actually composed in the late first century and was *not* included in the
Bible. In this account, Ezra is said to live in an era when "the world is in
darkness," when "the Law has been burned." Ezra requests the Lord to send
the Holy Spirit to him so that he might "write down everything that happened in the world from the beginning, the things that were written in
your Law" (14:20–22). He is told to collect writing tablets and to gather
five scribes, "these five because they have been trained to write rapidly,"
and to withdraw from society. Ezra is literally given wisdom to drink. He
then dictates, night and day for forty days, and the scribes write it all
down. And at the end the Lord says: "Make public the twenty-four books
that you wrote first and let the worthy and unholy read them, but keep the
seventy that were written last in order to give them to the wise among the
people. For in them is the spring of understanding" (43–47).

We gather from this that there was in the first Christian century a Bible
made up, like our own, of twenty-four books, and that the collection was
thought to be the work of the priest-scribe Ezra. These sacred books had
existed earlier but had been destroyed in whole or in part in the circumstances of the Exile, and Ezra, under the direct guidance of the Holy Spirit,
reconstituted them as written texts in the sixth century BCE. We also
learn of the putative existence, alongside the public texts, of a body of
esoterica—probably much like the apocalyptic visions that make up most
of 4 Ezra and the books of Enoch and Baruch—which were to be restricted to "the wise."

There is much earlier, if somewhat less circumstantial, evidence of what
may be a collection of sacred books. It is recorded in 2 Kings (22:3–23:3),
when sometime around 622 BCE or, at any rate, during the reign of King
Josiah, the high priest Hilkiah "found" a "scroll of the Law" (*sefer ha-
torah*) in the Temple. The expression "scroll" is singular, and there is no indication of its exact contents, though its name and location make it almost
certainly something that would later be called "Scripture." The same is
true of the next reference, in Nehemiah (8:1–8), when the priest-scribe
Ezra assembled in Jerusalem the Israelites who had been released from
their Babylonian Exile and read to them the "scroll of the Law of Moses,"
which they then solemnly affirmed. Again, we are not told the contents of

the scroll except that it was Torah and it was Mosaic, and that it was, by the manner and place of its formal public affirmation, the embodiment of the Covenant with Israel.

If we are looking for an actual *collection* of works sacred to the Israelites, the earliest is undoubtedly those included in the Greek translations done in Egypt from the third century BCE onward. What later came to be called the "Septuagint" comprised a broad collection of Jewish sacred books, far broader, in fact, than what was eventually the Jewish Bible. The collection was not formal since the books appear to have been assembled gradually, and all that is certain about the original third-century translation is that it contained (like the Josiah or Ezra "Torah" before it?) the five books of Moses, the so-called Pentateuch.

The next clue in the formation of our Bible is the broad and popular categorization of sacred writings under the rubric "the Law and the Prophets," with or without a third category called "the Writings" or the even more anonymous "others." Sometime about 132 BCE, we are told by the grandson and translator of Jesus Ben Sirah that this latter was devoted to "the Laws and the Prophets and other books of our fathers" (Ben Sirah prologue), which is suggestively close to the later rabbinic and standard division of the Bible into Torah, Prophets, and Writings. We still do not know, however, which or how many works were included under each of those heads. Josephus in the first century CE refers to twenty-two "justly accredited books" of the Jews, which is close to our own twenty-four but does not seem to suggest that the list was closed. In fact, religious writings with a claim to antiquity, religious authority, or both, are preserved from well into the second and third centuries CE, when the rise to prominence of the rival Christian movement and its own claim to sacred writings likely closed what had been a still rather open-ended category.

Reasonably clear from all these shreds of evidence is that the Jews had collected a number of sacred books, as well as more profane records—"Nehemiah collected the chronicles of the kings, the writings of the prophets, the works of David, and the [Persian] royal letters about sacred offerings." These writings, legitimate to call Scripture, were kept ceremonially in the Temple (2 Macc. 2:13), where, again according to Josephus, they were under the protective care of the priests. The practice of storing sacred records in that manner is reliably reported from the earliest stages of Israelite history. "Holy" is a frequent and invariable characterization of "the writings" and "the books." The written tablets of the Ten Commandments were stored in the Ark of the Covenant (Exod. 25:16), and subsequently the Ark, the tablets still within, was enshrined in Solomon's temple (1 Kings 8:6–9).

Those early collections, exact contents unspecified, were clearly the forerunners of our Bible, but there is no agreement on when or how the transformation took place. Absent any other clues, many are inclined to connect the "birth" of the Bible with the events described in 2 Kings 22:3–23:3. Thus, it was likely the high priest Hilkiah, the same who "found the scroll of the Law in the Temple of the Lord," sometime around 623 BCE, under the auspices or the direction of the king Josiah, had assembled in the Temple a collection of sacred writings. The initiative may have been intended to give authority and authenticity to Josiah's own broad religious reforms in Judea, and the collection probably contained, like all its later versions, a law book and an account of the history of the Israelites from Moses onward. More precisely, its contents may have been what modern historians call the "Deuteronomic history," that is, five books, a *pentateuch*, though not *our* Pentateuch. Josiah's Scripture may have begun with the newly found "Torah," that is, the present book of Deuteronomy, followed by Joshua, Judges, Samuel, and Kings (each of the last two regarded as a single book).

A series of gradual accretions probably followed. The first may have been the extension of the historical narrative to 561 BCE when King Jehoichin was released from his Babylonian captivity. This is described in 2 Kings 25:27–30, and the identical passage occurs at the end of Jeremiah, where we assume it was added at the same time. The next addition was more substantial. A whole new and more ambitious "Pentateuch" was assembled, namely, our present one, which begins with Genesis and ends with Deuteronomy, the book that once constituted the Israelite law but was now appended to a new expanded account. And to Jeremiah were added the further prophetic books of Isaiah and Ezekiel. This makes up a corpus of twelve books, five of the "Law" and seven of what were now being called "the Prophets." The "T" and "N" of Tanak were in place.

It is not certain when the next addition—another body of twelve books, what are now called the "Minor Prophets"—was made to this Bible of twelve books. This larger Bible of twenty-four books was finally enhanced by an addition of a very different type, another twelve-book corpus whose unity was so vague that it ended by being called simply "the Writings" (*Ketubim*). The obvious Hellenic tinge to the language and thought of most of the books included under this rubric, together with Daniel's references to current events under the Seleucids, make it likely that this last element of Tanak was added sometime in the late second century BCE.

Jewish Scripture was very early a treasured collection, but not yet a closed one, neither in its content nor indeed, in its text, as it certainly was by the end of the third or beginning of the fourth century CE. The New Testament still cites without discrimination books from both within and without what later came to be known as the Bible—Ben Sirah, for example, and Enoch—and the same is true of the sectaries at Qumran, who both copied and cited, *without discrimination*, writings that later the rabbis would judge noncanonical.

We may well be witnessing a gradual process of closure, of a collection of collections, so to speak. The first, "the Law," was certainly in place by Ezra's day, and perhaps much earlier. The second, "the Prophets," may have been assembled and agreed upon in the post-Exilic era, perhaps in the second century CE when Judah, called "the Maccabee," repeated Ezra's task of consolidating the sacred books of the Jews, and under somewhat similar circumstances, in this instance the Jewish persecution under Antiochus Epiphanes (2 Macc. 2:14). And significantly, there are no prophets recognized as "Biblical" after that date.

By the time of Jesus, the expression "the Law and the Prophets" seems to have gained wide currency as a descriptive term for Scripture. At that point the third category may have already been in the process of formation, not yet as "the Writings," but more likely as simply "the Psalms," which is regarded as a third category of Scripture in the Gospels (Luke 24:44), the Dead Sea Scrolls, and Philo of Alexandria. "The Psalms" did not, however, continue to serve as the definitive marker for the post-prophetic writings since those hymns were eventually joined by moral stories and collections of proverbial wisdom. "Writings" is a surrender to sacred shapelessness, and the mixed contents of that catchall category continued to disturb many Jews.

When the incremental process seems to have ended, and where we reach the limit of the books subsequently regarded as "the Bible," is in an early tradition (*baraita*) preserved in the Babylonian Talmud tractate *Baba Batra*, which cites the twenty-four books of our Bible and groups them into the now familiar Law, Prophets, and Writings. This tradition probably dates from the second century CE, and even then the matter was not quite settled; tradition remembers an ongoing debate in rabbinic circles about the sacredness of the books called Esther, the Song of Songs, Ecclesiastes, Proverbs, and, we surmise, the appropriateness of keeping in the collection the prophetic book called Ezekiel, which had already become the subject of considerable esoteric speculation.

If, then, we restate the question as who decided what was in the Bible, the answer is somewhere between "no one" and "everyone." The Jewish tradition consistently points to a rabbinic council meeting held in the Palestinian town of Yabneh sometime around 90 CE when a final decision was reportedly made on the books that were to constitute the Bible. The timing seems about right, but otherwise evidence for such a "council" is slim indeed. The rabbis of that era had neither the authority nor the organization to mandate the contents of Scripture or to make such a mandate effective. It more plausibly took a consensus, or, perhaps more accurately, a rolling consensus, to reach a decision on the contents of Holy Writ. It is often said that it was a Jewish community decision, but our inability to name names in the process does not mean that it was democratic. All the participants in the known discussions of the Bible's contents were rabbis, and if we do not have a lot of solid information about the individuals themselves, we do know something of their shared outlook.

What had been before the Great Roman War of 66–70 CE a very divided and sectarian Jewish society in Palestine emerged from that bloodbath as something far simpler. After 70 it was the pacifist and deliberately apolitical Pharisees who were, with Roman approbation, in control of religious life in Palestine, which is why they loom so large in the Gospels written during that same era. And if there were enough zealots abroad to provoke another insurrection against Rome in 132–135, the disastrous finale of that second adventure finally converted Jewish society into the inner-directed and quietist community that it remained for another thousand years.

At this point, the second century CE, it was the Pharisees, now long remote from political action, who were firmly guiding the path of post-Temple Judaism, and it was they, or certainly their direct spiritual descendants, the rabbis, who were debating the matter of Scripture and gave final shape to what we call the Bible. The second- and third-century rabbinic debates on the contents of Scripture reported in the Talmud and its related literature chiefly concerned "the Writings," and they introduce us to issues and reveal agenda we cannot discern in the case of the earlier "Law and the Prophets." Why were there objections to the books of Esther and Song of Songs? Why were other works from that same era, the third to the first century BCE and the century following, not permitted into "the Writings"? To say they were too late, or that Baruch and Enoch and the various "Ezras" offer prophecy after prophecy had ended in Israel, is simply to beg the question of why prophecy had ended. It has been plausibly suggested that their composition in Greek disqualified certain works like the Wisdom of Solomon and the books of Maccabees, while its Hebrew saved the apparently more profane Qoheleth/Ecclesiastes for the Bible.

More problematic than either of these criteria, yet closer to the heart of the debate, was the issue of sectarianism. Strictly speaking, there were no sects in pre-70 or Temple Judaism since there was no normative Judaism against which to measure them. But after the Exile the Jews do appear to have been divided, sometimes stridently, into apocalyptic and nonapocalyptic Jews, for example, some of them Messianists and some of them not; some willing to "hasten the End," others quietists. The authenticity of the priesthoods, with its consequent liturgical issues, also split the community, as did the modes and degrees of observance of the Law and its ideological backstory. Is *sola Scriptura* the rule or must the "tradition of the Fathers" be observed as well?

We know from the Dead Sea Scrolls that different Jewish groups had their own collections of books in the Second Temple era and that they included, between the generally accepted Scripture of the Pentateuch and the Prophets on one hand and their own openly sectarian writing—like the Qumran Manual of Discipline and the Christians' Gospels—on the other, a penumbra of writings that shared in the characteristics of those other two categories. These latter were, by their style and attribution, near-Scriptural; and, by their content and use, near-sectarian.

The second-century rabbinic debate was conducted by the Pharisees, the triumphant survivors from that discordant community of pre-70 days. They were attempting to discern, in a new, exclusionary context, what now constituted Scripture, but we cannot be sure of the criteria they used in any given case. The book called Jubilees, for example, was almost certainly ruled out on ideological grounds—that is, it had its origins in or was being used by a dissident group—but why was Qoheleth/Ecclesiastes included and Ben Sirah/Ecclesiasticus excluded? The exact reasons are not clear to us, but reasonably evident is that works were being *excluded* from the emerging category of "Scripture" because they did not square with Pharisaic/rabbinic opinion, or, now that the Pharisaic perspective was emerging as "normative Judaism," works that could now be justly characterized as sectarian. We know of one other "sect" that, like the Pharisees, escaped the catastrophe of the Roman wars, namely, the followers of Jesus of Nazareth, the newly dubbed "Christians," and they carry us directly into the heart of the question of the Jewish canon of Scripture.

The number of books that made up the Scriptural category called "the Writings" seems to have been growing slowly and unselfconsciously in the immediate pre-Christian era; there does not appear to have been any debate, at any rate, about what belonged in the Bible and what did not until the rabbis took it up in the second century CE. At that point certain Jewish "Writings" like Tobit and Esther and Ben Sirah were excluded. If we do not know the exclusionary reasons in each case, we can surmise why the discussion arose in the first place. Judaism was in upheaval. Two major insurrections against the Romans had been launched in Palestine and had been bloodily suppressed. The Temple lay in ruins and its attendant priests, who were also the guardians of the Jewish patrimony, had been rendered useless. Like Josiah and Ezra before them, the rabbis attempted to reconstitute Judaism and, as in those earlier attempts, the linchpin of the restoration was Scripture.

Earlier, there had been unmistakable signs of community disintegration, but in the second century CE there was also a threat from within. The new Jesus movement among the Jews survived the insurrections; indeed, it showed unmistakable signs of vitality across the Jewish Diaspora. The second century was critical for both Jews and Christians. The two communities were struggling through a painful disengagement as the followers of Jesus the Messiah were banished from, or fled, the synagogues where the movement had been born. And they took their Scriptures with them.

The original Scriptural issue between Jews and Christians was not that the Christians had their own "Scripture" in the so-called New Testament—the Jews could and did simply ignore such since it had no great textual circulation among Jews—but rather that they had their own copies of the

Bible, which the rabbis had to decide were Scripture or not in the material sense. More determinative for the formation of a Jewish restrictive canon, however, was the fact that the Christians used works from the generously "open" canon of the Septuagint and Qumran, and of Second Temple Judaism generally, in their demonstration that Jesus was the Messiah. Some of those texts the rabbis rejected at their source, which was the Greek translation called the Septuagint: its broad inclusion of works and equally broad translation techniques aided the Christians' arguments for the Messiahship of Jesus. In the end the rabbis disavowed the Septuagint and many of the books in it.

The books rejected by the rabbis are known to some as the "Apocrypha," a word that means "concealed" or "set aside," but in English has come to stand for "spurious" or "inauthentic." Neither the name nor the category has much to do with the rabbis, however. The so-called Apocrypha are an "Old Testament" phenomenon. The rabbis had not created a special category for such works; they had simply eliminated them from their Bible manuscripts when they narrowed the list of sacred books that were earlier included in the Septuagint or were being read at Qumran. Why? What new and more stringent criteria eliminated those books? The rabbis who made the decision(s) do not say and, absent other direct or decisive evidence, it is generally thought that it was the aggressive Scriptural posture of the Christians that led the other Jews, now under the leadership of the rabbis, to reject the Septuagint; to commission new and far more literal Greek versions of Scripture; and, as a corollary, to narrow the range of the books that they, and the Christians, regarded as authoritative.

A substantial support for this argument is the fact that the Christians declined to follow their example. Jerome, a scholar concerned with Scriptural authenticity, may have "sequestered" such works, but the Christian Church, which was devoted to the Septuagint, stayed with what it regarded as tradition: the Christians' Old Testament continued to include Jerome's "Apocrypha" with no discrimination regarding their authority. Not until the Reformation, and then only in the Western Reform Churches, did authenticity as represented by the rabbis' Bible reassert itself over the "tradition" represented by the Septuagint. The Apocrypha were first separated from the canonical books and then eventually banished from Protestant Bibles altogether. In a curious reflex of the rabbis' rejection of the "apocryphal" props to the messianic argument, the Reformers rejected the use of the same texts for the Roman Church's construction and defense of the dogma called "Purgatory."

The Making of a "New" Testament

Biblia, "books," is simply a descriptive term. "New Testament," in contrast, is, like its correlative, "Old Testament," argumentative. But while "Old Testament" is prima facie a label pinned somewhat dismissively by Christians on Jewish Scripture, the texts collected under the rubric "New Testament" attempt to make the argument not that there is a "New" Covenant—that is assumed in this Jewish context—but rather that it was initiated and embodied in Jesus of Nazareth and why it is the exclusive possession of his followers.

The New Testament collection of books was born of an idea, a thoroughly Jewish idea that had been lodged in Jewish consciousness since the time of the Babylonian Exile. That time of troubles witnessed some practical optimism that can be discerned in the restorative and reforming measures of Ezra and Nehemiah. There was an attempt to return to traditional normalcy: under Ezra's guidance the Covenant was reconfirmed, the Temple rebuilt, and the old rituals resumed. Nehemiah undertook the eminently practical project of rebuilding Jerusalem's city walls and then bringing people to live within them. And both leaders laid heavy emphasis on the purification of tribal identity: all the returnees who had taken foreign wives, that is, non-Jewish women, were forced to send away both their wives and any children born of such unions (Ezra 9–10:44; Nehemiah 13:1–3, 23–27), on the grounds, previously unstated but later made explicit by the rabbis on the basis of these passages, that "Jewish descent" was matrilineal.

This practical optimism led to the rebuilding of a Jewish community in Judea, one strong enough to survive and even apparently to thrive, until the Romans expelled it from Judea in 135 CE. But it did not prevent another, much darker form of optimism from appearing in Jewish circles in the centuries after that hopeful restoration. We know it from the literary form known as apocalyptic, the famous "unveiling" of the End-Time that describes the traumatic but glorious final days of the cosmos when Israel would receive its ultimate (and only?) validation. If this is optimism, it is born of a deeply disappointed hope in human means employed to achieve human ends, in short, in history. The hopeful pragmatism of Ezra and Nehemiah had come to naught; the glory days of the Maccabees faded into twilight with the last inconsequential Hasmoneans and into ruin with Herod and his heirs. Behind were the Greeks and ahead were only the Romans, who many felt were too heavy a historical burden for the Jews to bear; only a Deus ex machina and His instrumental Messiah could now save them.

The mushroom-cloudlike gloaming of the apocalypses began as a prophetic gleam in the days of the Exile itself. Even before the political and social efforts at restoration made in Jerusalem after the return, another brighter and more spiritual hope was expressed most distinctly in Jeremiah, the Grand Prophet of the Exile. "The days are coming," God is heard to say, "when I will cut a new covenant with the House of Israel and the House of Judah." "It will not be like the one made with the ancients," the Lord continues through his prophet. "This will be written in their hearts. . . . No longer shall they teach one another, . . . for they shall all know Me. . . . I will forgive them their iniquities and will remember their sins no more" (31:31–33).

This divine promise of a "new covenant," a redrawing of the foundation document of the Chosen People, is one of the basic elements of the Christians' construction of a self-identity in the years following Jesus' death. And, like much else in that construct, it is a Jewish idea. "Covenant," here rendered "testament" by way of the Septuagint's Greek translation of the Hebrew *berit* as *diatheke*—and eventually in Latin as *testamentum,* is the Abrahamic cornerstone of the Jewish self-identification as God's Chosen People. God's Covenant with Israel underwent frequent renewals and rethinkings in the long history of that people, but for the Christians this clarion text of Jeremiah was the seed from which grew both the Christians' notion of their own election and eventually also their collection of texts, called the "New Covenant" or, with a notable preference for the Latinate term, the "New Testament." Early on this theme of a new and redrawn Covenant began to be echoed by the followers of Jesus (2 Cor. 3:6; Gal. 4:24–26); indeed, it may even have been introduced by Jesus himself, who refers to a "new Covenant" to be sealed by his blood on the occasion of his Eucharistic supper with his followers on the night before his execution (Mark 14:4 and parallels).

The exegetical history of this text of Jeremiah and of others like it during the long Second Temple period until its reemergence in Jesus' circle is largely concealed from our eyes, but it is possible to draw some conclusions. The Christian case for Jesus as Messiah rested, as we have seen, on the understanding of the body of Biblical texts—"Biblical" in the sense of the broader, prerabbinic canon visible in the Septuagint and at Qumran. From our perspective that understanding looks peculiarly "Christian," that is, given the events of Jesus' life, his followers combed the available Jewish literature to find texts that might be construed in a messianic sense and applied them to Jesus. It is unlikely to have happened quite so. Jesus' followers were Jews, not Christians, and their exegesis would have to have been recognizably, and plausibly, Jewish. More, Jesus was not the only messianic claimant of those days, and so the "evidence" for such claims must have been widely and fervently discussed. The era was one of "open" reading of texts, as the *pesher* commentaries from Qumran reveal, but even in those circumstances, if the textual evidence for Jesus' Messiahship adduced from Jeremiah or Isaiah or the Psalms appeared eccentric or outlandish to Jews, it would soon have been dismissed as rubbish.

"New Testament," then, which we generally think of as a book or a collection of texts, is considerably more: it is certainly that book, but it is also a thesis, a profoundly Jewish thesis, and an argument to demonstrate the truth of that thesis. Christians used the notion of a "New Covenant" from early on to collect and bundle together the body of texts that were thought to both describe (as in the Gospels) and explain (as in Paul's letters) how the events of Jesus' life, both the happenings and his teachings, make it certain that through him God had indeed initiated the "New Covenant/Testament" of prophetic promise.

The New Testament is a brief composed of a set of four biographies— "Gospels" or "Good News"—where both the case and the evidence is set forth. The case, which is laid out most directly in Matthew's Gospel, is that Jesus of Nazareth was the promised Messiah, and it is based on his fulfillment of Biblical prophecies thought to refer to that familiar eschatological figure of Second Temple Judaism. The prophecies and the events of Jesus' own life are juxtaposed so that the reader may readily see the connection and make the intended inference: Jesus was the Messiah. But further evidence was required since this same Jesus had died the apparently unmessianic death of a convicted criminal. He had been executed by the Romans but with what must have been widely understood as the agreement, maybe the connivance, or perhaps even at the initiative, of Judaism's highest priestly authorities. Additional prophecies of a "suffering servant" were produced from Isaiah (52:12–53:13) to show that this too had been foretold of the Messiah. And there was even more stunning support for the messianic case: witnesses could testify that the crucified Jesus had risen from the dead!

The case is continued in the Acts of the Apostles, though now perhaps intended for the encouragement of Jesus' followers rather than to convince other Jews to follow him. What is set forth in Acts is history—its author, Luke, is the most self-conscious historian among the New Testament writers—but there is still an argument beneath the narrative: the success of the movement as recorded in Acts is visibly and undeniably the work of the Holy Spirit. Jesus was indeed the Messiah and God has validated him by the miraculous growth of the Christian assemblies (*ekklesiai*) around the Mediterranean.

Paul stays firmly on message in his letters, which follow Acts in the New Testament. The teachings and healing miracles that Jesus worked during his lifetime are not, in Paul's eyes, at the heart of Jesus' Messiahship. Instead, Jesus' resurrection is the central event of the Christian faith. Paul passes the fundamental testimony that he himself had received, namely, "that Christ died for our sins in accordance with the Scripture, and that he was buried, and that he was raised on the third day in accordance with the Scriptures," as was attested by numerous reliable witnesses, many of whom were still alive (1 Cor. 15:3–9).

But Paul was no longer writing for the "Christian" Jews of Jesus' original fellowship nor for unbelievers; his audience was the mixed Christian congregations of the Jewish Diaspora, some Jewish followers of Jesus but more and more of them Gentiles. So Jewish doubts and hesitations are posed and answered, not yet in a polemical mode—that will come later—but to solve the dilemma that a once Jewish and now Christian faith posed for Jew and Gentile alike. There are pastoral concerns too, as Paul sketches the first outlines of a Christian life, not as it might be lived in provincial Galilee or exclusively Jewish Jerusalem but in the cosmopolitan societies of Antioch and Athens and Rome. And behind the encouragement and the counsels and the cautions are the outlines of a theology, Paul's own version of what it now means to be a Chosen People on the Mediterranean stage large enough to hold Jew and Gentile alike.

The other letters of the New Testament collection attributed to John and Jude and Peter and James are in the same vein, but in a lower theological register and on a narrower pastoral stage. And the urgency is fading: there is not the same need that drove Paul flying to the barricades. And finally, there is the book of Revelation, the Christians' contribution to the Age of Apocalypse. This is the Messiah Fulfilled, the anticipated closure that the First Coming did not bring about, the final validation of God's new Chosen People. The case is closed.

The once strident debate about the provenance, and particularly the date, of the collection of books called the "New Testament" has quieted down into a discussion of what exactly is meant by the term of preference for it, the "canon." For some, "canon" has meant simply a more or less distinct collection of books, and in that sense the New Testament, or at least part of it, is an early second-century phenomenon. If greater distinction or definition is required, then the birth of the New Testament must be pushed back to the mid-third century. And finally, if by "canon" is meant an explicitly exclusionary collection—these books and no others, what everyone later recognized as the New Testament—then we are speaking of a fourth-century or even later New Testament.

The New Testament as it now stands, that is, a defined and exclusive collection of books recognized as both sacred and authoritative by the Christian authorities, is undoubtedly that latter, fourth-century creation, and it first appears as such, with a list of contents identical to the twenty-seven books in our New Testament, in a letter of the bishop Athanasius of Alexandria written in 367 CE. But another and perhaps more reliable approach to the reality of the New Testament is to inspect what was actually being published and read by Christians as their Scripture. And here the evidence is rather different. Despite the fact that one or another of the early Christian authorities may have raised doubts regarding a given work, most often the Letter to the Hebrews or the book of Revelation, almost all the preserved manuscript evidence down to the seventh century are versions of what has been called the "Canonical Edition," that is, the one in our present New Testaments. Though some may have questioned certain inclusions, all the works in our New Testament were already in the published edition in use among Christians, probably from the second century onward.

Once the terms are sorted out—collection, restricted, sacred, authoritative—and whether we are thinking about preserved manuscripts, or canonical "lists," or canonical "functions" such as being used in worship, or else simply cited as authoritative in theological discourse, or both, there is actually little disagreement on the details. Shortly after Jesus' death, it was understood that something called the "Good News" (Gk. *euangelion*; Lt. *evangelium*) was the primary witness to the belief of his followers. The "Good News" was a message, still an oral message when Paul was preaching and writing to Christian congregations in the 50s, but with the "Good News according to Mark," it had also become a *text*, written, it appears to almost everyone, sometime around 70 CE. Paul speaks of "Gospels" in the plural, and the title phrase "according to Mark" underlines the fact that there was more than one version of the "Good News" in circulation; in fact, modern scholarship has retrieved one such that had disappeared under the editorial hands of Matthew and Luke, the so-called Q.

By the late second century, or perhaps even earlier, the many Gospels had been reduced to the four now represented in the New Testament, those "according to" Matthew, Mark, Luke, and John. The earliest physical evidence from the papyri and codices of the Gospels seems to indicate that these four texts were bundled together as a single copy, whether for private Christian devotion or public liturgical worship. There are no other candidates and no debates, and Ireneus, the bishop of Lyons writing in the last decades of the second century, can serenely explain why these four are Gospels, and only these four. At about the same time, the Syrian Tatian composed a Gospel "harmony"—an arrangement of the Gospels along a single chronological line—based exclusively, and without discussion, on these four. Tatian's work in fact points in two directions: first, that the four "canonical" Gospels had already reached a position of preeminence among Christians, but, second, they were as yet not so absolute in their authority that they could not be combined in a "harmony."

Though the expression was in use, there is no direct evidence that first- and second-century Christians, when they spoke of a "New Covenant" or "New Testament," were referring to an actual body of texts. The habit of calling the Jewish collection of books the "Old Testament" set in earlier than the parallel Christian text collection, so that when early contrasts were drawn between an "Old Testament" and a "New," the former refers to the Bible and the second to Jesus' redemptive acts and teaching that rendered the Biblical Covenant and the books that described it "Old." The Gospels, which bore witness to the "New Covenant," did not yet constitute it.

This is not to say that the Gospels, or Paul's letters for that matter, were not collected texts and did not circulate as such. The four Gospels eventually included in the New Testament seem to have come together conceptually and materially toward the end of the second Christian century at the latest. And though they enjoyed an unmistakable preeminence among Christians, they were not the only Gospels in circulation. At the end of the second century, a Gospel of Peter was being cited, in orthodox circles, and Clement of Alexandria (d. ca. 215) had a veritable library of Gospels at his disposal, including the immensely popular Protoevangelium of James, which filled in many of the details of Jesus' birth and childhood. Matthew, Mark, Luke, and John were copied and bound as a unit, but they did not yet possess exclusive claim to the title of "Gospel."

Paul's letters, another major component of the New Testament, were written before our Gospels—they are, in fact, the first Christian texts we know of—and were circulating as a collection at least by the end of the first century, though we cannot be sure of the exact contents of such collections. Individual letters were being cited as authoritative and passing from church to church throughout the second century, and possibly much earlier since Paul himself had urged it (Col. 4:16). The first detailed information we have of the contents of a Pauline *collection* comes from Marcion (ca. 148 CE), who attempted to construct a "New Testament" by excluding everything except Luke's Gospel (edited) and Paul's letters. His collection had ten letters: Galatians, 1 and 2 Corinthians, Romans, 1 and 2 Thessalonians, "Laodiceans" (probably Ephesians), Colossians (possibly with Philemon), and Philippians. Galatians apart, the order is approximately that of descending length—the same, generally speaking, as the suras in the Quran. The suspicion is that Marcion inherited the descending length order, which has been connected with the fit of the letters onto a standard papyrus roll (*volumen*), and that it was he who moved Galatians up to the front for his own theological reasons. The more accurate order of descending length, which puts Romans at the head, then 1 and 2 Corinthians, Ephesians, and then Galatians in its "normal" position, followed by Philippians, Colossians, 1 and 2 Thessalonians, and Philemon, is the most common in the early manuscripts.

The earliest manuscript to testify to this order is a papyrus (p^{46}) from circa 200 CE. This manuscript also includes, however, after Romans, the Letter to the Hebrews, which some churches, mostly Western Latin ones, doubted was by Paul, though it seems to have been widely accepted in the East—Origen is one glaring exception—as its inclusion in this papyrus manuscript attests. Modern scholarship, whose only criterion is authenticity, tends to agree with the Latins, that the Letter to the Hebrews is Pauline rather than from Paul himself. The same kind of doubts have hovered over the so-called Pastoral Letters, those addressed to Timothy and Titus, which are not in p[46]. Finally, internal, chiefly stylistic differences between Ephesians and the undoubtedly authentic letters have led some to think that this letter too came from another, but very similar, pen.

The third collection in the New Testament is that of the so-called Catholic Letters, "catholic" in the sense that they were not addressed to any individual church but rather to all Christians universally. Each of the letters has its own career. Some, like 1 Peter and 1 John, were widely recognized and cited, while others are mentioned only here but not there among the ancient authorities. As a collection, they seem not to have finally come together until the end of the third century, well after both the Paul collection and that of the four Gospels, and even then questions continued to be asked about one or other of them. Why they were assembled in the first place is unknown. Three of the authors—Peter, James, and John—were certainly preeminent in the earliest Christian circles, and their writings may have been intended, it has been suspected, as a counter to the overwhelming influence of Paul. If so, the project cannot be considered a success.

The books that eventually made up this New Testament did not begin as Scripture, and none of the authors represented in it imagined himself writing a sequel to the Bible: for them, as for all contemporary Jews, "Scripture" was the Bible, as that was constituted in their day. What they were writing, however, were briefs for Jesus as Messiah, the eschatological savior and redeemer of Israel. As we have seen, the cornerstone of the case is presented in the four portraits of Jesus called Gospels where his life is laid out in a particular way to demonstrate to contemporary Jewish audiences that Jesus of Nazareth was the Messiah promised in Scripture's prophetic books and awaited by many in Palestine and the Diaspora. The clinching argument was, of course, Jesus' own resurrection from the dead, the proof of which—the living Jesus—was observed by many eyewitnesses whose testimony the Gospels and the rest of the New Testament adduces. Taken together, that was the original kerygma or "preaching" of the "Good

News," and to confirm the case, the Acts of the Apostles shows the unmistakable signs of divine favor at work in the new movement.

This, then, is what constitutes the New Testament: documents that argue, out of Biblical prophecy and the eyewitness testimony to his own marvelous deeds, that Jesus was the Jewish Messiah and then begin to spell out the consequences of that conviction. The case is closed, rather oddly perhaps, by a dramatic presentation of a favorite Second Temple Jewish theme, an apocalypse, which is attributed to a certain John who was quickly identified by Christians with the Apostle John and the author of the Fourth Gospel. The case was not so much closed—the argument with other unconvinced Jews went on—as there was a growing conviction among Christians in the ongoing second century that all the primary evidence was in.

There were other consequential developments. Almost from the beginning, the Jesus movement had a second, less obvious but no less attentive audience in the non-Jews—*goyyim*, as the Jews called them, or "Gentiles," as the Latinized Greek had it (Gk. *ethne* > Lt. *nationes, gentes*)—in Palestine and in even greater numbers in the Diaspora. They had found Judaism interesting or attractive, among other things for its monotheism, and were now drawn to this new and apparently more universalistic Jewish sect. Their presence, if not in Jesus' immediate circle, then among the earliest cadres of converts, is already attested to in the writings that will make up the New Testament. It is witnessed by the fact that Jesus' Aramaic teaching—he may have known Greek but he certainly did not use it for his message—was soon being presented in that more broadly intelligible Hellenic koine. Sympathetic Gentiles appear here and there in the Gospel narratives and the Acts of the Apostles. There is Paul's relentless insistence on appealing directly to Gentile audiences; the subtle but highly consequential passage from the concept of a Jewish "Messiah," which was a notion unintelligible to most non-Jews of the day and whose Greek translation, *Christos*, was soon no more than Jesus' name, to that of a universal Savior (*soter*), a familiar and attractive notion to the Mediterranean Hellenes of the first and second centuries; and, finally, the movement's own perhaps belated recognition of where the future lay: "Go and preach the Gospel to all nations" is the command tacked on to the end of Matthew's Gospel. The New Testament passed, then, from being a Jewish brief to being a universal call: an invitation for "all nations" to accept

Jesus as their "Lord"—the resonance is still Jewish—and as a fully Gentile-accredited "Savior."

If the Christians very soon after Jesus' death began to collect and circulate collections of Paul's letters, and only slightly later the four Gospels of Matthew, Mark, Luke, and John, when did they come to regard them as "Scripture," sacred writings on a par with what they were already calling the "Old Testament"? The earliest evidence has also to do with Paul rather than the Gospels. The author of 2 Peter, which was most likely written at the end of the first or the beginning of the second century CE, when the expectation of the Second Coming was already fading (3:4–6), says that some people were twisting Paul's letters, "as they do the other Scriptures" (3:15–16).

Two prominent figures, whose lives fall in the second half of the second century CE, the Latin Tertullian (ca. 160–225) and the Greek Clement of Alexandria (ca. 150–215), both testify to the authority of most of the books in our New Testament, and this to the exclusion of all other Gospels and letters, though Clement seems to regard (as did some others) the Shepherd of Hermas and the *Didache* or Teachings of the Apostles as authoritative as well. An even more detailed Greek source is the Scripture scholar and theologian Origen (ca. 185–254). Though we know his views only through the summary of the fourth-century Church historian Eusebius, who may have tampered with his remarks, Origen recognized that Christian Scriptural writings could already be divided into "accepted" or "recognized" (as authentic), "doubtful" or "disputed," and, finally, "heretical" or, less delicately, "rubbish." Hebrews, for example, is "accepted," though "only God knows who wrote it," whereas 2 Peter is "disputed." Later Eusebius himself, though he does not use the word "canon" (which becomes common only in the next decade or two), does indicate which writings were considered "disputed" in his day: the Acts of Paul, the Shepherd of Hermas, the Revelation of Peter, the Letter of Barnabas, the Teachings of the Apostles, and possibly—Eusebius is not sure about this—the Revelation of John.

And so we reach the era of the ecumenical "canon," the "closed" or restricted list of accepted Scripture, a judgment made and verified by Church authority. There can be, of course, no "ecumenical" canon until there is an "ecumenical" Church, not as a conceptual body—Paul had already introduced a sense of a corporate body of believers who are the "body of Christ"—but as an institutionalized one. Arguably that latter "Great Church" came into existence—was perhaps summoned into existence by Constantine in 325 CE—at the Council of Nicea to confront the threat of Arianism. As we have seen, various Christian writings had long been regarded as sacred to the Christians, and hence a Scripture, in the sense that they were used in public and private devotions, were recited as part of the liturgy, or were cited as authoritative in theological argument. But now, beginning with the imperial Christian age of the emperors Constantine (r. 306–337) and Theodosius (r. 379–395), and, not coincidentally, with the birth of the Great Church as both a notion and an operative institution, writings that had been descriptively regarded as "consensually accepted" (*homologoumena*) by Christian churches (*ekklesiai*) were now normatively "prescribed" by the Universal Church (*ekklesia katholike*).

The prescribed works frequently appeared in the form of lists now called, with a nod to their academic origins, "canons." The same word used for the "things measured" also served for the "measure" itself, and Christian writers discussed the "canons" in this latter sense, the criteria that lay behind the lists. Chief among those criteria was undoubtedly orthodoxy, the congruence of any given work with what were regarded as universal Christian beliefs. If that criterion is patently theological, the other chief earmark of canonicity was somewhat more historical: the work in question had also to be "Apostolic." It seems doubtful, however, that the churches, and now the Great Church, looked upon this latter as a strictly historical criterion. Where "Apostolic" might mean for us only and exclusively "eyewitness," the fourth-century and later designation of "Apostolic" more likely spoke to the spiritually guaranteed probity of the witness than to the mere act of witnessing. But "Apostolic" carried with it nonetheless an assurance that the document was in fact an early, and hence reliable, witness to the New Covenant.

The "Old" and the "New" in the Covenant

After Paul it was chiefly Marcion (d. ca. 160), a Christian at Rome, who brought the Bible back to the center of Christian consciousness. Paul had attempted to "neutralize" the Bible for his new Gentile converts: the Torah was necessary and proper for its time, but in the new age of redemption in

Christ, it was no longer required. Christ's blood had washed away sin and with it the need for the Torah's guidance. Marcion's stance was far more radical. While Paul was meditating the prescriptions of Leviticus and Deuteronomy, Marcion took dead aim on Genesis. Adam's disobedience did not introduce sin into the world; the cosmos was sinful, root and branch, from the outset. And so too was Yahweh, the God who created it. The Greeks regarded the cosmos as perfect; Paul, as spoiled; Marcion, simply as evil.

And the contents were different. As we have already seen, the Christians kept in their Old Testament what eventually came to be called the Apocrypha, the broad range of books that the Jews had originally regarded as authoritative but had in the end repudiated; down to the Reformation, the Christians' Old Testament was longer than the Jews' Bible, and the Roman Catholic and Eastern Orthodox versions remain so today. But that is not the only difference in the two Scriptures that should be, on many grounds, identical. In both the Jewish Bible and the Christian Old Testament, the books that make up the collection had been editorially arranged or ordered, just as the books in the New Testament and the suras in the Quran have. The large categorical arrangement in the Bible—Torah, Prophets, Writings—probably reflects the chronological order of their assembly: the Torah and Prophets collections were already firm and closed even as the Writings were still being added.

As in much else in the editorial process surrounding Scripture, there is no direct evidence of why the Christians rearranged the books of the Bible in the manner they now appear, whether they were simply following another, variant Jewish order that the rabbis later discarded along with the Apocrypha, or whether there was a deliberate decision to alter the sequence, to end suggestively with the prophetic books, which lead directly from the promises to their fulfillment in Jesus, rather than with the ideologically nondescript Writings, which add little or nothing to the Covenantal idea.

From all the evidence, Christians began to talk about the *idea* of an Old and a New Testament before they applied those terms to a set of texts. The term "Old Testament" referred to the text of the Jewish Bible before Christians began to think of their own texts as a collection on a par with the Bible and eventually, of course, as a *part* of the Bible, where the latter term comes to mean a book that includes *both* the Old and the New Testament.

Before the end of the second century, the bishop Melito of Sardis (d. ca. 190) said he went to Palestine "to learn accurately the books of the Old Covenant." Ireneus of Lyons (ca. 130–200) explicitly contrasts the two Covenants and in some instances seems to be referring to two sets of books, as in his remark vis-à-vis 2 Corinthians 7 that the Apostles "granted certain precepts in the New Covenant similar to what God did in the Old Covenant."

By the turn into the third century there is no longer any doubt that Christians are talking about two collections of texts when they use the terms "Old" and "New Covenant." Clement of Alexandria (ca. 150–215) cites Matthew as "the voice of God heard in the New Covenant," though the more scholarly and careful Origen (ca. 185–254) still sensed that the term was a novel one, "the so-called Old and New Covenant," as he puts it. Both Clement and Origen, writing Greek, like Melito and Ireneus before them, used the standard Septuagint-based word *diatheke* for "Covenant" as both a concept and a text. When Latins began to speak of it, they had to devise their own terminology. Tertullian (ca. 160–225) preferred the word *instrumentum* for Scripture—as Erasmus later would, briefly—but he remarked that there was another word current, "each instrument, or testament (*testamentum*), as it is more usual to call it," and that latter term became the common one in the European languages.

It is not Marcion's cosmic pessimism that concerns us here but rather its Scriptural corollary. For Marcion the Bible was a genuine revelation, but if read correctly, by which Marcion meant literally—the Jews concealed the malice of the story by reading it allegorically—it was a revelation of an evil world and evil Creator God. That evil had been undone by Jesus' redemptive work, and so the Christian should now repudiate both Yahweh and the Bible describing his works. Marcion rejected the Old Testament not because it was false but because it was all too true. In its place he put the New Covenant, not (yet) a collection of texts like the Bible, but a message, the "Good News" of Jesus' mission and work and teaching.

Jewish Scripture was from the beginning essential to Christian claims regarding Jesus, and over the centuries arguments between the Christians and the Jews continued to center precisely on the interpretation of these texts. The Scriptural argument even finds an echo in the Quran's own apparent claim (61:6) that Muhammad, here called "Ahmad," was likewise foretold in Scripture, now, of course, understood as *both* the Torah (*Tawrat*) and Gospel (*Injil*), the Quran's only names for the Jewish and Christian Scriptures.

Marcion's self-assigned task of rearranging Scripture was probably impossible at that point, and its failure is reflected in the history of the Church. Even as Marcion was writing, Jews and Christians were separating in belief, in ritual, in their calendars. Christians left the synagogue, but they never left the Bible or severed the ties that bound their faith to the Jewish Scripture. They did, however, rename it. If Christianity was a New Covenant/Testament, then Judaism was the Old, enshrined in a Scripture that God himself had rendered not so much false—God's Word is never false—as passé by the New Testament of His son and the collection of works that bear witness to him, which the Christians likewise regarded as "Bible." Jesus had begun the process by anticipating his own death as the inauguration of a "New Covenant," and Paul completed it by designating the now "first" or "former" covenant as irredeemably "old."

The Christians' Old Testament was a different book from what the Jews read as their Bible. First, the Christians were reading it in translation, in the Greek Septuagint translation in the East, in Jerome's Latin so-called Vulgate version in the West. Many Jews were using translations as well, but they were quite different ones, more literal than the Christians' and always controlled by the rabbis' understanding of the Hebrew original. The Christians' knowledge of the Hebrew Bible diminished considerably after Jerome and did not revive until the polemicists of the late Middle Ages deemed it useful and the humanists of the Renaissance as necessary.

The Hebrew Bible and the Christians' translated versions also differ in their order. The Christians moved Chronicles from the end of the Bible to a position immediately following its twin, the two books of Kings, and this collection of histories was then closed with Ezra-Nehemiah, also promoted forward from its position close to the end of the Writings. The Writings, which in the Christian Old Testament included the non-Biblical books of Tobit, Esther, Maccabees, and others, comes immediately after the historical books. And finally there are the Prophets, from the Major Isaiah to the Minor Malachi, with Lamentations and Baruch spliced in after Jeremiah, and the apocryphally enhanced Daniel following Ezekiel. The Eastern Church's differs from the Western's chiefly in that it reads the Minor Prophets before the Major and so ends the Old Testament with Daniel rather than Malachi.

We have already witnessed the Christians' claim that Jesus of Nazareth, a Jewish man who was born in the troubled last days of King Herod (d. 4 BCE) and who, sometime around 28–30 CE, was executed by Pontius Pilate—one of the governors of what had become the Roman province of Judea—was the promised Messiah of Israel. The Christians' case rested on what has been termed a "strong reading" of various prophetic texts in the Bible, chiefly (60 percent) from the Psalms, Isaiah, and Deuteronomy, and on Jesus' fulfillment of them in his life and death. There were other claimants to Messiahship before and after Jesus, and those other claims too were inevitably grounded in the same or similar texts, many of them Biblical and many from the apocalyptic literature that had grown out of the same Scriptural soil.

It was, then, the Christian claim of Jesus' Messiahship, and the Scriptural argument used, from the Gospels onward, to support it, that tied Christians firmly to the Jewish Bible even in the face of powerful centrifugal forces. Christians of the second and third centuries, when their *religio* was no longer regarded as a type of Judaism by the Jews, or the Romans, or themselves, attempted to separate themselves from their former coreligionists by institutionalizing in Christian life what Paul had already sketched in Christian ideology in his Letter to the Romans. What was in Paul's eyes an obsolescent Torah, a tutor dismissed when the child grew into a man (Gal. 3:24–25), became for some Christians a dead letter and for others an encumbrance or an incubus.

We know that Marcion argued the rejection of the Jewish Bible, and we know why; what we do not know is how exactly he accomplished this formidable task. We are told that he banished Matthew's Gospel (along with Mark and John), where the argument for Jesus' fulfillment of the Biblical prophecies is most forcefully made. Marcion also took the editorial blue pencil to Luke: he removed from that Gospel all those Biblical passages that Luke, like Mark, adduced to demonstrate Jesus' Messiahship. He also cut all evidence of Jesus' humanity: his genealogy, the Nativity story, references to his family. But Marcion's problem runs deeper than that. In Luke, as in the other Gospels, the Bible is constantly on Jesus' tongue, as we might expect of any Jewish preacher of that time and place: twenty-three of the thirty-six books of the Bible, including all of the Pentateuch, Isaiah, Jeremiah, and Ezekiel as well as the Minor Prophets. To omit the Bible from the Gospel was to omit a substantial part of Jesus' message.

But what was the Bible? The premodern Christian tradition was not always aware—and we are scarcely better informed—of the first- and second-century Jewish debate about the contents of the Bible that led from the expansive view of the Septuagint and Qumran to the narrower canon of the rabbis of the third and fourth centuries. Christians left the Jewish mother ship in effect in the second century, and left it, moreover, in its Diaspora version, where the Greek Septuagint translation *was* Scripture and its reading in the synagogue was sometimes not even accompanied by the Hebrew original. But on two famous occasions at least some Christians were made critically aware of the difference between what they regarded as the Bible and what the Jews considered as Tanak.

The first occurred in the flurry of Christian scholarly interest in Hebrew initiated by the editorial work of the Egyptian scholar Origen (ca. 185–254). The fruit of Origen's labors was the enormous and cumbersome Hexapla, a six-columned edition of the Bible that juxtaposed the Septuagint with the original Hebrew and threw into the mix a number of later Jewish versions in Greek. We shall look more closely at the work of Jerome (ca. 340–420); it is enough here to note that he was a Latinist who had been working in Rome at the behest of Pope Damasus on improving the older Latin versions of the Old Testament, moved to the Middle East in 386, and took up the monastic life in Bethlehem. In the Christian library at Caesarea in Palestine he discovered Origen's own copy of the Hexapla, which he removed to his own library. The Hexapla graphically revealed what Jerome already knew, that not only the old Latin versions but the Septuagint itself had often strayed far from the Hebrew text then in use. He proposed to remedy the defect by basing his latest Latin translation not on the Septuagint but on the Hebrew itself.

Jerome discovered something else as well in his investigation of the Hebrew text of the Bible: what the Christians were calling their "Old Testament," which was in effect the Septuagint, included books the Jews did not regard as Scripture, namely, Tobit, Judith, Wisdom of Solomon, Ecclesiasticus/Ben Sirah, 1 and 2 Maccabees, and Baruch. And there were discrepancies in the texts of Esther and Daniel. At this point Jerome was deeply committed to allowing himself to be ruled by the Hebrew in both textual and what we would call "canonical" matters. He removed the "extraneous" books—which he labeled "apocrypha" or "set aside"—from his new Latin translation/edition of the Old Testament and he rearranged the order of the rest to more closely conform to that of the Hebrew Bible.

Jerome's re-Judaizing of the Jewish Bible did not take. The Septuagint's hold on Christianity's emerging Scriptural culture was too powerful to be pried loose even by Jerome. Augustine had argued that very point with Jerome, that it was more conducive to the unity of the Church that Christians, whether Greek-speaking Easterners or Latin-speaking Westerners, agree on what was Scripture and that the Septuagint provided the appropriate basis for such agreement. Jerome was not convinced, but in the end he had no control over the matter: copyists of the Latin edition soon began to restore Jerome's carefully "set aside" books to the main body of the Old Testament, where they remained down to the Reformation.

The Reformers, as we have seen, reverted to the contents of the Jewish Bible, in part because, like Jerome, they preferred authenticity to comity—a preference strongly buttressed by the growing influence of the humanists with their strong text-critical biases—and in part by the same kinds of theological perspectives that had winnowed the New Testament to begin with. The Reform rejection of Purgatory encouraged a rejection of Maccabees, where the doctrine found its principal proof text, just as Luther's embrace of a Pauline justification through faith led to his famous disparagement of the Letter of James—a modest enough statement of the case for good works—as "a letter of straw." The Protestant Old Testament looks more like the Jewish Bible, but not entirely, not necessarily, for Jewish reasons.

The Collection of the Quran

Muslims do not often speak of the "canon" of Scripture, not, certainly, in the sense that such discussions go on among Jews and Christians. The canons of both the Bible and the New Testament were in the end understood as restrictive or exclusionary lists of books included in the Scripture. For Muslims there is but one Book. When Muhammad's audience demanded of him a miracle to demonstrate that his pronouncements were truly divine revelations, the Prophet responded with a challenge: if you think what I say is the work of man, *you* bring a sura or Quran like it (2:23; 10:38; 11:13)! None did so. There are no pseudepigraphic Qurans, no Muslim apocrypha.

But the Quran is, for all that, a collection, and so the notion of exclusion-inclusion, if not the word "canon," does come into play. Were all the recollections of Muhammad's pronouncements authentic? Were there pronouncements, suras, as they came to be called, that were neglected or forgotten? These are two quite separate issues, the first of authenticity, the second of completeness, but they both have to do with the text of the Quran, or, since it has many parts—114 in the final count—the *collection* of the Quran.

Muslims have long had in their hands a standard text of the Quran, standard in the sense that the written consonantal text is invariable—in Arabic only the consonants are "written" and the vowels indicated by marks and symbols—while some variations of vocalization and pronunciation are permitted. This is the text reportedly prepared under the caliph Uthman sometime about 650 CE. While Uthman's text is thought to represent the base of the present Quran, it was a far from perfect guide for Muslims of that or the immediately following generations since it was written in a primitive and imperfect writing system without the diacritics that bring clarity to the consonant signs. It has been called "an elaborate mnemonic device" rather than anything we might identify as a text edition. Only when a fully articulated Arabic writing system was introduced at the turn into the eighth century did the real differences between local ways of "reading" the Quran became apparent. It took another century or more for those differences to be resolved, at least to the point that seven local variants were acknowledged as acceptable.

Today there are two widely used printed "editions" of the Quran that differ chiefly, albeit slightly, only in the numbering of the verses. The first is by the German scholar Gustav Flügel and was originally published in Leipzig in 1834; the other was published in Egypt in 1924 under commission from King Fu'ad and has been widely accepted as standard in the Muslim world. It chose one of the "readings" traditionally in use at Kufa and so rendered that the now de facto standard Muslim version of the Quran. Neither the German nor the Egyptian text represents what is called in Western circles a "critical edition," that is, one wherein all the extant manuscripts are arranged into families, variants traced backward closer and closer to the earliest redaction, and finally, in the face of the testimony of the antiquity of the texts and the likelihood of the variants, an edition is produced that represents the editor(s)' best judgment on what constituted the original text, with a notation of the variants and their sources.

This notion of what constitutes a critical edition is a Western scholarly construct with antecedents in Hellenistic Alexandria and perfected in nineteenth-century European academic circles. It provided the template for just such editions of the Bible and the New Testament, and Western scholars have attempted to do the same for the Quran for well over a century. A series of historical accidents and the daunting nature of the enterprise—mere access to the manuscripts appears almost as difficult as discovering where they are—have made its completion, at this juncture, seem extremely remote, and anyone working on the Quran has of necessity to use either of the two standard printed editions. For their part, Muslims are content with the integrity of the text they now possess, as well as with the authenticity of the accounts of how it came to them.

Muslim authors appear to know far more about the process by which the Quran was assembled or "collected" than do their Jewish or Christian counterparts about the canonization of the Bible and the New Testament. But there is no greater certitude in the accounts. According to the available Arab Muslim sources, all of them dating from a century or more after the event, there were three early attempts at "collecting" the Quran, that is, bringing the various incomplete versions in circulation among Muslims into a single authoritative ensemble. The first two caliphs, Abu Bakr (r. 632–634) and Umar (r. 634–644), are both said to have attempted such a collection, though apparently with only partial success, and only under the third caliph, Uthman (r. 644–656), was the project completed.

What happened on each of those three occasions is remarkably similar—close enough, at any rate, to suggest to some that we are here dealing with three different versions of the selfsame tradition. Why should that occur? Why tell the same story three times with only the names changed? One reason is that a later generation of Muslims were unsure exactly who was responsible and so they uncertainly attributed the collecting to each of the first three successors of the Prophet. Another is that the assembling actually occurred under Uthman, but because of his later unpopularity in many circles, the story was spread abroad that the far more respectable Umar or, better still, the venerable Abu Bakr had actually initiated the process.

As usual in such circumstances, the Western critical approach is to read the multiplicity of contradictory traditions as a sign that the facts were either unknown to or being manipulated by the early Muslims. If forced to choose, most Western students of Islam have opted for the Uthman story on the quite plausible grounds that no one would have invented such an important accomplishment for such an unpopular man. There have been far more radical suggestions, however. One is that Muhammad himself had "collected" the Quran and that later Muslims deliberately fogged that fact with these stories of caliphal intervention so lawyers might more easily manipulate the text. Another quite contrary theory is that the Quran was still in a state of editorial flux as late as the end of the seventh century, and that all stories of earlier recensions were an attempt to place the cachet of antiquity on an edition of much more recent vintage. Muslim scholarship, whether medieval or modern, tends, like traditional Christian treatments of the Gospels, to harmonize the traditions. Thus, according to the Muslims, we do not have three differing accounts of one event but, rather, various accounts of a single evolutionary process: what was begun under Abu Bakr and Umar was completed under Uthman.

Before we ask what precisely it was that began under Abu Bakr, we must take another look at the Quran itself, the now standard Quran, as a whole. It is divided, as we have seen, into 114 suras or chapters. The origins of the word *sura* are unknown, but it occurs in the body of the Quran itself (e.g., in 10:38; 11:13; 28:49), in contexts where the word can mean either "a revelation" or "a part of a revelation." After an opening sura that is clearly a prayer—the clearest example of such, perhaps, in the entire Quran—the suras are arranged in what can be generally discerned as a descending order of length. Attached to each sura is a name, chosen not randomly, it would appear, nor by any single discernible criterion. This name is followed by an indication, "Mecca" or "Medina," to denote its place of origin in Muhammad's career; and, finally, there is an indication of the number of verses, in Arabic *ayas*. The two latter notations are probably later additions, but the name of the sura may go far back into the tradition, and so too the ordering of the whole.

A later Muslim dogma asserted what is called the doctrine of the "inimitability" of the Quran, namely, that not merely the Quran's content but its style and diction signal its divine origin. A Muslim dogma is not like a Christian one in that there is no Islamic body or individual competent to define any given proposition as an essential part of the faith; Muslim "dogma" is, rather, a hardened consensus, as this one is. Another such consensual dogma is that the Quran is the eternal and uncreated Word of God, but these qualities have never been extended to cover either the order or the arrangement of the version we possess since Muslims have long conceded that both those operations took place after the Prophet's death.

Whatever the literal or metaphorical truth of the judgment of divine origins, the construction of the text shows all too clearly the presence of very mortal editors; and, in the opinion of many, less than skillful ones at that. "Perfunctory in the linking of disparate materials, and given to the repetition of whole passages in variant versions" is one Western verdict on the Quran, which has also been described, more famously, as "a true *corpus vile*; no one cares how much it is chopped up." Or, we might emend, equally plausibly, no one dared touch texts that were regarded as the revealed Word of God and that had already accumulated into a kind of sacred sorites, which the editors were reluctant to disturb in any substantial way. How precisely does one edit revelation, particularly when it is in the form of a mixed discourse—mixed in mood, style, and length—that had proceeded at different times and places from the mouth of a single individual, and he the Envoy of God?

The condition of the Quran, the Quran that emerged from Uthman's supposed editorial atelier, is, with all its rough seams and patches, evidence that the evolutionary process may well have been the actual one: that the material of the Quran was continuously being collected from the time of Muhammad's death in 632 down to what seems to be signaled as the end of the collection process sometime about 650 CE, during the caliphate of Uthman. None of those "redactions" was, however, quite as "official" as the later tradition painted them, which would explain the literally thousands of variants that have shown up in the Quranic citations by authors writing in the early centuries of Islam, in inscriptions on monuments, in papyrus fragments, and now, more recently, even in complete early manuscripts of the Quran.

The official version of how the work of collection began attributes to Muhammad's close associate (and the eventual second caliph) Umar ibn al-Khattab a concern that those who had memorized the Quran—what we are led to think of as an official group called "the Reciters" (*al-qurra*)—were being killed in large numbers in battles against apostates in central Arabia a year or so after Muhammad's death. And so he asked Abu Bakr, another close associate and Muhammad's immediate successor as head of the Muslim community, to sponsor a collection of all the known fragments of the Quran, "whether," as the famous phrase goes, "written on palm leaves or flat stones or the hearts of men." The work was entrusted to Zayd ibn Thabit, Muhammad's amanuensis, who had presumably been responsible for writing down some of the revelations during the Prophet's lifetime. Zayd wrote out the material on (unbound) "sheets," in Arabic, *suhuf*, the same word used in the Quran to describe the revealed books of Moses and Abraham. The resultant text was passed on from Abu Bakr to his caliphal successor Umar, and then, at the latter's death in 644 CE, to his daughter Hafsa, who was also one of Muhammad's widows.

Even if the story of a compilation under Abu Bakr is true, there were other, less complete collections of the Quran in some of the other centers to which Islam had spread in Syria and Iraq. We know very little about them except consistent traditions that (1) they were written texts; (2) they had readings different from those later found in Uthman's text, though none of them has proven to be very significant; (3) they contained material not in the Uthmanic text, evidence that our Quran, while authentic, is not necessarily complete; and (4) they were not arranged in chronological order, a good indication that even the first generation of Muslims was little concerned with the chronology of the suras.

Finally, we arrive at the Uthmanic recension. The date is about 650 CE, and this time the alleged motive for the "collection" is a dispute among the different Muslim army units serving in Armenia over the correct recitation of the Quran in their prayers. So, the story goes, Uthman once again summoned Zayd ibn Thabit and two other Meccans to prepare a definitive text. They got hold of the "sheets" entrusted to Hafsa bint Umar and collated them with other material, now, presumably, most of it written. There is an additional element in the story here: the commission was instructed, in case of doubts about the correct form of words, to follow the dialect of the Quraysh, the paramount tribe of Mecca, and the one to which Muhammad himself had belonged. When the work was completed, Uthman, who ruled his rapidly expanding empire from Medina, sent copies to Kufa and Basra in Iraq, to Damascus, and to Mecca and ordered all other versions destroyed. Even those who accept the story cannot fail to note first, that our Quran is not, in fact, in the Quraysh dialect, and second, that the story of the destruction of all other versions is also contradicted in fact; the latter was probably a fillip added to give increased authority to Uthman's version.

All the evidence indicates that the process of fixing the text of Islam's

Sacred Book went on after Uthman's collection, chiefly through improvements in the manner of writing Arabic. But the caliph's enterprise was thought to have accomplished two important things in addition to establishing a "written consonantal outline": first, it stabilized the content of each sura, and second, it arranged the suras in order, the same content and the same order we find in our present Quran.

If Uthman's "edition" of the Quran stabilized the contents of the suras or chapters, did it also create them? The suras vary widely in length, from the two verses of sura 112 to the 286 verses of sura 2. Moreover, many of the suras are transparently composite. If we take the very early Meccan sura 74, for example, we note that verse 26 affirms that one of Muhammad's opponents will be flung into "the burning." This latter is apparently a new word or usage, since it is immediately followed (v. 27) by the stereotyped phrase used to signal a gloss: "What will explain to you what 'the burning' is?" There quickly follow verses characterizing "the burning" for the audience. The last of these (v. 30) says "over it are nineteen." Nineteen what? And why nineteen? The same questions must have occurred to others in Mecca, and perhaps in Medina as well, since verse 31 is a long, rambling, and quite combative rejoinder to those who had made an issue over "nineteen." The verse is obviously intrusive, a later insertion in a wholly different style from what precedes and follows. There are many such in the Quran. Finally, there occurs at verse 32 what appears to be a seam in the composition, a series of oaths that typically begin the early Meccan suras and that may here represent the beginning of a new pronouncement.

Not all the suras of the Quran are composites, of course. Among the longer ones, suras 12, 19, and 26, for example, show signs of finished, even polished composition; among the shorter, suras like 87 and 104 are obvious examples of single units. But many others of what we have called the "chapters" of the Quran are in fact composites and pose to the historian the larger question of the unity of the work and the variety within it. On its own testimony, the entire Quran is certainly to be thought of as constituting a book, quite like those of the Jews and the Christians (3:3–4). And yet, again by its own witness, it was "sent down" to the Prophet piecemeal (17:106; 25:32). At first glance we might think that the "divisions" and the "well-ordered stages" referred to in the last cited text might refer to the suras, the 114 well-marked divisions into which the Quran is currently divided. But the suras themselves are divided into verses (*aya*s), and it is conceivable that these latter might be the unit of revelation; indeed, all three Arabic terms, *qur'an, sura,* and *aya,* are used in the text to describe a unit of revelation.

The possibility that the Quran was revealed verse by single verse may be ruled out almost immediately since the verses are often bound together by a repetitive assonance, to form what appear to be in many instances what we might call a strophe, a unit of poetical composition, though here of a very loose type and of various lengths and rhythms. Were these strophes, then, the short, original units of revelation? It would appear not since the line of thought often spills over from strophe to strophe. Strophism, the sudden shift of assonance or rhythm into either a totally different line of thought or prose diction, may indicate, in the first case, the end of a revelational unit or, in the second, the presence of an interpolation.

Although assonance and rhythm are useful indicators for studying many of the earliest suras, these criteria desert us when we pass into the later Meccan period and the entire body of Medina suras. We can still see sudden shifts in thought or focus that may indicate different revelational "moments," but no longer by the external criteria of assonance and rhythm. And absent those indicators, the very division into verses begins to be suspect, particularly when we discover that the division of the text into verses does not appear in the very earliest manuscripts of the Quran.

The abrupt changes of subject, diction, rhythm, and rhyme that strongly suggest a pasteup of Muhammad's pronouncements occur throughout the Quran. There are, in short, more than 114 "revelations" in the Quran, a fact apparent to Muslim as well as non-Muslim students of the text, though they disagree who is responsible for such editing. One Muslim tradition from Ibn Abbas (d. 688), a nephew of the Prophet, has Muhammad instructing his scribe after the revelation of some verses, "put those verses in the sura in which such-and-such is mentioned." The report thus shows Muhammad as his own editor, a view that runs counter to the general Muslim tradition, and it has been argued that such an odd tradition can have no other purpose than to deflect criticism from the Uthmanic recension, which must, in fact, have edited the contents of the suras.

Among Western critics—the Muslims' theological aesthetic of the "inimitability" of the Quran bars them from this type of analysis—the judgment that many of the suras are pastiches, while general, is by no means unanimous, and a case has been made that at least the Meccan suras represent structured unities, and that their composition as such was the work of Muhammad. It is difficult to know how far the editorial work extended, but the second point seems correct: it is difficult to imagine any scribe or collector, even under caliphal mandate, "editing" the Word of God, unless there was Muhammad's own precedent to encourage him. As for the "unity" of the suras, both sides in the debate, those who wish to dissolve them into small units—a couple of verses, at most—and those who argue for some degree of intrinsic unity to the suras, may be correct.

Even if we except the clear interpolations, the early revelations do give the appearance of having been assembled, though without a great deal of regard for logic or consistency. Two motives suggest themselves. The first is liturgical. Very early on, in sura 73:1–5, Muhammad himself is instructed to spend part of the night "reciting the Recitation in measured fashion." The injunction does not refer here to the public announcement of the Quran—it is, after all, night—but rather to a liturgical action. Even more clearly, sura 29:45 commands Muhammad to "follow what has been sent to you of the Book by inspiration and establish prayer," where the first command appears to refer to the public promulgation of God's revealed message, and the second to its use in liturgical prayer. In short, the early Muslims prayed the Quran after they had heard it recited by the Prophet, and for this purpose some of the pronouncements may have been joined to make units appropriate for liturgical repetition, where neither internal logic nor consistency is demanded if the words are indeed from God.

The second motive has left no such telltale signs in the text itself, but we know with some certainty that large parts of the Quran were memorized—we are assured that some individuals had memorized it all—and to accomplish this, or at least facilitate it, some assemblage was required. The smaller units were joined together in some rough fashion to form larger ones with some internal integrity. In both instances, whether for liturgical purposes or memorization, the "editor" was doubtless Muhammad, and it was he too who must later have inserted prose clarifications or annotations into some of these already assembled units.

Today the Quran is often memorized as a whole, but we must assume that originally the revelations would have been memorized as they poured forth piecemeal from the Prophet's mouth. And since there were, as we shall see, repeat performances of the suras as well as signs within that they were emended, possibly by the Prophet himself, it seems quite likely that the revelations were memorized only when Muhammad judged them ready for memorization and repetition by the believers, and under his supervision. This may explain the seemingly senseless order of the suras according to their (nearly) descending length: the order made no difference since there never was a chronological order to the suras as units of liturgical recitation.

The present suras, most of them perhaps, do not to seem to represent units of revelation from another perspective. Many seem quite too long for any performance setting we can imagine—sura 2 is 286 verses long!—and many others show signs of the junctures where different revelations have been joined. And in one instance, suras 105 and 106, what was a single sura has somewhat puzzlingly been divided into two, rendering the first obscure and the second unintelligible.

There are, then, any number of signs of editorial activity within the Book, something that must have already been obvious to its original audience since the Quran—which is very sensitive to criticism—itself seems to refer to it. In sura 75 (16–18), in lines which seem an intrusion since they are addressed to Muhammad personally and have no relevance to a Meccan audience, God—if it is God speaking and not Muhammad—tells the Prophet not to hasten his delivery since "Ours is the collection of it [the Quran] and Ours the reciting of it. When We recite it, you follow the reciting of it. And afterward Ours is the explaining of it." Thus God recites and Muhammad follows His example. But God also "collects" or "assembles" the revelation and, we assume, here too Muhammad follows His lead. If "collection" refers to the assembling of the discrete units of revelation into suras, we can observe some of the points of juncture. The rhyme or assonance scheme is suddenly altered within suras, often accompanied by equally abrupt changes of subject. There are breaks in syntax, and pronouns sometimes do not agree with their antecedents. Somebody was working on the text, and without much concern for concealing his work.

The Quran also addresses anonymous charges that Muhammad had somehow "altered" his revelation, though the complaint appears to refer to his changing of position, or putting forth contradictory positions, rather than to careless editing. The Quran's response is threefold, though spread out across a number of suras. The first (2:106 and cf. 87:6) is a straightforward admission that the Prophet had indeed forgotten some of what had been sent down to him. The second is quite remarkable: God has on occasion permitted Satan to suggest (certainly not reveal!) certain verses, which God later removes from the Quran (22:52).

⊗⟨⊗⟩ | *Note: The Satanic Verses.*

We would know little of what to make of these so-called Satanic verses except that a twelfth-century commentator offhandedly gives us an example. Muhammad, his mission failing, was hoping for something conciliatory from his Lord to win over the stubbornly unbelieving Meccans. Satan obliged by casting into the Prophet's mind some verses saying in effect that it was possible to worship the One True God and at the same time venerate the three goddesses called "the Daughters of God." God of course intervened, and the offending verses were removed from sura 22:52, whose present verses are all agreeably orthodox. But not, we may add, from the minds of the Meccans. Why did this subject come up? Were there more "withdrawn" verses, "revealed" but then withdrawn from the Quran by the Prophet, his critics must certainly have said— enough of them to provoke the skepticism behind this explanation?

Finally, there is an explanation for Quranic alterations that has no parallel in the other Scriptures and has had profound effects on Islamic law. God, it is explained (16:101), sometimes abrogates or cancels parts of the Quran and puts in something better, but without necessarily removing the cancelled verses. This astonishing statement that some (unspecified) verses of the Quran no longer apply, if it seems to have had little effect on Islamic theology, which chose not to deal with the notion of God changing His own revelation, did get the attention of the lawyers who used "abrogation," as perhaps Muhammad himself was doing, to resolve the Quran's apparent contradictions.

The charge to which these passages were responding was obviously that the alterations signaled a change in the Quran's direction or, in the view of the Meccan skeptics, who were not much interested in theology, that Muhammad was waffling or at least trimming his sails to shifting local breezes. Changes there certainly were in the Quran, at least in the one we now have in our hands. The present order of the suras is generally thought to be the work of later editors, as well as the name and other title matter at the heads of the suras, including the "mysterious letters" that appear in combination at the head of only twenty-nine of them. The early Muslims believed, however, that the arrangement of the revealed matter into suras, or parts of suras, was the work of Muhammad himself. Most moderns are inclined to agree. Would anyone but the Prophet have dared to have followed the first nineteen poetic verses of sura 73 with the lump of prose that is verse 20? To insert the Medina-like verses 1–11 into the Meccan sura 29, or verses 29–30 into Meccan sura 53?

The answer may well be "yes," however, if we look upon all such as precisely the kinds of changes that would be made in a literary-textual context rather than in an oral one. Would a poet-editor so blatantly violate his own rhyme, assonance, or metrical scheme? So violently interrupt the stylistic or conceptual form of a piece? Rather, the editing appears done with a text editor's blue pencil, and we can be reasonably certain that Muhammad possessed neither the metaphorical blue pencil nor the ability to use one. If this editing was textual, as it seems it must have been, it was done by someone other than the Prophet of Islam.

For the present we cannot reconstitute out of our Quran the original revelations, or at least their original Quranic form. The earliest suras are quite brief (3–5 lines), but they grow longer even at Mecca, whether from Muhammad's growing skill in the medium or his increasing confidence in the message and in himself. This was, after all, the reluctant man who waited two or three years after his first revelation before venturing into public with it. We cannot ascertain if there was some conscious or unconscious limit to what he could receive or perhaps to what his followers could memorize on any given occasion. The *Iliad* and the *Odyssey*, both longer than the whole Quran, were not recited in one session, and there too an editor, in this instance a very literary editor and not just a scissors-and-paste artist like the one who glued together various suras of the Quran, refashioned the original recitation units into "books" so skillfully that we can no longer discern them.

These are essentially editorial questions posed in connection with the earliest putting together of the Quran, a process that lasted most of Muhammad's prophetic career. His death inaugurated a new process, an attempt, or perhaps attempts, at a collection of all the suras created by the Prophet and their arrangement in some kind of order, an order that had not existed theretofore. Eventually we shall have to address the even more fundamental issue of the size and shape and the manner of the revelations, the words that proceeded from the mouth of the Prophet that constituted the *Urstoff* of both the suras and Islam.

For the moment, however, we return to the two "canonical" questions with which we began. Is everything in the Quran authentically from the mouth of Muhammad? Muslims answer resoundingly "yes," and non-Muslims have found no evidence to the contrary: there is no sign of serious interpolations in the Quran. There is evidence of insertions, but they all, or almost all, appear to be from Muhammad himself. The evidence surrounding the other question—whether the Quran is complete—is equally strong. The Muslim tradition insists—and, the reasoning goes, no one would invent such a troubling notion—that there were either in circulation or in early Muslims' recollections pronouncements from Muhammad that were understood as revelation but were not included in Uthman's text of the Quran. In short, abundant anecdotal testimony indicates our Quran is not complete. But it is certainly closed, as God had intended, and there were no known Muslim attempts to reopen the corpus and restore, in whatever degree was possible, the missing parts.

If we stand back and regard the processes that led to the final stages of Holy Scripture, the books we hold in our hands, it is transparently clear that what went on with regard to the Quran is quite different from the parallel process with the Bible and the New Testament. The latter two are complex assemblages shaped by an idea (the Covenant, Messiahship), and the community of believers had to discern and decide which individual works witnessed the idea and so belonged in the complex and which did not. The issue was one of authenticity. For the Muslims, the issue in the collection of the Quran was one of accuracy. The Jewish and Christian canonists created a collection; the Muslims, a book. Though others may have begun the task before them, they scrutinized and assembled the Prophet's message, word by vocalized word, verse by stopped verse, strophe by unified strophe, sura by edited sura; and then they arranged and identified all the parts they had in effect made.

Chapter 3

Reciters, Rhapsodes, and Scribes

How the Bible Reached Us

ॐ⟨⑥⟩ॐ

W e have now seen what is *in* Scripture. We have looked briefly at its material contents and then at the assembled parts that make it up, whether they are called books, as in the Bible and the New Testament, or suras, as they are named in the Quran. And some explanations have been put forward as to when and how and why these collections came into existence. When we attempt to probe deeper, to look at the parts themselves and ask where they came from or how and when *they* were composed, the answers become progressively more difficult. Not only is the evidence slimmer; the protective dogmatic mantle around both questions and answers grows thicker and firmer.

The believers have, of course, a ready answer to where these writings, these collections of parts, came from. "From God" is one Jewish (and Christian) response to the question as it refers to the Bible, and much the same answer is forthcoming when the question is posed to Christians and Muslims regarding the New Testament and the Quran. God does indeed have a great deal to say in the Bible, particularly early in the collection. But the voices of His interlocutors are also loud and clear throughout, and there is, besides, an authorial voice of a narrator, who is sometimes identified—"These hymns are David's"; "This Wisdom is Solomon's"— but just as often is not, not at least in the text, though later generations of Jews thought they knew exactly who had "written," or better, composed, each book of the Bible.

Although many of the books of the Bible and all of those of the New Testament have authors' names attached to them, the Quran has no such ascription. It calls itself both a "Recitation" (*qur'an*) and a "Book" (*kitab*). The first suggests not an author but a performer, the one who recites. Though there is no doubt in anyone's mind that the reciter was Muhammad, Muslims do not call it "The Recitation of Muhammad" since for them the emphasis is not on a "Recitation by" but a "Recitation from," and there is equally no doubt that the "Recitation" was from God. Thus, while Jews and Christians have no hesitation in ascribing human authors to all the books included in their multivolumed Scripture, Muslims steadfastly refuse to do so.

These differences translate themselves into differing explanations of how God communicates with His creatures. In terms of directness or immediacy, at one end of the scale stand the Muslims, who believe that God sends down verbal messages to His chosen prophet, who then *repeats* them exactly as he heard them. At the other end of the scale is the Christian view that the authors are inspired by God, more specifically, the Holy Spirit, to write down the story of a revelation. In Christianity Jesus is, of course, the formal revelation and not the words of Scripture, which are simply, albeit inerrantly, *about* Jesus.

The Matter of Authorship

Jewish tradition readily concedes both the divine and the human element in the Tanak. The issue of origins does not seem to have been of much concern or interest in the era when the Bible was being assembled and shaped, but when Jews later gave thought to the matter of revelation, they regarded the authorship of most of the books of the finished Scripture somewhat on the Christian model, that is, the books from Joshua to 2 Kings and all the books collected in the "Writings" were "inspired" like the Gospels rather than "revealed" like the Quran. Where Quran-like revelation occurs in the Bible is in the stretch from Exodus 20 ("God spoke all these words") to the end of Numbers, which are presumably everything Moses heard on Sinai and then pronounced to the Israelites, as we would now express it, as well as inscribing them in his books.

Somewhat more ambiguous are the prophets' books in the Bible. Did the prophets pronounce and then have written down exactly what they heard, or were they "inspired" to deliver a message that was then couched in their own terms? Their manner of expression—"and God said . . ."—may make us incline toward the former, but it must be remembered that all the prophets are given author's credits in the books preserved in their names. "The prophecies of Isaiah" is as natural an expression for the Jew or the Christian as "the recitation of Muhammad" is unlikely for the Muslim.

When we turn to the Biblical books themselves, we note that some of them do have authors' names attached to them, as already remarked. The traditional attribution of authors to books of the Bible is in some cases fairly obvious (David for the Psalms, Ezekiel for his own book), but in others there is a recognition by Jews that there were some other (and very well known!) editors at work. Thus, according to the rabbis who attempted to straighten out the matter of authorship, "Samuel wrote his own book and the books of Judges and Ruth. . . . Jeremiah wrote his own book and the book of Kings and Lamentations. Ezekiel and his group wrote Isaiah, Proverbs, and the Song of Songs. The men of the Great Synagogue wrote Ezekiel, the Twelve (Minor Prophets), Daniel, and Esther." These facile and interesting attributions did not attract much notice from either Jews or Christians, perhaps because there seemed so little at stake, and one guess, if it made sense, was quite as good as another. But one attribution that did provoke comment was the most fundamental of all and cast its divinely derived authority over all the other books in the collection. That was the identification of Moses as the author of all five books that make up the initial five-volume Pentateuch.

Early Jewish literary polemic with the Gentiles, like those of Philo and Josephus, seems mostly directed to clearing up Gentile misconceptions about Jews or to protesting to the Gentiles their treatment of Jews or the abridgment of recognized Jewish privileges. But the Christians quickly became engaged with pagan intellectuals on a somewhat different level. These latter, many of whom were the Christians' former colleagues or classmates, had apparently struck directly at the authority of what both Jews and Christians regarded as Scripture, that is, the Bible. Philo, the profoundly Hellenized Alexandrian Jew of the late first century BCE, could solemnly instruct his readers that their hero (and his!), Plato, may well have borrowed material for his *Timaeus* from the earlier Jewish author Moses. Two centuries later, Origen, another Alexandrian intellectual, but this time a Christian, had to answer, or rather, to dismiss, pagan allegations that Moses could not have been the author of the Pentateuch to begin with, that the whole thing was a recent forgery. But the pagans eventually disappeared from both the streets and the university, and, with them, the problem of Scripture authorship, at least for the moment.

The issue of the author of the Pentateuch arose again, however, and this time not from the skeptical goyyim but from within the Jewish community itself. The Arabized Spaniards Ibn Yashush (d. 1056) in the eleventh century and Abraham ibn Ezra (1089–1164) in the twelfth both found material in the Five Books that seemed to postdate Moses in either content or style, and more of it than merely the already notorious last verse of Deuteronomy that tells of the death of Moses. But the furthest they were willing to go was to suggest that the offending passages must have been later interpolations in Moses' writings. By the fifteenth century Christians were expressing some of the same reservations, but in the sixteenth century, when Europe's new breed of humanists were casting a harshly critical light on ancient texts, including that of the Scripture, Andreas Karlstadt (1480–1541), a radical reformer and the most prominent of the Protestant Biblical scholars, expressed fundamental doubts about the Mosaic authorship of the Pentateuch.

This was a serious challenge to Scripture and there were various attempts at saving Mosaic authorship, and so the authority of what he had written, by positing the existence of a series of later, anonymous, and freewheeling, editors of the Mosaic original. By the next century there were, however, open denials of Mosaic authorship of the Pentateuch: the agnostic Thomas Hobbes (d. 1679) in England, the Jew Baruch Spinoza (d. 1677) in Holland, and the Catholic Richard Simon (d. 1712) in France all denied that Moses was the author of anything we now read in the Bible. Spinoza was excommunicated by his Sephardic community for his views and Simon's work was put on the Church's *Index of Prohibited Books*, but the damage had been done: the issue of Biblical authorship was formally open to critical discussion.

The Higher Criticism of the Bible

That discussion began in earnest in the nineteenth century, chiefly in liberal Protestant circles in German universities, and though it began with the Bible, the critical approach to Scripture was soon turned in the direction of first the New Testament and then the Quran. By the early twentieth century there were in Europe and North America numerous practitioners of the "Higher Criticism" of Scripture and a growing body of scholarly artifacts—dictionaries, concordances, grammars, and encyclopedias—as well as collections of archaeological and ethnographic data to assist in the enterprise.

The Higher Criticism was understood to be the application of rational criteria borrowed from literary and historical critics of classical texts to the texts that the believers called Scripture. For the Higher Critics, however, most of whom were believers and some even churchmen, Scripture in this context was no more than another collection of ancient documents, no different from the *Iliad* or the *Histories* of Livy. No matter that the critical project had not always been carried out either dispassionately or even rationally; or that Scripture was *not* Livy but works in which there had been an infinity of human investment, a matter, literally, of Eternal Life or Death.

Though the Higher Criticism was begun by Protestants, Jews and even, belatedly, Roman Catholics joined in this critical-analytical approach to Scripture; indeed, Jews are now the lead scholars in the Higher (Middle and Lower) Criticism of the Bible, though Christians continue to be actively engaged in it. Christians dominate in New Testament criticism, in recent decades chiefly American Christians and most of them from Evangelical backgrounds. Jews too have become increasingly drawn to the critical analysis of what are arguably Jewish documents in the New Testament, or at least documents about an important Jew, namely, the Gospels. Jews and Christians alike have now addressed the Quran in critical terms for more than a century and a half, but not so the Muslims. Nor have the Muslims interested themselves in either the Bible or the Gospels. The ideological mantle around those two Scriptures is still too dense and too intimidating—as it still is to many Jews and Christians—to allow them to be approached as simply another set of documents.

Few modern students of the Bible would agree with the rabbis' identification of the authors of the books that make it up. Indeed, many would prefer to avoid the question of whether such individuals actually existed, much less wrote the books of the Bible. The Bible's human "authors," if that is even the appropriate term, which seems unlikely, are anonymous;

attention is now focused instead on a later generation of Israelites, scribes, and likewise mostly anonymous, who "fashioned" or "redacted" the books as we now have them.

But if anonymous, or corporate, or community "authorship" is likely in the instance of historical annals like Samuel, Kings, or Chronicles, and even more convincing when it is a question of mythic accounts like Genesis, or such distant tales as Exodus, there is no good reason not to think that David was the actual author of most, or many, or some, of the psalms attributed to him in the Bible, that the person of Ezekiel stands behind the prophecies attributed to him, or Jeremiah behind his, or to deny that there is at least one "real" Isaiah behind the two or three prophets whose work has been discerned in the book that bears that name.

Is it possible to proceed any further? An early nucleus of the Bible may have been constituted, as we have seen, by the series of books running from Genesis down to the section of Kings describing the discovery of a "scroll of the Law" in the Jerusalem Temple during the reign of King Josiah. While most students of the matter are content simply to have disengaged that core, some few are willing to ask who assembled this particular version of "Deuteronomic history"; or perhaps, since the era was one of relatively widespread literacy in both courtly and religious circles, where scribes did service for both, who "wrote" this extraordinary collection of works.

Composing and Performing

The founders and followers of the Higher Criticism were above all searching for documentary sources for the books of the Bible. We, however, have a wispier matter at hand: we are inquiring after the authors of those books. In the context we are now examining, it must be insisted, the designation "author" has nothing to do with writing. Composers living in an oral culture, like that in which the oldest books of our Bible came into existence, worked first of all in their heads, and in private, and then completed the process of composing in the course of performing, and reperforming, their work. At the outset the composer and the performer were the same, and then, as a piece became better known, it might find its way into the local or tribal or ethnic repertoire and be performed, or repeated, by others who were not its maker.

The oral performer, the one whose work is good enough to survive, does not, of course, create out of nothing. There is already in existence a body of performed tradition that can be drawn upon and a complex of conventions that will formally shape the work. That tradition consists in a pool of experience-tested language and diction, of frames and formulas, themes and tropes that the performer can, and indeed must, employ. All those formal elements are also conventions he or she will be expected to observe. There doubtless are absolute innovators among them, but the oral composer-performers to whom we are here referring stood at the peak of a tradition, not at its beginnings. Our performers were all professionals; they were members of a guild of long standing.

The performance of such orally composed pieces was, of course, highly variable. Whether the performer is the composer or a "reciter" who is performing what is in effect a "cover" version of the piece, each performance of a work will differ from the one that has preceded it and the one that will follow. Tradition may have restrained the performer of the sacred from taking too many liberties, as we would call them, with a known piece, but audience reaction and the performer's own virtuosity and desire to please and impress the audience were powerful incentives to "improve" the piece in performance. Just as they are for a jazz musician or a bel canto soprano, riffs, trills, and cadenzas are always available for those skilled or daring enough to try them.

We cannot see the ancient composer at work, of course; we have only the work itself, not Homer but the *Iliad*; not Ezekiel but only his Collected Prophecies. Nor do we have the work in its original oral form, but only in a written transcription, the latter the work of scribes who not only transcribed the oral original but also, we believe, transformed it. In the oral tradition the composer-performer was succeeded by the reciter-performer and then, with the onset of a literary tradition where professionals knew how to write, the reciter was replaced by another link in the transmission chain, the scribal transcriber-editor. It is the anonymous scribes of the nascent literary tradition who transcribed, shaped, and transformed the oral text and are the closest we have to "authors" of the books in our Bible: it is they who created, out of earlier materials, the base text of what we now read.

The Scribes

As it concerns Scripture, the earliest scribes were the *sofers*, the professionals in Israelite society who were responsible not merely for the copying of the sacred texts but also for their exegesis. The priests were the primary guardians of the Law in Israel, but after the return from the Babylonian Exile, the scribe emerged not as a distinct competitor but as a form of professional specialist on the Scriptural texts and their contents, first within the priesthoods—most of the earliest known scribes were of priestly descent—and then, when the priesthoods went into functional eclipse after the destruction of the Temple in 70 CE, as a distinct profession that was useful for profane, chiefly administrative, matters as well as for more sacred tasks relating to Scripture.

There are two Biblical scribes with particularly high profiles. The first is Ezra, the priestly scribe who played a pivotal role in the restoration of the Jewish community after the return from the Babylonian Exile. His work is described in the Biblical book Ezra-Nehemiah, where he is signaled as the initiator of the restoration of the Covenant through a public reading of the Law in Jerusalem (Neh. 8:1–7), a role the rabbis later underlined and enlarged. That was only the beginning of his career. A number of apocalyptic books that appeared later in Second Temple times bore his name as their author, though the attribution has long been rejected. The other celebrated scribe is Baruch, who is named and acknowledged by the prophet Jeremiah (37) as his amanuensis and collaborator, and he too had his name attached to a visionary apocalypse in a later era.

Apocalypses aside, we know of the professional work of the scribes from two main sources. We can inspect their product and methods firsthand in the scrolls from Qumran and elsewhere in the Judean desert, scribal evidence that dates from the third century BCE down to the first. We can learn *about* them from the highly detailed rabbinic attempts to regulate their practices. The rabbis of the Mishnah and Talmud were profoundly concerned with the accuracy of Scripture, and the chief instruments in the production of Scripture were the scribes. From both sources, the prescriptions and the actual work product, we can conclude that the Israelite "scribe" was far more than a copyist of texts; he was expected to be not merely careful in the reproduction of the texts but intelligent and educated in their *matter* as well. From the Judean scrolls we can observe that the scribes who produced those texts operated with considerable liberty. They not only divided the texts *ad sensum* according to their own lights; they also modified Scripture as they proceeded, sometimes in trivial matters, but sometimes more substantially.

It was this scribal freedom that the rabbis were attempting to curb, not so much by controlling the scribes as by controlling the text. Two textual worlds existed side by side at the time and in the place of the New Testament's own coming into being. On one hand, there was the scribe as editor, transcribing and transmitting texts, sacred as well as profane, with the freedom to emend, alter, and adjust; on the other, there was emerging, from about 250 BCE onward, a fixed and definitive text of Scripture. The Judean scrolls from Qumran and elsewhere from the third century BCE to the first CE enable us to chart the development of both of these tendencies. The earliest copies of the Bible at Qumran show not only that there was as yet no fixed list of books that made up the Bible—in more modern terms, that the canon was still open—but that the text of any given book was also not yet fixed, that is, there was no accepted or standardized way of either writing or reading the text. We were already aware of that fact, though in a more indirect way. As we can read between the lines of their versions, whoever were translating the Bible into Greek in Egypt from the third century onward had before them a number of different Hebrew texts. Now, with the discoveries at Qumran, we have just such Hebrew texts before us as well.

From Recitation to Writing

But the process was not yet complete. With a written tradition came new concerns for accuracy. And concerns became anxiety with the appearance, now in writing, of textual variations in the work of generations of editor-scribes, some working serially, some in parallel, as at Qumran. Such variations had not disturbed either the composer or the reciter of oral texts, but in an increasingly literate society they spurred efforts to produce a *textus receptus*, a relatively fixed written text. The final stage, the one that finally delivered the Bible text into our hands, was the work of genuine literary text editors. The oral tradition, with its performer- and audience-driven variety, was left behind; the new mantra was accuracy, the hallmark of a genuine literary tradition. In Biblical terms this was the age of the masoretes, the scribal guardians of the Biblical *text*.

We cannot follow all of these stages with any great degree of accuracy as they pertain to the Bible. The most we can hope for the first stage—that of the oral composition of various parts of the Bible, of the units that lie below the editorial level of the disengaged "documents" called J and E, for example—is to construct an outline from shreds of evidence and the experience of other oral traditions and the models drawn from them. The second stage in Biblical development, the passage of the earlier orally composed and transmitted material into writing, we know happened but are reduced to conjecture why and when and how. The third stage in the making of our Bible, the fixing of the written text, is the best-known since literate societies leave their traces scattered wholesale behind them. And throughout this process we are always moving backward. The evidence we do have, our Bible, is the product of the final fixing with only traces of an earlier, more fluid text buried in the writing. Of the original oral texts, the ones whose authors we are seeking, we have nothing.

It is obvious that neither the Jews nor the Christians thought of the "books" in their Scripture as documents in the Higher Criticism sense of a piece of value-neutral written evidence for a historical event or person. Rather, their books were "witnesses" sworn, so to speak, under the most solemn of oaths, to testify at a more than human tribunal. Nor did they refer to books in quite the same manner as we now do. For us a book is something that is inscribed, printed, bound. The ancients, whether in Israel or Arabia, had a somewhat simpler notion of a "book" as something inscribed or written down, though of course without the corollaries of printing or binding. Writing is ancient, printing is not, and bookmaking, as we shall see, falls somewhere in-between. But if the ancient peoples knew of a book as something written, their own "Sacred Books" did not begin that way. The original forms, or better, the original contents, of what we now call the Bible, the New Testament, and the Quran were not written down at all. "Scripture," "writing," paradoxically began as speech: speech delivered, speech remembered, speech recorded, before it became the Written Word, the "Book."

But writing did become attached to the Word very early on. Books were sacred objects among people who could not read them. There were royal "books" recording royal decrees on parchments, papyrus, bricks, stones, and walls, and though not many could read in what were still overwhelmingly oral societies, the point was taken: this is the royal will; pay heed! And not unnaturally, in consequence, there were thought to be heavenly books inscribed with divine decrees, God's will or the dooms of Fate. The Quran provides a clear and striking example of a famously illiterate prophet imagining his own oral "recitations" as a "book," even though his followers could not have read it even if he had been able to write it. "Book" in the Quran is indeed something inscribed, but in heaven, on a "closely guarded tablet," to which Muhammad is giving voice. But it is something more. His pronouncements are also a "Book" in the sense of the Jewish and Christian "Books" he and his audience may in fact have seen and even viewed carried in the solemn liturgical manner favored by the Jews and the Eastern Christians.

The Quran came into existence in a seventh-century Western Arabian world that may have seen or heard of books but, as far as we can tell, had neither produced nor read them. The same is likely true of the Israelites who stand behind—"composed" is still a step beyond them—the earliest "books" of the Bible, the Pentateuch or "Five Books of Moses": Genesis, Exodus, Leviticus, Numbers, Deuteronomy. These five make up what the rabbis later called "Torah," and to which were added, as previously mentioned, the two large categories of "Prophets" (Joshua through Malachi) and "Writings" or Everything Else. We, who are more sensitive to literary genres than to theology and who take great pains not to confuse theology with history, might divide it differently by separating the rabbis' "Prophets" into "Histories" and "Prophets." Or we might do as the Israelites themselves did before the Exile. They joined Joshua-Kings to the Pentateuch and thought about the whole of it—we do not know what they called it—as sacred tradition.

Authors behind the Authors

These various ways of categorizing the Biblical books may conceal the fact that there is a distinct unity running through them, at least till we arrive at the miscellany of the Writings. Genesis opens with a general account of Creation and the earliest history of humankind (1–11). This is followed by the Covenant story featuring, in lively and dramatic fashion, Abraham and his wife Sarah and their descendants (12–35). The narrative then takes a new turn as the sons of Jacob/Israel, Abraham's great-grandchildren, expand (36) into the *Benei Israel*, the extended clan group that embarks on what appears to us as the Epic of Egypt (Gen. 37–Exod. 19). That tale of success, reversal of fortune, and providential escape from the tyranny of the Pharaoh into the wilderness of Sinai is interrupted—essentially sidetracked—by a very detailed description of the laws given on Mount Sinai by God to Moses, the hero of the Exodus from Egypt and now God's chosen prophet (Exod. 20–end of Deut.).

After this very long "digression" and the death of Moses at the end of Deuteronomy, the chronological-historical narrative resumes with the Conquest and Settlement of Canaan or How This Land Became Ours (Joshua–Judges). In Samuel we leave the tribal world of Exodus, Joshua, and Judges and enter a different, or rather, an evolved, world, that of a chronicled monarchy whose heroes (and villains) are the Israelite kings and their descendants. This is patently royal history, though with a difference. This is no familiar stately royal procession through Samuel and Kings. The kings are certainly praised for their achievements: David, the victorious conqueror of Philistia and Jerusalem; Solomon, the wise and prodigious builder of temples, palaces, and an empire. But the Israelite royals are also the subjects of a tabloidlike treatment filled with sex and violence and dark and reprehensible doings.

These are purely literary-descriptive characterizations of what lies before us in the Bible and are patent to any reader who does not rest too heavily on the Bible's division into books. But critics who have probed more deeply into what lies behind these earliest Biblical books are thought to have discovered more fundamental building blocks for the Pentateuch. This manner of probing is called "source criticism" and its most widely held result is termed the "documentary hypothesis." This holds that at some point an editor stitched together a number of divergent accounts—they are called "documents"—to form our Pentateuch, but not so skillfully that the seams cannot be detected and the constituent units identified, separated, and studied. The invitation to do just that is issued in the very opening chapters of Genesis, where there is one account of Creation in chapter 1 and another, quite different version in chapters 2 and 3, a fact that has provoked harmonizing or conciliatory comment from endless chains of rabbis and Christian theologians.

But the chief and salient clue to what is afoot in the Bible is revealed by something else. The God of the Bible, who, we are told there, created the universe and then, somewhat later, concluded a pact or covenant with one of His creatures named Abraham, provided his name, Yahweh, to one of his later devotees, the leader and prophet called Moses (Exod. 3:14). It is a rather odd name perhaps, "I am that I am," and it is not His only one. Although the deity is often designated as "Yahweh" in the Pentateuch, He also appears there as "Elohim," a name that is not only an alternative to Yahweh but disconcertingly plural: God, the ancient world's most defiantly monotheistic deity, is also called "the Gods."

The Bible's plural "Gods" has produced far more wonder among modern scholars than it did among ancient or medieval worshipers of Yahweh. Those latter simply created something called a "plural of majesty" to explain the matter and moved on. But this rather peculiar movement between one divine name and another throughout the Pentateuch, together with other clues, like the telling of the same story of Creation twice, and somewhat differently, in the book of Genesis, raised an interesting possibility. Could it be, nineteenth-century German scholarship asked, that what we have are really two different sources that have been somewhat ineptly joined together into a single narrative, one in which God is called "Yahweh" and the other in which he is called "Elohim"? The scholars, who were by now looking upon the Bible as a scripture rather than the Scripture, answered their own question in the affirmative. The question and the answer lie at the heart of the documentary hypothesis, which, in one form or another, provides the most universal explanation of where the Bible came from.

Enter J, E, and Company

Now that they had caught the scent, the source critics began to separate out the text on this basis and labeled the two resulting "documents," one as E for Elohim and the other as J (Yahweh is spelled with a "J" in German, the Sacred Tongue of the nineteenth-century critics). The remainder of the Pentateuch, what cannot be assigned to E or J, appears to place a strong emphasis on Temple and ritual matters. It has been identified as the contribution of a later priestly editor or editors and dubbed P for "priestly."

Finally, all the critics agreed that Deuteronomy was a later addition to the first four books and so it seemed fair to call it D and list it as a fourth "source" for the Pentateuch.

There are diverse variations on the theme—Had E and J come together before P was added to the mix? Was there an EJP before D was tacked on?—but the general thrust of source criticism was to make the Pentateuch into an edition; not the creation of an author but the product of an anonymous redactor from a later, perhaps much later, era. The documentary hypothesis left in a shambles the traditional notion of the Five Books of Moses, and indeed of Moses as an author altogether. Editing, not authorship, was the issue for the source critics, but the authorship question was still on the table. If P had a community or group ring to it from the outset, what of J and E? Were their authors—let us call them "J" and "E"— individuals or groups? All the evidence is internal, of course, but there is enough of it for one modern literary critic to argue that "J," for one, was a quite distinctive personality and, what is more, a woman.

If "J" was a woman, she was no bardic chanteuse but a genuine bluestocking with pen firmly in hand. When the nineteenth-century critics said "documents," they meant precisely texts. In the seventh century BCE redactors of the expanded Pentateuch were already working with written documents and so too were the earlier editors who joined J and E, and perhaps P, into the Genesis–Numbers quartet. Before them, the supposed ninth-century "southerner" "J" composed a written document, as did the eighth-century "northerner" "E." None of this archaeological text excavation leads us back to anything earlier than the written sources, however. We are shown successive generations of editors cutting and pasting written accounts into ever larger wholes that grow by that process of redactional accretion into our Biblical books.

But if some Biblical seams are visible, others are more difficult to detect, most notably the passage of the Biblical materials, choose whatever literary unit you will, from an oral form to a written one. Everything we know about Israelite and comparable societies tells us that a great deal of the Bible, particularly the early books, but portions of the later ones as well, must have issued from an oral tradition. That is, they were oral compositions, inevitably and invariably linked with oral performance, even though we cannot tell when or where, in time or place or in our text, their transformation from recited account to written text took place.

The Writing Begins

Finding the juncture between the oral and the written, or better, the *era* when the Bible began to be written down—the steps between oral and written were, as elsewhere, very gradual—is a matter of inference. When were there both the means and the motive to commit the oral traditions regarding Creation, the Covenant, and the Israelite past to writing? Many of the sensibilities of the Biblical text as we now possess it seem to speak of the post-Exilic period, an analysis that has led some to date the writing down of the Bible to the Persian era (ca. 500–300 BCE) or even the Hellenistic period (ca. 300–150 BCE).

But on the evidence from both Israel and elsewhere in the Fertile Crescent, that cultural transformation seems to taken place much earlier, as early as the days of the Israelite king Hezekiah (715–687 BCE), when Israel, along with the rest of Middle East, underwent an observable urbanization. With urbanization, and the birth of both an urban bureaucracy and a royal chancery, the use of writing began to spread, together with a rise in numbers of those who could do it and the need to employ it for matters royal, religious, and economic. The matter is clear in Judea; in the seventh century there is a notable increase in Hebrew inscriptions and that provides the context of Josiah's already remarked promotion of a *book* of the Law to the head of his reforms.

That nascent urbanization all but disappeared with the depopulation of Judea during the Exile, but royal literacy survived in the form of the literary projects encouraged and supported by the House of Judah in exile, an activity reflected in the Biblical books of Zechariah and Haggai and, most importantly, in Ezra-Nehemiah.

But the royal scribes of the Exile had been trained in Aramaic, not Hebrew, and the consequence of this becomes apparent in the sharp decline of preserved Hebrew inscriptions (and the increasing number of Aramaic ones) in post-Exilic Judea. Books were now composed as such rather than transcribed from existing oral material. Esther and Daniel and Qoheleth/Ecclesiastes all bear the linguistic and literary stamp of the Hellenistic era. But as for the rest, the matter of the Bible was in the hands of the priests after the Israelites' return from the Exile, and it was they who put the finishing touches on the collection called the Bible.

The oral tradition, which was the original one among the Israelites, was not dead, however, in that increasingly literate society. That same Hellenistic period saw the rise of at least one faction, the Pharisees, who used the tension between the oral tradition, which they professed to control, and the written, Biblical tradition wardened by the priests, to challenge the authority of the latter.

Jeremiah

Some few of the Biblical books may have begun precisely as that, written compositions intended for publication. Jeremiah provides two clear examples. In one place in his book (50:60–64) he dictates a prediction of the destruction in store for Babylon, which an Israelite will carry in writing to the Exile community there. More pointedly, we may have in Jeremiah 36 a description of the very book we now have before us. The prophet dictates to his scribe Baruch, who writes down, "from the mouth of Jeremiah," on a tablet, all the prophecies he has uttered. When the Israelite king hears of this, he orders Jeremiah and Baruch to come and read him the scroll. Jeremiah and Baruch, who presumably would have done the "reading," go into hiding, but the king gets his hands on the "book" of Jeremiah, listens to a reading of it and, angered by the grim forecasts in it, cuts the scroll into strips—separates the sewn-together pages of the scroll?—and has them burned. No matter. Jeremiah dictates from memory a second copy, which, whatever else we can say about it, was assuredly not identical with the first.

Jeremiah's life falls in the late seventh or early sixth century BCE in a society that was clearly both oral and literate. There is no reason to think Jeremiah himself could not write, but he certainly did not "compose"—one is never quite sure of the correct word, short of "prophesy," for what prophets do—his prophecies in writing. He was an oral bard-poet like Muhammad, who composed and then pronounced/performed—more ambiguity—his prophecies orally. But Jeremiah was also enough of a child of his times to wish his work to be committed to writing. In this way it would be delivered to specific persons or places in a form other than memorization. The same is said of Muhammad by the much later Muslim tradition, which alleged that the prophet of Islam had his pronouncement committed to writing, but, as we shall see, there are strong grounds for thinking that Muhammad, more than a millennium after Jeremiah, lived in a society even less literate than the Israelite prophet's.

Writing, if not yet written composition, was on the mind of Jeremiah at the time of the Exile, and was certainly so for every Biblical figure after him, particularly as the Jews came into contact with the elites of another highly literate society, that of the Hellenes. The Greeks had their own "Scripture," the Homeric epics, which had passed from oral to written presentation, perhaps at about the same time that Jeremiah was dictating to Baruch; indeed, the Hellenized Jews were soon writing their own epics. Where our more serious problem arises is in moving backward and exploring the oral-literary divide of an earlier era.

The Bible as we now have it is a collection of books regarded as in some manner representing the sacred tradition of the Jewish people. If "in some manner" masks a theological-cultural criterion that gives the Biblical collection its identity, there are different notions at work in the smaller collections within the Bible: Torah, Prophets, and Writings. Torah, from Genesis to Kings, appears too organic, to have too much thrust and purpose to be termed simply a "collection." There is an idea here, a Covenant/Israel idea, that has been extended backward to the very Creation of the world and forward into the history of the polity called Israel and of its kings and that had the Law dropped into its heart. The growth of Torah thus appears to be more from within than by accretion: the idea has been expanded to include broader vistas. Prophets, in contrast, is, as the title indicates, a genuine collection, the assembly of works regarded in that light, while Writings is, and again the name somewhat fecklessly confesses it, quite simply a collection, perhaps of whatever was thought fit to join the company of the already recognized and ideologically stamped Torah and Prophets.

Who "Wrote" the Books?

Our concern here has not been with these larger collections but with the origins and authorship of their constituent parts, and, in the first instance, of the individual Biblical books. Some of these come fully and convincingly identified, like the books of the various prophets, though it is clear that even here a fairly heavy editorial hand has lumped some diverse poetical material under the name of "Isaiah." There are two or three fairly distinct

"Isaiahs," for example, in that book named after but one of them. And the variegated textual history of Jeremiah among the finds at Qumran leads us to conclude that even when there was one author, his text was not fixed until much later. Yet, some books are transparent collections, like Psalms. David may indeed have been the author of some of them—the tradition insists they are all his—but we are far more certain that they are hymns of various types than that they were composed by that Israelite king. Ruth and Esther shout out their anonymity of authorship. They passed through many hands, or tellings, before they reached us in their written form. Such timeless stories do not have authors, nor do we know—or need to know—the identity of the skilled scribe who passed them on to us. They were included in the Bible for their content rather than their authorship.

As for the rest, from the Torah, which was thought to have been written by Moses, to Ezra-Nehemiah, whose ascribed authors were historical personages who actually could have written the books ascribed to them, we can sometimes glimpse their sources, like E and J in the Pentateuch, for example. But if E and J were subsumed by an editor into the Pentateuch, it is equally likely that even older traditions were integrated into E and J, and that "E" and "J" were individuals who were, like the editors who wove them into the Pentateuch, a combination of author and scribe: a scribe in the sense of copying and using older traditions, some oral and some written (like the "Book of the Wars of Yahweh" and the "Chronicles of the King" mentioned in the text), and an author in his making a new whole greater than its older, reused parts and by reason of its uniform style, rhetoric, and *tendenz,* Biblical scholarship's word for "spin."

Thus we can describe the author-ity of the various books of the Bible on the basis of the compositional and stylistic traits that each manifests, and thanks to source criticism, it is even possible in certain cases to go back a further step and describe the style of a "J." But we cannot yet tell whether E and J were written documents (as the source critics supposed) or oral traditions. Both types of "document," the oral and the written, may betray a style that displays the features of both a performance and a text. Writers who composed written works still betray the stylistic traits and features of the oral performer. Macpherson could convincingly write "Ossian" and George Gershwin "Porgy and Bess" in a style and an idiom that was neither theirs nor their cultures'. But unlike Macpherson and Gershwin, the authors of Biblical books were not conscious antiquarians. They lived in the transitional world between an oral and a literary culture and could still function, to a degree, in each. In Biblical-era terms, they lived between the late monarchy of the eighth century, when writing began to be common in some circles, and the Hellenistic third century, when writing began to prevail. Literacy did not arrive of a sudden and destroy all orality: the writer of tales did not slay the singer of tales with a single blow. For long centuries the two lived in what has been described as a world where oral and literary coexisted and interacted. More, literary authors, writers as we call them, were quite capable of reproducing elements of the oral style that had preceded them.

Writing in Scripture

"Writing"—usually and more specifically, objects with writing on them—appears early in the Scripture tradition. What are manifestly the oldest parts of Bible and the Quran both make fairly frequent reference to it. But the reference is not to something that lies ready to hand. "Writing" is rather an object with power, a manifestation of royal or divine authority, for example, or of a guild of sages whose jealously guarded skill manifests their control of the hidden, the mysterious, the dangerous. References to writing in an oral performance do not mean, in short, that either the author(s) of a work or the people listening to it could read or write.

It is that mixed or transitional era of orality and literacy that produced much, if not all, of our Bible; late books like Esther, Daniel, and Ecclesiastes date from Hellenistic times, when the oral and the literary jostled against each other, poetry and folktale against the annals of kings, royal decrees, writs of divorce, and letters: sources were listened to and archives consulted (read) in the making of our Bible. But even in a Hellenistic book like Daniel (after 185 CE), in an era when literacy was becoming relatively common, writing had lost none of its odd power or "glamour." The "moving finger" writes on the wall of the palace and moves on. None can read it (5:7) save the Israelite wise man Daniel. He "reads" it and it is, in translation, a nonsense jingle of Aramaic coinage, but for the Persian king in the story it is pure magic.

The juncture of the two worlds is illustrated in a famous passage in Deuteronomy, a book that was likely the product of the late monarchical era, the reign of King Josiah, when writing and reading skills were becoming somewhat more widespread in royal and scribal circles. The Israelites are told (6:4–9) by God to write upon their doorposts the words that God will dictate to them. The passage tells us as little about the ancient Israelites' ability to write and read as it does about those same skills vis-à-vis Hebrew on the part of modern Jews who post the same words in mezuzahs on their doorjambs. Rather, it reveals a belief in the apotropaic power of writing, even in the late monarchy, when some did know how to write; in this instance, the writing averts the Angel of Death.

References to writing or to written documents become increasingly common in the later Biblical books like Chronicles, Esther, and Ezra-Nehemiah, but scattered through almost all the books are indications that the Torah at least was regarded as a written document, even though exceedingly few could read it. Deuteronomy 19:18 mandates that the Israelite king must write—presumably have written for himself—a copy of the Torah, which he is to carry about with him and "read." Likely it is Torah excerpts or slogans that the king has with him, even in battle, just as the early Muslims pinned "copies" of the Quran—here too likely just some verses—to their lances at the battle of Siffin in 680 CE. A copy of the Torah was reportedly found in the Temple in Josiah's day (2 Kings 22:8)—modern scholars think it was Deuteronomy—and in Nehemiah (13:1) the Levites are bade read from the "Document of Moses" and the people, who presumably could not read, to listen to them.

By sometime in the Second Temple period—it is impossible to be more precise—the whole of the Bible was "safely" committed to writing, which is surely one element in why the Biblical canon was closing at that juncture. But the decisive turn from the oral to the literary era was equally instrumental in writing finis to prophecy in Israel. It was not merely the prophets' mouths that were stopped in Second Temple times—the next prophet would appear only in the fully oral society of seventh-century Mecca—the oral tradition itself had reached a point not of extinction but of deterioration, and though there would continue to be objections to committing sacred matters to writing, in the Mediterranean world the written word was replacing the living voice as a guerdon of authenticity. There could be no clearer signal than the passage in Deuteronomy (31:24). Earlier God had written the Law on tablets for Moses to announce to the Israelites; here He dictates it to the now literate Moses, who is commanded to write it down on tablets.

As we have seen, a number of larger blocks of literary units go into the Bible. There is in the first instance Israel's "foundation myth," the epic tale that stretches from Abraham (with a prologue on Creation and the early history of humankind) down to the decline of the Davidic monarchy. There are also collections of hymns, like the Psalms, an extended song-poem like the Song of Songs, an extensive collection of prophetic books from Isaiah to Malachi, and, from later days, anthologies of wisdom sayings and a potpourri of stories, romantic, moral, and exemplary.

In each Biblical instance the issue of authorship presents itself differently. To start with the latest, the ingredients in the Bible's collection of wisdom sayings and stories in the Writings appear to be oral in origin, with many folk and popular wisdom prototypes but with the heavy (yet skillful) impress of a writer's hand. With the prophets and hymns we have moved somewhat closer to the oral composer-performer (whose names are attached), but here too the material has been reworked by a scribal editor. Isaiah (6) and Jeremiah (36) in fact tell us exactly how it came about, and Jeremiah even provides the name of his scribe, Baruch. In all these instances the units are discrete and reasonably small. But the story of Israel's foundations, which is epic in its scope and properties, extends from Genesis to the second book of Kings.

The Levites

This long Israelite epic, which is related as history and not as a poetical or dramatic story, does not have the smooth unity of the *Iliad* or the *Odyssey* with their central heroes and a war or a road trip to give them coherence and so suggest in each case a single author's work. Both the hero and the theme of the Israelite epic is Israel, the people and the idea. The hero is not God; it is this people's relationship to their God. This must have been the work of many hands, or rather, of many anonymous mouths. It was a history told—or chanted, or sung—and retold over many centuries from we know not when until it began to be written down in something like its final, and present, form under the last Israelite monarchs before the Exile. But the Bible from Genesis to 2 Kings is not a wild growth thrown together as circumstances permitted or dictated. Its unity of theme, motifs, and purpose says it was the product of a controlled transmission.

302

קֹהֶלֶת בֶּן־דָּוִד מֶלֶךְ
בִּירוּשָׁלָ͏ִם׃ הֲבֵל הֲבָלִים
אָמַר קֹהֶלֶת
הֲבֵל הֲבָלִים הַכֹּל
הָבֶל׃ מַה־יִּתְרוֹן לָ͏וֹ
לָאָדָם בְּכָל־עֲמָלוֹ
שֶׁיַּעֲמֹל תַּחַת הַשָּׁ

הַשֶּׁמֶשׁ׃ דּוֹר הֹלֵךְ
וְדוֹר בָּא וְהָאָרֶץ לְ͏וֹ
לְעוֹלָם עֹמָדֶת׃ וְזָרַח
הַשֶּׁמֶשׁ וּבָא הַשָּׁמֶשׁ
וְאֶל־מְקוֹמוֹ שׁוֹאֵף
זוֹרֵחַ הוּא שָׁ͏ם׃ הוֹלֵךְ
אֶל־דָּרוֹם וְסוֹבֵב

אֶל־צָפוֹן סוֹבֵב סֹבֵב
הוֹלֵךְ הָרוּחַ וְעַל־
סְבִיבֹתָיו שָׁב הָרוּחַ׃
כָּל־הַנְּחָלִים הֹלְכִים
אֶל־הַיָּם וְהַיָּם אֵינֶנּוּ
מָלֵא אֶל־מְקוֹם לְ͏וֹ
שֶׁהַנְּחָלִים הֹלְכִים

הוֹלֶ͏ךְ ד׳ הֵם בְּטַעְמַם ... וְהֵירוּחֵיהֶן ... זֶהֵר הֹלֵךְ דּוֹר בָּא ... כְּשֵׁוְ͏וֹ ... אֲשֶׁר יָ͏וֹתֵּר הֹלֵךְ ... כְּשֵׁהַסְּפֵר הֹלֵךְ לֹא חֶסֶר ... כִּי הֹלֵךְ הָ͏אָדָם ... יְ͏רֵא ... בֵּית עֹלָמִ͏וֹ ... הֹלֵךְ לְ͏דָרֵי לְ͏שֵׁמָרֵיו וְהַב שַׁמַּט ... שֶׁמָּשׁ ... טּ ... חֵל הַמְ͏דְ͏רֵ͏עַת ... פ טּ הֵירֵיע אֹרֵת הֹלֵךְ עֹזָהֹלֵל ... ע׳ חֵל קֹהֶלֶת חֵסֵר ... בֹּ͏נֹב ... תָּמִים וְסֵמֵרֵיתַן ... הֹלֵךְ תָּמִים ... וְ͏תַּגַּעֵל ... שָׁ͏ךְ ... וְ͏חֵ͏יְ͏תַ כִּי בְּ͏שֵׂר הַבָּ͏ה ... רוּחַ הֹלֵךְ ... חַל בְּ͏שַׁ͏ל הֹ͏ל ...

Plate 1. *Duke of Sussex German Pentateuch*: beginning of the Book of Ecclesiastes

נמרוד וחכבתו משליכין את אברהם בכבשן ואש וילשין זאימד עזרזתם נזח רו, ויח

Plate 2. The Golden Haggadah: scenes from Genesis (Adam and Eve)

אדסיקורא שפות ולהיות ולבהמות   אירסואשתו ערומים

נחואשתו ובני יוצאים מן התיבה   ויקר לך יטן גרן עיר ויהדל   ליחיל מהנקן וותר

Plate 3. The Golden Haggadah: scenes from Genesis (the Tower of Babel)

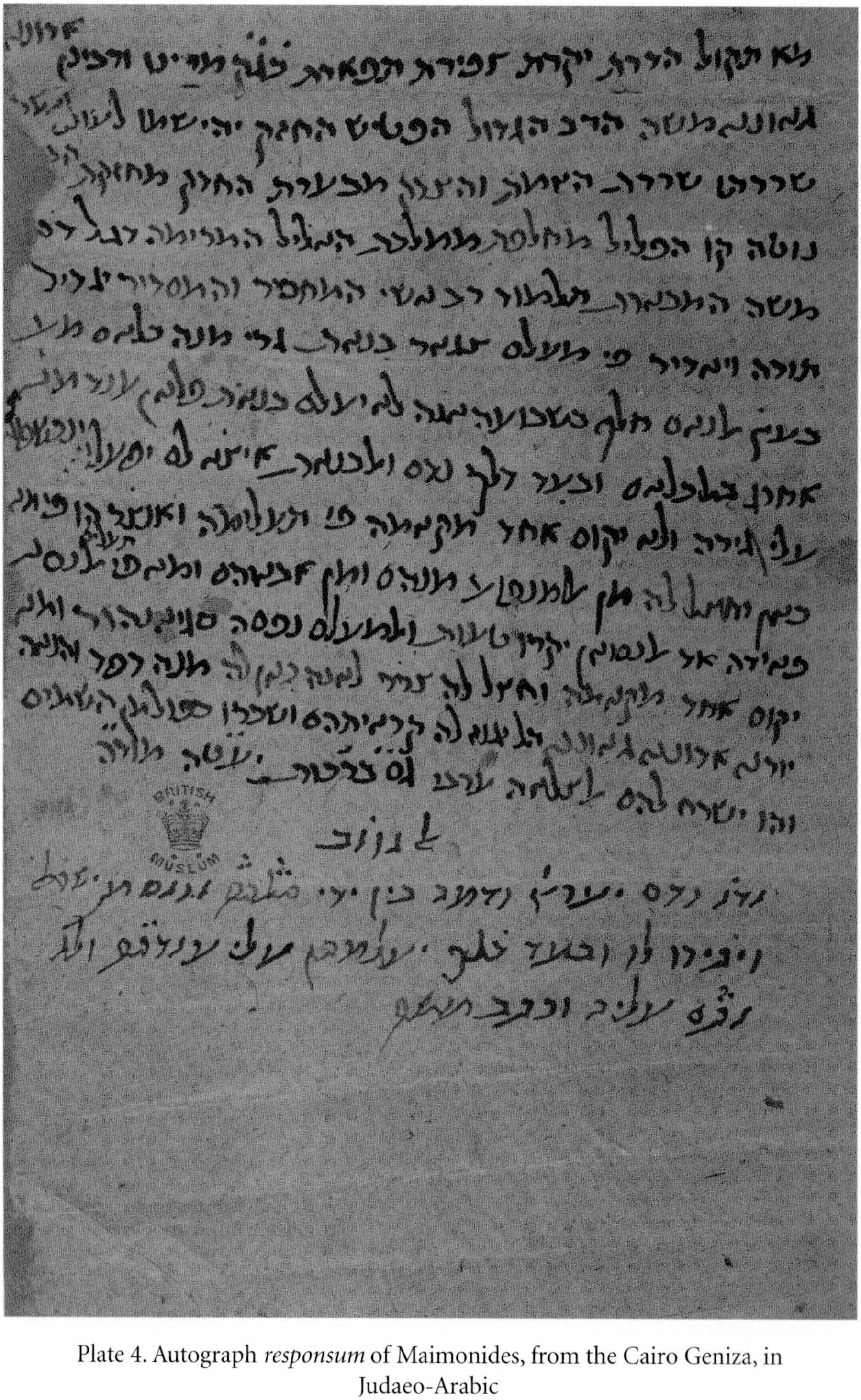

Plate 4. Autograph *responsum* of Maimonides, from the Cairo Geniza, in Judaeo-Arabic

ועתה הנה לנו עצה ' דבר מקובל ' נרצה ' ונשמור דברי פיך ומוצא ' שפתיך לא
יפול דבר ארצה ' ויאמר שמענו נא קטיני ' האזינו קולי כבוני ' לכו ונעלה אל
הריס ונבואה עד עיר היונה ' מקוטרת מור ולבונה ' הר המור גבעת הלבונה
' ושם תמצאו מרגוע ' ואכלתם לכול ושבוע ' ותגבלו מצרה ומקטוב ' שמענו
אלי ואכלו טוב ' ויאמר הגד לנו טוב הארץ העבליה ' האמינה היה אם רוח '
ומה מעלת יושביה וגריה ' זקיכ'ה וכעריה '

צידת הארי שואל הצבי מעלת הארץ וערכה ' והצבי משיבו בעניין וכהלכה '

ויאמר קבלה היא בדינו
מאבותינו ' וכך
אמרו רבותינו ' הדר בארץ
ישראל דומה כמי שיש לו אלה
בחבלו ' והדר בחוצה לארץ
דומה כמי שאין לו ' וכל מי
מעביל ומעיד על מאמר זה
ומסכים' אוירא דארץ ישראל
מחכים' ואמרו לעולם ידור
אדם בארץ ישראל אפילו
מעיב גויס בעיריס ' ואל
ידור בחוצה לארץ ואפילו
בעיר שרובה ישראל דריס '
ואמרו להתגלל בקדושתה ו

ולהשתבח ' כל הקבור בארץ ישראל כאילו קבור תחת המזבח ' ונשאלו אל החכוניס
הקדמוניס ' גוי צדיק שמיר לאמויס ' היתחייב לילך בחוצה לארץ למות יבוס '
ועל דרך התיומה התעבוס ' ואמרו אחיו של זה נשא גויה ' ברוך המקוס אמר הרגנ
בסדייה ' ואמר כל המהלך ד' אמות בא" מובטח לו שהוא בן עולס הבא' יחיה
ויזכה בלי שמץ ודכה ' ועל זה תקנו רבותינו ' לומר ביום מנוחתינו ' מעניין כונת
לבבנו ותחוויינו ' רחס על צין כי היא ביג חיינו ' ואמרו דבר ברור להודיינו '
מציון מכלל יפי ה'הופיע'ואמרו דבר אשר לכל מסכיל לא נעלס יק" יושבת כ
בארצעית של עולם ' וירושלים באמצע א" והיא הנקראת הטרך' ובית המקדם
באמצע ירושלים ' במחולת הימחניס ' ההיכל באמצע בית המקדם' והארון

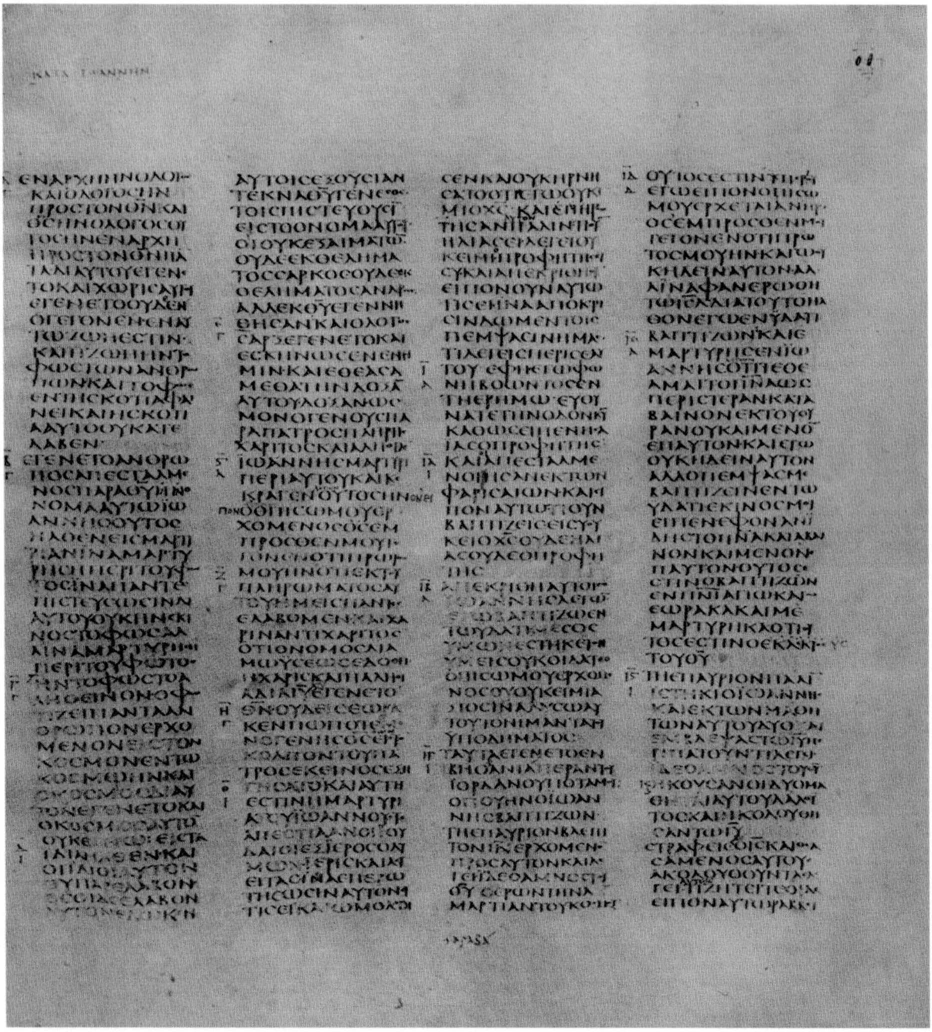

Plate 6. *Codex Sinaiticus*: beginning of St. John's Gospel

Plate 7. *Octateuch*: an illustration of Christ in Glory

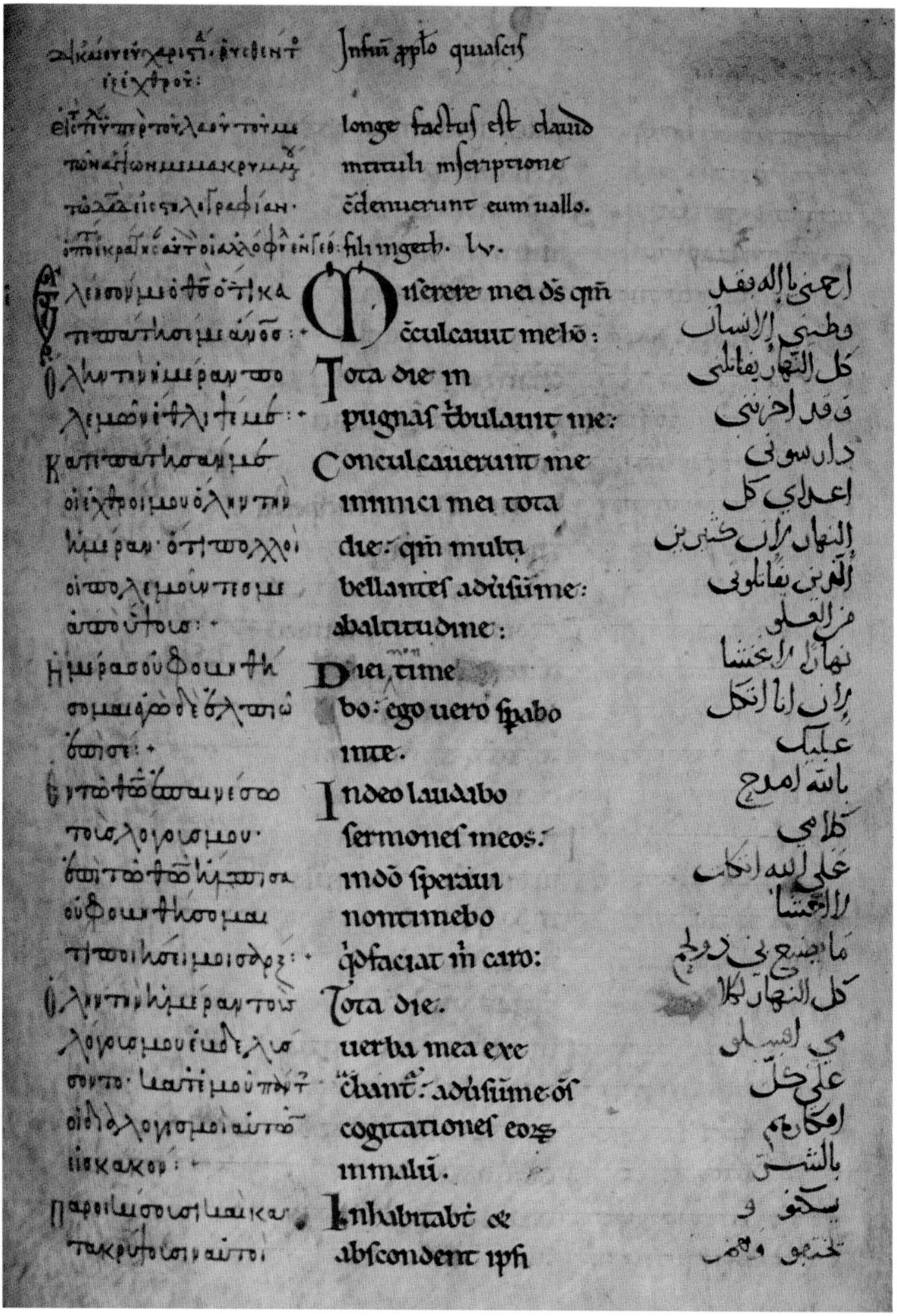

longe factus est dauid
tituli inscriptione
tenuerunt eum uallo.
filii ingeth. lv.

Miserere mei ds qm
cculcauit me ho :
Tota die in
pugnas tbulauit me:
Conculcauerunt me
inimici mei tota
die: qm multi
bellantes adusume:
abaltitudine:
Diei time
bo: ego uero spabo
inte.
Indeo laudabo
sermones meos:
moo speraui
nontimebo
qofaciat in caro:
Tota die.
uerba mea exe
chant: adusume oes
cogitationes eo~
inmalu.
Inhabitabt et
abscondent ipsi

Plate 8. *Harley Psalter*: Psalm 55, in Greek, Latin, and Arabic

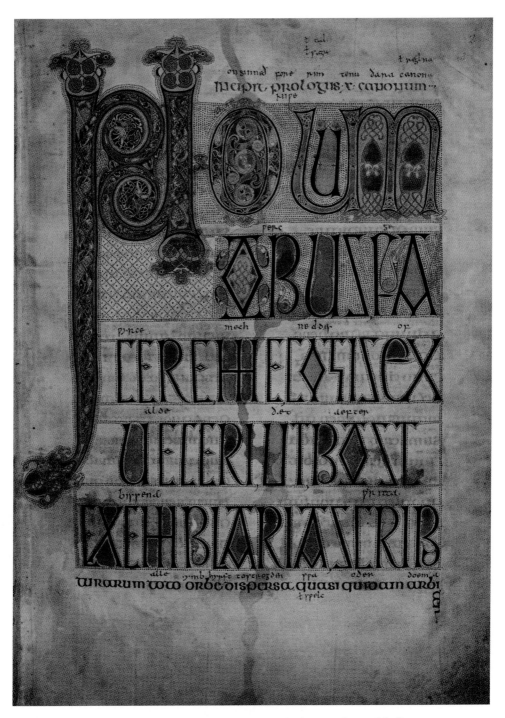

Plate 9. *Lindisfarne Gospels*: text, with decorated initial "N"

Plate 10. *Silos Apocalypse*: the woman clothed with the sun; the seven-headed dragon attacked by St. Michael and his angels

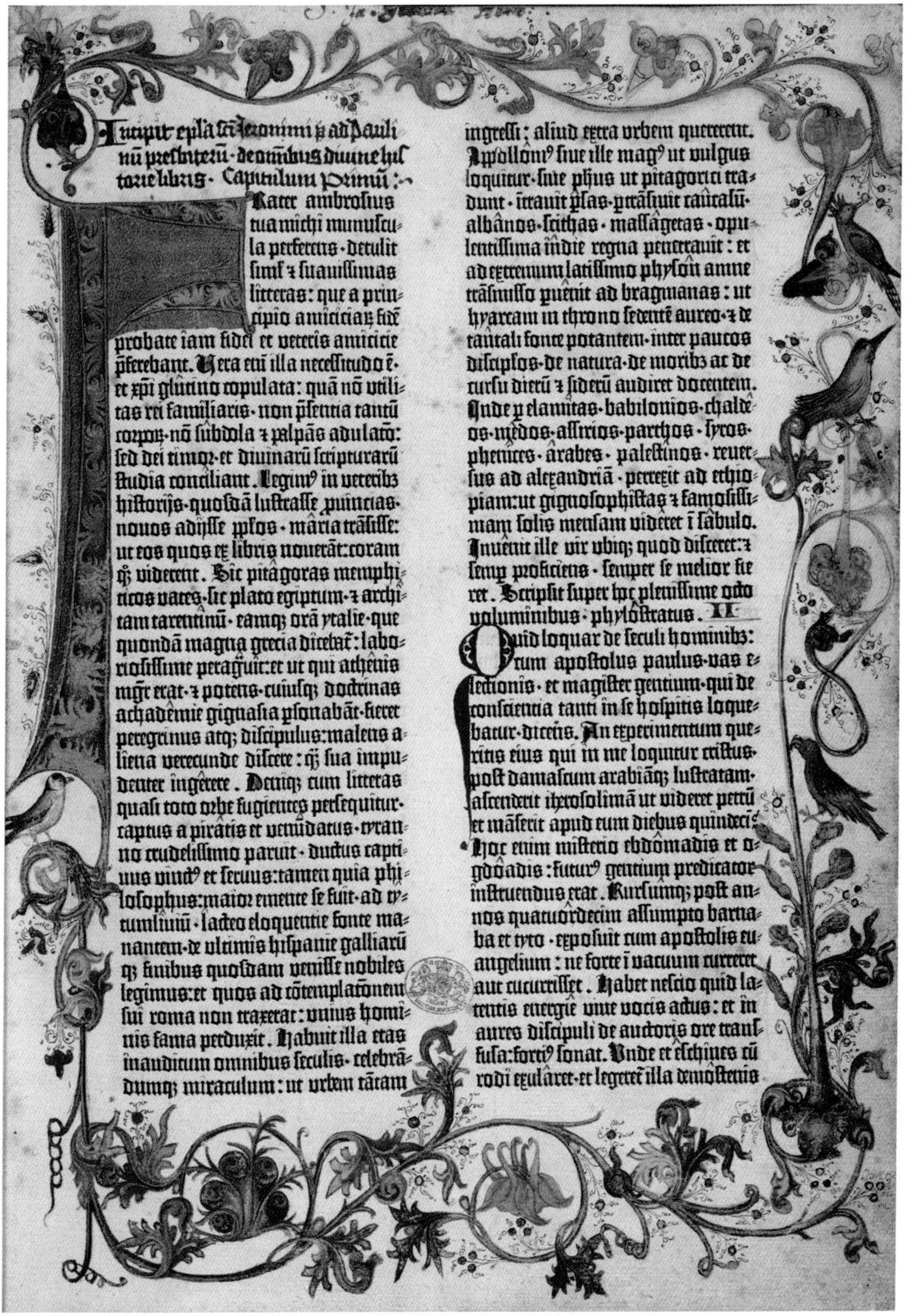

Plate 12. *The Bedford Hours*: the exit from the Ark and the drunkenness of Noah

Plate 13. Calligraphic specimen of Hadith: eighteenth century

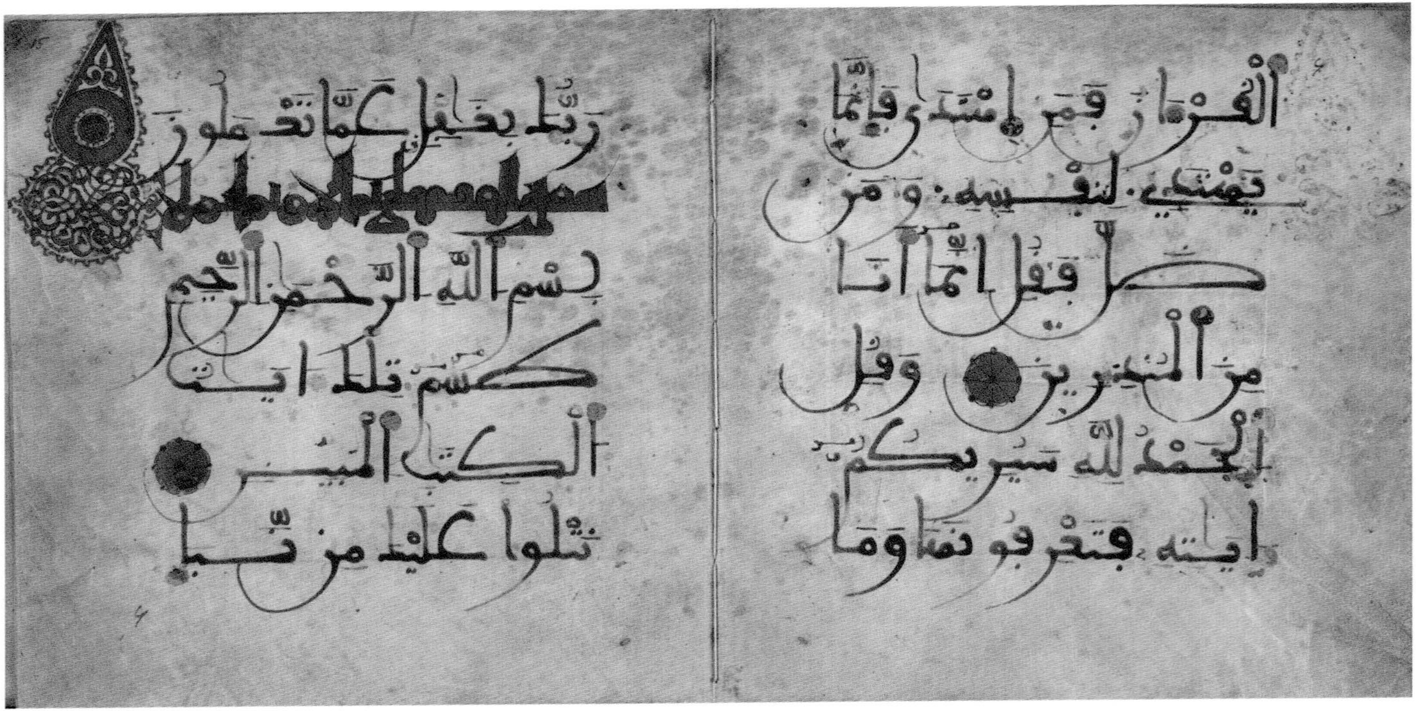

Plate 14. Pages from an elaborately decorated Qur'an

Plate 15. A hajj pilgrimage certificate; Mecca, 15th century

Plate 16. Decorated text page from Sultan Baybars' Qur'an

Were there such transmitters in Israel who were not simply rhapsodes or *rawi*s on the Greek or Arab model but a more unified and purposeful guild? One plausible candidate might be the Levites, the singers and teachers of Israel, Temple servants who were bound to no particular tribal perspective or territory (Deut. 33:8–11). And it may well have been the Levites who began to commit the "Epic of Israel" to writing after the Babylonian destruction of the Temple—a likely site where they would have performed their recitations—and the dispersion of the people into Exile. The Levites were not the authors of the tale; the identity of the actual authors, the singer-bards who first gave voice to these stories, are lost to memory, as often happens in the oral tradition. Later Jews undoubtedly had it fundamentally right in thinking that Moses was the "author" of the Pentateuchal heart of the story. But if the Levites did not create the parts of the story, they were "authors" in another important sense: it was they who tended and shaped the growth of the tradition and who gave coherence and unity to this narrative made up of some many different stories and elements.

If we try to look behind the Levites, and then behind the work of "E" and "J" and the other alphabetic authors whose work can be discerned in the Pentateuch, we are attempting to peer into the opaque anonymity of the oral tradition. We can find the historians' sources readily enough. Certain repeated stories in Genesis and Exodus that tell of the sister who is also a wife and others about the displaced firstborn heir in favor of another have their origins in the Hurrian society, with their center at Harran, through which Abraham and his family would have passed on their trek from "Ur of the Chaldees" to the land of Canaan. Again, a great deal of the legal material in the Torah is similar to what can be found in the ancient law codes of Mesopotamia. But these are parallels, or even borrowings from one society by another, or, it might be argued, the sources the author of the Biblical account used in his own work. And if they are of considerable interest to the cultural historian, they do not bring us much closer to the author or to his original work.

The Masoretes

Now, finally, we must look forward. From 700 CE onward we have two types of Hebrew Biblical manuscripts. Physically the two types are quite distinct: one is a *codex*, leaves of writing material joined at one edge—in effect, our "book"; the other, a *volumen* or roll, sheets of writing material joined at top and bottom and rolled up, often on a wooden spool. But there are more basic differences within. The medieval Hebrew codex—a technical innovation to which the Jews came very late in the day—has inscribed on it a consonantal text signed with a series of symbols (dots and lines) and a variety of verbal annotations concerning that text. The roll consists only of a consonantal text. Which is really the Jewish Scripture? Modern, and Western, sensibilities might very well choose the more complete and more determined codex text since it is, *por sopuesto*, closer to the original revelation. But the choice is likely incorrect. In a very powerful sense the volumen, the unadorned, conservative consonantal *Sefer Torah* used in the synagogue service is more genuinely Scripture, at least as concerns a written text. *These* were the Lord's words, viewed through all the deficiencies of a human script; all else are human stage directions.

The impressive collection of such stage directions that we find in Hebrew codices down to the introduction of printing (which carried accuracy off in a somewhat different direction), the shower of prompts, advice, and warnings that flow through and around the Hebrew consonantal text, is called the "tradition" (*masorah*). It is the work product of the last generation of scribal editors working on the Bible. The distant original performer has now migrated across a spectrum of transmission from reciter-perfomers to editor-perfomers to scribe-editors and now finally to genuine literary editors whose sole concern was to preserve the text. This final generation of Biblical editors are called "traditionists" (*masoretes*), and their goal was that of every literary culture—accuracy—and, since they were also rabbis, accuracy in the transmission of the Word of God.

We cannot be sure when this masoretic tradition of attempting to fix the written text began—perhaps in the era of the Maccabees with Jewish exposure to the Hellenic preoccupation with textual matters—but when it comes into clear view it is associated with established rabbinic schools in Palestine and Babylonia, in the same places and in the same prolific era, circa 500 CE, that produced the Talmuds. These were rabbi editors, and from their approach to Scripture we can deduce a number of presuppositions. The first is that a consonantal Hebrew text of the Bible had by then been established—a half millennium after the textual variety we find at Qumran—and that all could agree on this baseline of Scripture. The second factor operating in the masoretes' work is the conviction that the Biblical text should not be altered, not merely in its written consonantal form, the *ketib*, which was no longer an issue, but even as a vocalized text, the *qere*, that is, how the consonants should be read. The masoretes were now working in an environment where the values of a literary culture had become paramount.

How the masoretes accomplished their goal of a stabilized text was by writing down the directions. They adorned the text before them, first with a series of signs and symbols to signify the correct vocalization and accentuation of each of the inscribed consonants. These were written interlineally, above and below the consonantal baseline. Then, in the lateral margins, on the tops and bottoms of pages, and even at the end of the codex were further annotations to ensure not only that the text would be recited correctly but that it would be copied with the utmost accuracy. Scribal pitfalls—nasty homonyms, peculiar spellings, difficult or misleading words—were all displayed for the guidance of the next scribe to take up the work. The result was an extraordinary *apparatus criticus* that guaranteed an equally extraordinary degree of stability in the Sacred Scripture.

Not all the masoretic versions were identical, of course, since the rabbis who produced them were working in different school traditions. A scholarly consensus was almost certainly developing in academic circles regarding the different masorahs. That consensus was settling on the masorah of the Tiberian master Aaron ben Asher (d. ca. 960 CE), which is the one replicated in the oldest complete Hebrew manuscript of the Bible, dated 1009 CE, discovered in Cairo and now housed in St. Petersburg. That particular masorah received an extremely influential endorsement by Maimonides (d. 1204), the Spanish physician, philosopher, and Torah expert then resident in Egypt. The masorah he preferred to use, he wrote, was one that had been refined by the notable Aaron ben Asher. Maimonides either had or had consulted a copy of this masorah, which he remarked was kept in Jerusalem, where it was used as a standard. That selfsame codex, vocalized by Ben Asher himself in Tiberias in 920, appears to have been preserved intact in an Aleppo synagogue until 1948, when Arab-Jewish problems in the city caused it to "disappear." It has since "reappeared in Israel," no longer quite intact—about one-third of it is missing.

With Ben Asher and the Aleppo Codex we have reached an important stage in the history of the Bible. The Book is now not only closed—the rabbis had accomplished that four or five centuries earlier—but the text is fixed. The oral Word of God has been reduced to writing. The fixing has not been in the consonants, which had been established at some earlier point, but in their vocalization. We do not know who had devised the Hebrew consonantal *aleph-beth*; likely no one, since the process is so clearly evolutionary. Nor do we have names for the authors of its vocalic refinement, which made possible a more accurate representation of the sound of spoken or, in our case, recited Hebrew. What we do know is that by 900 CE or somewhat earlier, the Jewish scribes we have been calling masoretes had devised a system of annotation sophisticated enough to enable them to convert sound into sign. The Bible, the living Word of God, could now be read off the page.

Chapter 4

The Reporters

The Good News and How We Got It

∂⁄6∖∂

The world of the Bible and that of Jesus are the same world; or, to put it in another and more accurate fashion, Jesus was born into a society that was creating the Bible in its final—that is, its written—form. He was, of course, remote from the actual Biblical origins, when the stories of Creation and Israel and her kings were being sung for the first time, or even from the days when the prophets were still reciting their messages. Jesus' contemporaries were rather the scribal "editors" working on written Biblical texts. The best known of them to us are those working at Qumran on the edge of the Dead Sea during Jesus' own lifetime. Qumran and the Essenes are never mentioned in the Gospels, but "scribes" (*grammatikoi*) are a presence in Jesus' life and they file in and out of the Gospel narratives.

Jesus: The Setting

We must imagine the setting. Purely descriptively, Jesus was an itinerant preacher who went about in Galilee with a circle of followers, who traveled with him. He preached and taught in various venues from inside synagogues to spontaneous outdoor gatherings, and changing public audiences listened, questioned, and went their way. Whatever the literacy of Jesus himself or of his followers in that relatively literate Palestinian society—the Jews as a group were more literate than their contemporaries around the Mediterranean—there is no indication that Jesus committed any part of his teachings to writing, or even that his follower-companions wrote them down during his lifetime. This was in the years circa 26–28 CE, when Jesus was active, first in rural and agricultural Galilee—he seems to have made a point of avoiding the largest, and most Hellenized, cities of Tiberias and Sepphoris—and then finally, and briefly, in Jerusalem.

With the passing of some twenty-five years after his death sometime around 28 CE, we no longer have merely to imagine Jesus. We begin to possess not so much recollections of him—the author never met his Redeemer—as references to Jesus in the letters of one of his highly literate followers, Paul, raised a Hellenized Jew of the Diaspora (in Tarsus, in Cilicia) and, more recently, a rabbinic student in Jerusalem. Paul's letters, which are rapid, idiosyncratic, and either written or dictated (Gal. 6:11; Rom. 16:22), make no claim to be from a Jesus eyewitness, but they do lay abundant claim to be from an "Apostle" and so an authentic and authoritative witness to Jesus. Paul's letters cause no great literary problems. As a writer he makes perfect sense, as does the epistolary genre he preferred. We have other such letters from antiquity—a whole drawer full in Latin from Cicero—and Paul's, if somewhat quirkier, are not very different from them, particularly if we overlook the extraordinary things he was saying in them.

The Gospels

It is those letters that tell us there were already "Gospels" in circulation even before Paul began his correspondence in the 50s. We learn firsthand that the "Good News" had been proclaimed across Palestine, Syria, and what are now Anatolia and Greece (1 Cor. 1:10–17). Jews and Gentiles had heard—or read—accounts of Jesus and had believed. Paul did not pretend he was writing Gospels, and we can see in Acts, written another twenty-five years later, the Apostles and others preaching in forms that may soon have developed into Gospels. Peter's speech in Acts (2:14–36) is one such, where the Jesus event is presented, and argued, in summary, and, as we shall see, Peter himself may have been in part responsible for expanding the capsule "preaching version" of the Good News into the "narrative version," that is, into Gospels like ours.

Perhaps ten years after Paul finished writing there appears our first narrative account of Jesus, the "Gospel according to Mark," as it is described by its title, and that very title suggests there were already other versions of that Good News. There are two others, quite similar to Mark's, that the Church recognized as "canonical," one described as "according to Matthew" and another "according to Luke." We do not know exactly when these latter two works appeared, but long enough after Mark—ten or twenty years perhaps—for copies of Mark's Gospel to have been in circulation and used by both.

Extracting Q

That source scenario is based on an earlier finding. Modern scholarship has concluded, chiefly on stylistic grounds, that Mark was the earliest Gospel—the traditional Church order put Matthew first, where he stands in all New Testaments—and it continues to be a near-unanimous opinion among those who study the matter: Mark is shorter, simpler, and more straightforward in both diction and narrative and hence more "primitive" than the others. It is an important conclusion since the foundations of redaction criticism, the search for the Gospels' sources, rest on the conviction that Mark is the earliest of the canonical Gospels.

Thus, if we lay side by side the texts of all three Synoptics—Mark, Matthew, and Luke—all of whom generally reproduce the same series of Jesus events in the same chronological order, it quickly appears that Matthew and Luke must have verbally reproduced (though with certain interesting editorial variations) a great deal of the material already in (the earlier) Mark. What is more, it also reveals that they share *almost verbatim*, but again with emendations, some 235 verses *not* in Mark. The conclusion to explain this coincidence of material was (and remains) that just as Matthew and Luke were using Mark in writing their own Gospels, they were also both drawing on another shared source, which each of them copied in his own somewhat individual way.

This conclusion marks the birth of Q—from the German *Quelle*, the hypothesized "source" that Matthew and Luke must have been using, along with Mark and other material, in composing their Gospels. No one has seen Q, of course; if it once existed, it has long since disappeared, leaving no trace save its ghostly skeleton in Matthew and Luke. But an inspection of those shared non-Markan verses tells us something of what was in it and what it must have been like. Their source was, we discover, not a narrative like Mark but a collection of Jesus' *logia,* the aphoristic sayings and parables characteristic of his teaching style; there is no trace in Q of the man who was arrested, executed, and then experienced alive by witnesses on the third day after his death.

And finally, let us not overlook the fact that Matthew and Luke each has material proper to his Gospel alone, acquired possibly as an eyewitness in Matthew's instance, from an eyewitness such as Mary in Luke's case, as is sometimes said, or in oral or written form from a source or sources unknown.

Dating the Gospels

There is no absolute dating of the four canonical Gospels save that they were produced after Jesus' death, which would place them after 28 CE, itself only a probable date. The next peg on which to hang them is the Roman destruction of the Jerusalem Temple in 70 CE. It is thought that that prodigious event is echoed in Mark, judged to be the earliest of our Gospels. If so, Mark was probably composed shortly after 70 CE, long enough, in any event, for Jesus' message to have passed from Aramaic to Greek and to have been written down (see below). The dating at 70 CE is not terribly firm, however. If Mark 13, which is a prophecy by Jesus, does refer to the destruction of Jerusalem, it is a remarkably oblique allusion to an event that was catastrophic for the Jews—including Jesus' followers— and one that had moreover been predicted by Jesus himself and figured in his trial!

Matthew and Luke are dated from Mark, allowing time, as has been said, for them to use copies of Mark. They also seem to reflect a worsening of relations between Jesus' followers and their fellow Jews, particularly the Pharisees (Matthew), which would fit the state of affairs circa 80–90, when the Pharisees were the new religious rulers of the Palestinian Jews. John too is dated relatively. Its author had, according to Church tradition, apparently read the other three (and chose not to follow them), and his view of Jesus is so theological and the Christians' dealing with the Jews so troubled that it seems to reflect later, more developed—and perhaps more Gentile—understanding of the role of Jesus, one current circa 100 CE.

And yet! The troubles between Christians and Jews portrayed in Matthew's and John's Gospels are no worse than what Paul experienced in the 50s. Nor is John's theology of the Christ, his "Christology," any loftier than Paul's. If we did not know with certainty that Paul wrote his letters in the late 50s, we might well have made him, on the theological evidence, a contemporary of John. Should we now make John a contemporary of Paul?

John

It should be immediately noted that the Gospel "according to John" was regarded by the early Christians as equally authentic and authoritative as the other three, though it is quite different from them. If the other three Gospels give us a comfortably "synoptic" view of Jesus' life, with roughly the same events in roughly the same time frame, John's Gospel had something else in mind. Some early Christian authorities thought they knew what it was. When he saw that the Synoptics had covered the "bodily" or "material" aspects of Jesus' life, John, it is claimed, set himself to writing a "spiritual" Gospel. "Spiritual" is an apt description of what is inside its covers, beginning with its famous prologue that meditates on Jesus as the "Word," and indeed, as the "Word made flesh" (1:1–14). But there is more. The aphoristic Jesus of the Synoptics is subsumed in John into a Jesus who pronounces long, formal discourses. John alters the chronology of the other three—Jesus dies here on the eve of Passover rather than, as in the other three, on the day of the feast, which is hardly a slip of the pen—and he omits incidents reported by the others and includes others unknown to the Synoptics, like the marriage feast at Cana (2:1–11), which he pointedly says is Jesus' first miracle, and like Jesus' long and interesting encounter with a Samaritan woman (4:1–30). And yet, for all his "spirituality" and deviance from the Synoptic "historicist" tradition, John shows equal, if not greater, interest in the topography and circumstances of contemporary Palestine.

The Gospels as Documents

In much the same way they had dealt with the Jewish Bible, the nineteenth century's standard-bearers of the Higher Criticism took to regarding the

New Testament books purely and simply as documents rather than as inspired Scripture. The same documentary approach that had once spied J and its analogues under the apparent unity of the Pentateuch now led some New Testament scholars to discern Mark and Q lying only partially digested in the texts of Matthew and Luke, and prompted still others to discover an older collection of miracles, the so-called Signs Source beneath John. But Mark and Q were already written texts—the borrowing is too verbal to be otherwise than textual—when they lay before Matthew and Luke. Was it possible to push ever further and close the two-decade gap between Jesus' voice and the collections of his sayings in Q? Between Jesus and Mark and Q there was a change in language from Jesus' native Aramaic to the Gospels' Greek as well as a change in medium from Jesus' oral teaching, to its oral (re)collection, to its written form in the Gospel of Mark and probably in Q as well.

From Aramaic to Greek

Were there any Aramaic Gospels? An early and widespread Christian tradition, first made explicit in a work by the early Christian writer Papias (ca. 60–130), as reported by the fourth-century Church historian Eusebius (d. ca. 340), suggests there were "Matthew collected the sayings [of the Lord] in Hebrew [Aramaic] and each interpreted [translated?] them as best he could." A third-century Christian authority maintained that Matthew was the author of a "Hebrew" Gospel. Given the verbal borrowing, there is no doubt that whoever wrote "according to Matthew" was already using a Greek Mark and a Greek Q in composing his (Greek) Gospel. But it is not impossible that there was another Aramaic source associated with Matthew, and that it was incorporated into canonical Matthew, and carried the name, and of course the authority, of the Apostle with it.

We have a fairly good idea where the Greek Gospels originated, even if not quite the ones we have in our hands. Though Jesus may have known some Greek—carpentry made him and Joseph artisans, not peasants, and even Peter the fisherman seems to have picked up Greek readily enough— there can be little doubt that he was preaching and teaching in Aramaic to his Galilean audiences. But as the "movement" spread to Jerusalem it began to include in its number the so-called Hellenists, the Hellenized Jews from the Diaspora who lived in Jerusalem and had their own synagogues there (Acts 6:9). They appear early in the Acts of the Apostles (6:1), and one of their number, Stephen, who was publicly preaching the Risen Jesus in Jerusalem in Greek, provided the new movement with its first "witness" or martyr when his audience of fellow Hellenists turned on him and stoned him to death for blasphemy (7:57–60).

No one had to translate Stephen's speech, which was in effect the first known Greek version of the "Good News." There was no need—nor any sign—of intermediaries between those Greek-speaking Jews and the Apostles, nor did anyone have to "translate" Jesus for those of the Jerusalem "Hellenists" who had heard him in the flesh. The Hellenists were doubtless bilingual and so heard him in one language, Aramaic, and passed on their witness in another, Greek. The canonical Gospels are the undoubted legacy of those same Hellenists who were on the streets of Jerusalem in the 30s preaching the message of the resurrected Jesus to their fellow Jews in the lingua franca of the Diaspora, common or koine Greek.

The other passage, that from the oral tradition, Jesus' "performance" and its framing in a narrative, to a written text, must have been equally quick and easy in highly literate Palestine. Again, it is Papias, as reported by Eusebius, who gives us a glimpse into the way it was thought to have happened. According to Papias, Mark was the "interpreter" of Peter, we guess among the Greek-speaking Jews in Rome, where Peter ended his days. And, Papias continues, "he wrote down accurately everything that he [Peter] remembered, though not in order, of the things either said or done by the Word. For he [Mark] had neither heard the Lord nor been his follower, but afterward, as I said, was a follower of Peter, who adapted his [Jesus'] teachings as anecdotes [or "as needed"] but had no intention of giving an ordered account."

New Approaches

Papias somewhat oddly appears to be offering a historical criticism, that Mark's work, a gospel, was not written in the manner of history, with an orderly sequence of events. But that was acceptable, Papias notes, as was the fact that Mark himself was neither a disciple nor an eyewitness to

Jesus—which was grievously important in this matter of Christian authenticity—because he set down "accurately" in writing what had come to him from Peter, who was both an eyewitness to Jesus—particularly in the matter of the resurrected Jesus (1 Cor. 15:3–7)—and a Jesus "follower," that is, one who shared in the Messiah's private as well as public teaching. And if the translation "adapted his teachings as anecdotes" (*pros tas chreias*) is correct, it may have been Peter who began to shape the teachings of Jesus into the story of Jesus. In Q we can perhaps see the beginning of that process and in canonical Mark the end of it, where the teachings are fully embedded in a narrative setting as the "Good News."

Q was obviously *collected* (though with some editorial retouching, some would insist) whereas the canonical Gospels were all equally obviously *composed*, that is, they were literary productions using known literary techniques and with an author's intent and purpose directing the effort. By the beginning of the twentieth century an emphasis on the teachings had led to what is now called form criticism, and an analysis of the author's intent to redaction criticism. Form criticism, which had perfected its methods on the Biblical Psalms, attempted first to decompose the Gospels into their component forms (parable, miracle story, pronouncement, etc.), and then to determine how the literary "laws" governing such forms operated in the Gospels. It was an effort to discern the basic literary units within the Gospels, the pericopes, in something close to their original state. Redaction criticism looks rather at sources—the ghosts of "J" and family hover prominently here—and attempts to determine what the "author" had done with (or to) them in the course of producing the finished work. Thus, Matthew not only improves Mark's Greek, we observe, but he introduces into his own retelling of Mark the powerful notion of Jesus' fulfillment of the Biblical prophecies as well as sharpened conflict with the Pharisees and, in the end, with the Jews: the chilling cry "May his blood be upon us and upon our children" is Matthew's editorial addition to Mark's narrative.

If it was somewhat disconcerting to discover that Matthew and Luke were tailoring their sources on Jesus, it was even more troubling to be told that even Mark, whose Gospel had been regarded as the most primitive and the closest to the "historical" Jesus, had also shaped his account to fit his own agenda. If that was true, as some firmly believe today, there is no source for Jesus save Q, a collection of his sayings. The narrative Gospel of

Mark has thus become the modern battlefield for the possession of Jesus, or perhaps, the last line of defense in the religio-scholarly struggle to save the historical Jesus.

Community Authorship

Form criticism seemed to focus attention on the authors of the Gospels but from a perspective that was far more interested in oral rather than literary forms and so regarded the production of the Gospels as a species of "folk literature." The result was the authorship of the Gospels came increasingly to be understood as the product of a community, the new, more polite version of the somewhat tarnished "folk" or "Volk" of earlier critics, rather than due to an individual's effort. Thus, it was not an individual named Matthew who wrote the Gospel—no one was any longer quite sure who "Matthew" was in any event—but a "Matthean community." To discern who they were (and when and where they were active) one has to read between the Gospel's lines, whence seemed to emerge a group of scarcely Hellenized Jewish followers of Jesus—but Hellenized enough to need a Greek Gospel—who were, circa 80 or 90 CE, under increasing pressure from the new Pharisaic rulers of post-70 Palestinian Judaism. And the same is true of the "Johannine community" who are thought by some to have created, out of some old traditions, to be sure, the Fourth Gospel, but who were far more remote in time from the original events and so, by intimation, from the reality of Jesus. The Johannine community, those bold theologians allegedly behind the Fourth Gospel, had been "driven out of the synagogue," as the Gospel claims, and perhaps out of some Christian fellowships as well.

The one Gospel whose author has most resisted expansion and assimilation into a "community" has been that "according to Luke," which obviously and unabashedly smells of the inkpot. The authorial voice of Acts, which enters the text in person as "we" (he and Paul in 16:11), the "Luke" of the "Gospel according to . . . ," was identified without ancient demur as a converted Gentile physician, a native of Antioch, it was said, and obviously a follower and sometime companion of Paul. What is certain is that whoever wrote the Acts as "we" also wrote the Third Gospel and moreover conceived of the two as a single literary work. The Church, however, which obviously cared more for witness than for literature, separated the two parts: volume 1 was put with the Gospels after Mark and before John, while volume 2, the Acts, was postponed to a place after John's Gospel and before Paul's letters.

All the Gospels have prologues of a sort—John's (1:1–14) is nothing short of a theological manifesto—but Luke's (1:1–4) is professedly literary, as is its counterpart that begins Acts (1:1–2). In the first he indicates both the method and the purpose of the work that follows. "Many others have composed narratives" of Jesus' life—presumably Gospels, almost certainly including Mark, but probably not including the near-contemporary Matthew—but the author will take up the narrative task anew because he has done considerable research on the subject—"the events that have transpired in our midst"—and will set them out "just as those who were eyewitnesses and present at the Word delivered them to us." And the purpose, he instructs his patron Theophilus, is "that you may grasp firmly the significance of the tradition (*paradosis*, the "handing on") when you have been instructed." There was no community at work here: Theophilus had underwritten the work and Luke was delivering the results.

Paul and the Rest

The other works in the New Testament collection pose few literary problems apart from the personal identification of the authors. Early on Christians wondered if Paul had really written the Letter to the Hebrews, and modern critics have moved a few other of the canonical Pauline letters to the category of "doubtful." But "John" is the most uncertain of all, in part because three different works are attributed to "John"—a Gospel, a couple of letters, and the book of Revelation or Apocalypse—and no one, ancient or modern, is terribly sure that they are all from the same man. A very early and quite creditable Christian tradition going back to Polycarp (d. ca. 155 CE), a "follower" of John, and passed on by Ireneus of Lyons (ca. 130–200) makes the author of the Fourth Gospel to be John, son of Zebedee and the same "beloved disciple" who rested on Jesus' breast at the Last Supper (John 13:23). Many modern critics have surrendered judgment on that point; they prefer instead to speak, as we have seen, of a "Johannine community" that "created" the Fourth Gospel out of narrative and perhaps oral traditions to address its own current concerns at the turn of the first Christian century. It may also have produced the three stylistically similar "Johannine" letters, two of which describe themselves as being from "the Elder." Finally, there were doubts in the past and there are almost universal doubts today that whoever was responsible for the Fourth Gospel and/or the letters ascribed to John was the same "John" (Rev. 1:1) who wrote the Apocalypse, the last piece collected into the New Testament.

With Revelation we leave the professedly historical world of the Gospels, Acts, and letters to enter into the realm of futuristic imagination, one of the favorite genres of Second Temple Jews, at least until Armageddon almost descended on them from the hands of the Romans. Earlier Jewish authors had summoned up venerable figures of the Biblical past, notably Enoch, Baruch, and Ezra, to lift the veil (*apocalypsein*) and to serve as guides through the days of dread and glory that will constitute the End-Time. In them the evil launch a last terrible offensive, but in the end God intervenes, the last of His many appearances ex machina and, either Himself or through an emissary, crushes His foes and exalts His saints. It is all there in the New Testament's own vivid version. The emissary is of course Jesus, whose "Second Coming" (*parousia*) completes the work of the First, which inaugurated the Messianic Age. There is not much need for commentary here. The book of Revelation was composed, in writing and, like all the rest of the New Testament, in Greek, by an author. He was called "John the Elder." Beyond that we cannot go.

The Apocryphal Gospels

The witnesses to the risen Jesus, and so to the faith that he was Messiah and Savior, are essentially the men the Gospels name "the Twelve," the Apostles called by Jesus to play a critical role in the eschatological Kingdom. But that End-Time took a form different from what had apparently been anticipated by Jesus' followers, and after Jesus' departure the Apostles rather quickly lost their eschatological function and became instead the carriers of the Word in the reconceived Messianic Age and, as we have seen, the primary witnesses to Jesus' life and teachings and deeds, the historical anchors of the new faith.

Four of the Twelve—or Thirteen, if we include Paul among the Apostles, as the early Church did—had their testimony enshrined in Gospels: Peter (via Mark), Matthew, John, and Paul (via Luke). But what of the others, the Andrews, Jameses, and Phillips? The Acts of the Apostles do not tell us much about them, but the early churches eventually produced a lavish literature of the "Acts" or deeds of these other, neglected pillars of the Jesus movement. And there appeared as well a number of Gospels attributed to these "other" Apostles. The churches chose not to include any of these Gospels in the New Testament canon; rather, they were "set aside" or described as "reserved" (*apocrypha*).

There is very little direct testimony to these apocryphal or "reserved" Christian Gospels. The overwhelming number of them are known either from manuscript fragments or merely by titles that occur in lists compiled by early Christian writers whether from experience or by hearsay. The reason is fairly obvious: it required neither bans nor book burning to limit the circulation of the apocrypha. The Christian churches first agreed, and then the Great Church insisted, on the unique authenticity of Matthew, Mark, Luke, and John. The results are apparent in the number and diffusion of the manuscript copies of the four Gospels that have survived. Copying was an expensive and laborious task, and the churches' consensus must have rather quickly driven the other gospels out of circulation.

The churches came to their decision on authenticity by that kind of silent and mutual agreement that baffles anyone trying to describe the process of Scriptural canonization. In this instance, they agreed that these four Gospels, and these four alone, bore authentic testimony to Jesus, both the man and his message. What made them so? In part it was the attribution "according to . . ." in their titles—which is why the authors' names are in the title to begin with. The very titles announced, in effect, that the testimony of these four was thought to be either directly derived from apostolic eyewitnesses (Matthew, John) to the Good News of Jesus or else based on such (Mark on Peter, Luke on Paul). Indeed, some early manuscript editions of the Gospels recognized that distinction: they bound the Gospels in the order Matthew, John (the Apostles), followed by Luke and Mark (Apostle-derived). In either case, the Good News thus came from unimpeachable sources, a fact apparently that everyone knew and agreed on without benefit of a show of hands. As for the Apocrypha, all we can say is that they were not thought to be authoritative by reason of either their alleged attribution—Peter did *not* write this Gospel or Thomas that—their contents, or simply their late appearance, after the Four had already achieved their canonical distinction.

But if the apocryphal Gospels were not judged authentic, which meant, among other things, exclusion from Christian liturgical worship—the canonical Gospels and Paul were read at every Eucharistic celebration—it did not mean they were necessarily false or offensive or dangerous. Some were in fact judged exactly that—the Gospels labeled "Gnostic" were part of the documentation of that early heresy—but others simply responded to the Christian appetite for more details about the life of the Redeemer and enjoyed an occasional or local role as the stuff of piety. The so-called Protoevangelium of James (the basis of many a detail in the standard Christmas story) and the Infancy Gospel of Thomas fall into this category. In both those instances we are in the province of legend building, extensions of the same legendary accounts of Jesus' birth and childhood (inserted?) in Matthew and Luke.

The four canonical Gospels are all what may be termed "narrative Gospels," that is, the essential elements regarding Jesus are told in the form of a story that unfolds in a chronological and topographical line: Jesus' ministry in Galilee through Jesus' last days in Jerusalem. In two instances (Matthew and Luke) there are some preliminary details or stories about events surrounding his birth and early years, and in all four a postscript regarding what people witnessed after his death. Embedded in this storytelling are sayings and teachings of Jesus, usually grouped together as units.

Thomas and His Twin

As we have seen, Q was "extracted" from Matthew and Luke by nineteenth-century New Testament scholarship. There the matter rested, one of the assured findings of modern Gospel criticism. A previously unknown source had been adduced from Matthew and Luke, and a comparison of those two Gospels with the sources they were using enabled critics to understand more fully how the Gospels were composed and the editorial tendencies and agenda of their authors, including, of course, those of Mark and Q. No doubts were cast on the authenticity of the contents of Q: they were as authentic as the Gospels that used them, even though the churches never thought to use or canonize Q in its original form, perhaps because it was not a "Gospel." But then in 1945 the full text of an *apocryphon* that had been known only in Greek fragments and as the "Gospel of Thomas" was discovered, albeit in a Coptic translation, in a fourth-century Christian library at Nag Hammadi in Egypt. And this Gospel, for so it calls itself, is, like Q, a collection of the logia or sayings of Jesus. It was assuredly not the long-lost Q but something very like it, and very soon a synergistic field began to develop between the two collections. If Thomas was a Gospel, should not its sister sayings-collection Q also be thought of as a Gospel? And if Q, the source of Matthew and Luke, was authentic, and arguably *more* authentic than the two works that used it, might not Thomas also be authentic, even though the Christian churches had said not?

One obvious consequence of the mating of Q and Thomas was to raise the issue of the historical relevancy of first, this new category of "sayings Gospel," which Q, arguably even earlier than Mark, gave grounds for thinking was the original Gospel type, and second, more generally, the entire category of apocryphal Gospels. The early Church, which was certainly history-minded but not much concerned with historical criticism as we understand it, could take or leave those other Gospels as historical sources for the life of Jesus. For edification, enlightenment, or entertainment, the early Christians might read the Apocrypha; for authentic witness to their Savior, they turned to the canonical Gospels. But by all accounts, "authentic witness" rests on far more of a theological judgment than does "reliable source." What was being asked, all theology, and so the Church's judgment, aside, was whether any of the so-called apocryphal Gospels might be genuine and independent sources for the life of the historical Jesus. It is a question never posed by the early Christians, who preferred "witness" to "source" and for whom the "historical Jesus" and the "Christ of faith," to use the distinction favored by modern study, were one and the same person.

The question is much debated and remains unresolved, particularly in the case of the Gospel of Thomas. Most of the apocryphal Gospels are transparent reworkings of the Synoptics, but claims for an early date for Thomas and a historicity independent of the canonical Gospels is most strenuously argued, particularly since it has the parallel buttress of the undoubtedly early and undoubtedly authentic Q. And from this has arisen another contention, that these "sayings Gospels" were the original testimony or sources on Jesus, that they preceded the narrative, and hence more "editorialized" or, less politely, slanted, view of Mark and the others. It has been argued, in consequence, that with Q and Thomas—the elision is easy—we are in the presence of, or at least as close as we can expect to be to, the "real" Jesus, and that Mark and the other "stories" are the creation of the Church. If this is allowed, the "real" Jesus was first, foremost, and finally a Galilean preacher/teacher—a Cynic philosopher, a peasant revolutionary, or a "tweedy poetaster" on various reconstructions—but certainly not a dying and resurrected Redeemer.

The debate has focused new interest and attention on the apocryphal Gospels, which are, however, but poorly attested by actual texts. All we have are one or possibly two bits of papyrus for the Gospel of Peter or a translation into Coptic by an unknown hand at an unknown date for that of Thomas. And if the late date of some seems inconvenient for a genuine source on Jesus—again, Thomas provides the premier example—the apocryphal Gospel can be "redacted" back—shorn of its later additions—to a more acceptably primitive core. But the attention has been nonetheless useful. Besides enlarging the "Quest of the Historical Jesus," it has also cast a new light on the early Church, the *Sitz im Leben* or historical setting for the making of the apocryphal Gospels, and what they do not tell us about Jesus, they certainly do about the beliefs (and disbeliefs!) of the Christians who composed or assembled them.

Chapter 5

The Poet in Performance

The Composition of the Quran

ᢙᠻᢗ

Although we have not quite answered the question of who the authors of the Bible or the New Testament were, we have gotten reasonably close to the original stages of the works and understood something of their composition. To attempt something similar with regard to the Quran, to answer how it was composed, we have to rely on the Book itself, and chiefly on its signs rather than on its statements. Once we have identified these latter, we can then attempt better to understand them in the light of the now considerable evidence, and theory, available from other works produced in the same kind of oral culture in which the Quran appeared.

The Revelations

The Muslim tradition that arose in the wake of the Quran professedly tells us nothing directly about the making of the Book since it does not believe that in its original form it was either "made" or "composed"; indeed, Muslims could not quite decide whether the Quran was even created. It was not, they finally decided, despite the enormous theological difficulties that flowed from that position. What all Muslims knew as a certainty was that the Quran came from God and was delivered to the Prophet in the words we still find there. In addition, the Muslim tradition tells us what it knew, or thought it knew, of how Muhammad *received* the Quran, how it came to be written down, and, as we have already seen, how it was finally "collected" into a standard text, an event thought to have occurred less than twenty years after the Prophet's death.

Missing from our biographical texts on Muhammad, as well as from the Quran itself, are any references to a preliminary discourse whereby the Prophet explained to the Meccans what had happened to him and what it was that he was about to recite. Just as in the Christian case the "Good News" had been preached in some form and already embraced by the Galatians and the Thessalonians before Paul began to explain it to them, so it may well be that Muhammad had preached Islam to the Meccans before he recited the Quran to them and that the "Recitation" itself was, like its Syriac prototype, a *qeryana*, a liturgical *lectio* intended for those who had already "submitted" and who formed the first congregation of believers. The Quran by its content suggests otherwise, however. Its Meccan suras, which are arguably the most liturgical, are manifestly addressed to an audience of nonbelievers, and it was unbelievers who accused Muhammad of being a poet as they listened to (and watched) him "recite."

The Quran is silent on Muhammad's experience of revelation. The only description of what might have been a revelation event occurs in the early Meccan sura 53 (1–8). Muhammad feels constrained to convince the skeptics that he has not "wandered"—the same word used by God to describe Muhammad's state before his Lord set him morally aright (93:7). To do so he here adduces two personal experiences that were explicitly intended to quell doubts about his prophetic authenticity. First, time and place unspecified, there appeared to him a heavenly figure described as "one of mighty power." Initially it was seen on the distant horizon, but then considerably closer, a hundred yards distant perhaps, and then "He revealed to His servant what He revealed." The second time Muhammad witnessed the same figure on a more specific landscape, by a "garden of the dwelling" and "near the sidra tree." Some think this is a matter of heavenly geography, a vision attached to an exaltation, but the lack of any explanation of what are to us, and in fact to the Muslim tradition, unknown places argues rather that it was a matter of very local geography, neighborhood sites that the Meccans knew very well. And then, the passage continues, "he saw one of the greatest signs of his Lord." Despite later Muslim legend, nothing here or elsewhere in the Quran makes us think that Muhammad ever mounted to heaven; indeed, the Quran suggests quite the opposite (6:35; 17:90–93).

These two experiences described in the Quran are explicitly visions, visual appearances by God to His "servant"—only later (2:97) was Gabriel called into service as an intermediary—while the Quran itself was on the face of it an oral/aural revelation: God's words were pronounced to the

Prophet and were to be pronounced anew by Muhammad for the benefit of humankind. But how did Muhammad receive this elaborate message? Sura 42 (51–52) sets out some of the possibilities, albeit in a very general way, and it is the most specific evidence on revelation that we have from the Quran: "It is not fitting," the text says, "for a human being that God should speak to him except by revelation (*wahy*), or from behind a veil, or He sends a messenger who reveals by His permission what He will."

The crucial word here is the Arabic verb *ahwa*, and its noun *wahy*, whose semantic range in the Quran extends from "prompt" or "inspire" (from within) to the more specific "reveal" (from without). Muhammad had experienced both senses of the word. He is "prompted" to follow the faith of Abraham (16:123) just as that patriarch was to embrace monotheism. But the message of monotheism was "revealed" to him (41:6, etc.), just as it had been "revealed" to other prophets (21:25; 29:65). Indeed, the Quran itself has been "revealed" to Muhammad (12:3; 20:114; 42:7). To say that the Quran was simply suggested to Muhammad, or even to say that he was "inspired" to recite it, the way the Christians came to believe the evangelists were inspired to write the Gospels, is to back off the Muslims' original and pervasive contention that the words of the Quran are the *ipsissima verba Dei*.

The double range of *wahy* as both inspiration and revelation and a chronological arrangement of its occurrences—again, it should be noted how important a chronological ordering of the suras is to all attempts to learn anything about the Quran or the Prophet—opens another possibility. Did Muhammad's own understanding of what he was experiencing move from the mantic poet's inner "inspiration" to a verbal "revelation," just as the (apparent) figure of God in sura 53 becomes in sura 2 (97) an attestation for Gabriel following on Muhammad's exposure to Jewish traditions at Medina? And should we not see the changing notions across the Quran as another way of expressing the difference between the inspired "poetic" suras of Mecca and the revealed "prosaic" suras of Medina?

Biography and the Quran

There is much in the Quran to baffle the reader, but the text, even as we now have it, whether written or printed, stands closer to its original author than most of what we have in either the Bible or the New Testament. The "authors" of the books of the Bible are lost to us, and even the indistinct "J" and "E" are revealed to be editors of a text rather than its composers. The ascribed authors of the Gospels, each of whom has a somewhat distinctive voice, are all enveloped in an opaque tradition or else turn out to be another anonymous collector of logia like the unknown figures who stand behind Q and the Gospel of Thomas. In the Pauline letters, however, and in the Quran, we stand face to face not merely with a voice but with a full-throated personality. Again, the question of inspiration does not concern us here, though it is claimed for both men: in our context, the letters (the authentic ones) come from the pen of Paul, the Quran from the mouth of Muhammad. Both works are marked by a distinctive personal style, and for both men we have an external tradition that supplies details on the life of these two propagators and champions of the new faith, or perhaps of an old faith renewed.

There are, of course, considerable differences between the two cases. The Pauline letters are marbled with autobiographical detail: Paul had no hesitation standing in front of his work. Muhammad, in contrast, is all but totally concealed behind the Quran. There may be brief (auto)biographical hints in suras 80 (1–10) and 93 (6–8), but otherwise the Quran passes over this anonymous "servant," as Muhammad is called there—the name "Muhammad" occurs only four times in the whole Quran (3:144; 33:40; 47:3; 48:29)—with only the briefest regard. As for the external information, Paul's apostolic career is traced, not always in agreement with what is in his own letters, by a younger contemporary and one of his own followers, Luke, who dedicates a good part of his Acts of the Apostles to the acts of this rather late-coming Apostle. Acts was probably written in the 80s, twenty years after Paul's death. Muhammad's standard biography, which doubtless absorbed earlier collections of traditions about the Prophet, dates from Baghdad a century and a half later, a world of event and consequence away from the Mecca and Medina of Muhammad.

Named or not, Muhammad's voice is vibrantly present in the Quran, as are the suggestive outlines of his personality, though we find few details of his life or his doings. For these we must turn to a biography, and to what has become the standard Life, the one assembled in Baghdad in the 750s out of older materials by Muhammad ibn Ishaq (d. 768). Thus, if the Quran—like the New Testament's Q—is a collection of Muhammad's lo-

gia, then the Muhammad "Mark"—the narrative setting of those logia—
was postponed to a century later. Or more. Indeed, Ibn Ishaq's *Life of the
Envoy of God* has struck a number of modern scholars as composed precisely as a Muslim Gospel to meet the challenges of eighth- and ninth-
century Baghdad's aggressive Christian community. And what was true of
Ibn Ishaq's (now lost) original is even truer of the cut-down (and cleaned-
up!) version we have from the editorial workshop of one Ibn Hisham (d.
833) and whatever else we can retrieve from its secondhand use by later
Muslim historians.

But it is not merely for biography that we consult this biohistorical tradition. More importantly perhaps, the *Life* professes to give us the "occasions of revelation," as the Muslims called them: the circumstances surrounding the revelation of at least some of the suras of the Quran. Indeed,
this subset of Prophetic biography constitutes an entire genre of medieval
Muslim biographical exegesis or, as we may suspect, of exegetical biography, since they appear more often to be describing, or imagining, as we do,
events in the Prophet's life that might plausibly explain the Quran. On this
somewhat uncertain historical foundation an imposing edifice of Muslim
Quran commentary has been erected, a construction as essential as it is
suspect.

It has been justly said that the Quran is unintelligible without some
knowledge of Muhammad's life and prophetic experience. And we must
immediately add that that knowledge comes uniquely from the biographical tradition since the Quran itself has little or nothing to say on the subject. Without knowing, for example (from the *Life* and complementary
traditions), that the Quran was dictated by God to Muhammad, who is
simply reciting the words he had heard, we would be hard-pressed in
many instances to determine who was speaking, or to whom, amid the
text's welter of floating pronouns. On the basis of that (later) information,
we can infer that in direct discourse God is usually the speaker, even
though the speaker refers to Himself now as "I," now as "We" or "He"/"Him"
or obliquely as "my Lord," and even though Muhammad himself appears
to be the speaker in some places (81:15–21; 84:16–19; 92:14–21). Muhammad, we likewise infer, is the one addressed throughout by "you" (sing.)
or, more obliquely, as "His servant," while the plural "you" refers to the audience of the moment, the Meccans, the Medinese, or even, where the theology dictates, all of humankind.

The same later Muslim authorities who tell us these things also supply a great many details on the reception, writing down, and collection of the Quran. They provide, moreover, like most medieval Arab-Muslim historical writing, chains of authorities by which the information, almost all of which professes to be based on eyewitness testimony, reached the author. Muslims accept most of the contents of this historical-biographical information at face value, but non-Muslims are far more skeptical of both the chain of tradents and the information they claim to transmit. Some of this latter is doubtlessly authentic, though no one has devised a convincing means of separating the nutritious wheat from the acres of blowing chaff. Many of the traditions are patently self-serving, or else bent on explaining, just as we are, the circumstances surrounding the appearance of the Quran, without, however, admitting, as we do, that it is a matter of very few facts and much surmise.

ॐ๏๏ *Note: The "Apostolic Witness" in Islam.*

Just as testimony regarding Jesus rested firmly on the witness of the Apostles, that on Muhammad rests finally on the eyewitness testimony of the Prophet's Muslim contemporaries. But where the number of Jesus' Apostles is ideologically determined by their serving as representatives of the Twelve Tribes of Israel in the eschatological Kingdom, there is no such limitation in Islam. The "witnesses" to the Prophet, his "Companions," as the Muslim tradition called them, are defined as all who were alive, men and women, even children according to some, in the Prophet's presence. None of these worthies composed a Muhammad "Gospel"; their testimony to the Prophet is found rather in the hundreds of thousands of "Prophetic reports" (*hadith*) that were in circulation in the ninth and tenth centuries. It is from these, to which the Muslims granted, as we have seen, canonical status, that the true Muhammad "Gospels" were composed, the *Lives* by Muhammad ibn Ishaq and others.

What make the surmises of modern scholarship worth reading is that their conclusions can now find support in the comparative study of the oral tradition. For the Muslim the Quran is incomparable in not only the exalted sense of being without compare, but also, and this is central here, that it *should not* be placed next to, compared to, or illuminated from, any other merely human work. More, the Muslim theory of revelation, that what was "sent down" from God to His chosen prophet was both the message and the medium, that is, the language and diction down to the last anacoluthon, blocks all recourse to historical contingency. Here are none of the "constraints of history" that guide critical approaches to other Scriptures (to the pain of many believers!) or the notion of conditioning that enables some Scripturalists to escape the iron bed of the Divine Will. Conditioning, the circumscription of the Message by the limits imposed by the historical circumstances of revelation, the hocceity of the time, the place, and the messenger—save, perhaps, that the Prophet sometimes forgets what has been sent him (2:91)—has no place in the Muslim scheme of revelation: God's omnipotence trumps historical contingency as surely as God's Decree trumps human free will in Muslim theology.

Approaching the Quran

We must proceed, then, without direct help from Muslim historians, philologists, and literary scholars for whom Quran criticism, as that term is understood in non-Muslim circles, is not only unknown but unthinkable. Muslims have devoted a great deal of skill and energy to Quranic exegesis and, usually in connection with that, explanations of the Quran's language, style, and themes. But little or no effort has been made to explore how or whence this remarkable Book/book may have come about, or Muhammad's own role in producing—a spectacularly wrong word for Muslims—the Quran. But even from a purely secular point of view, the Muslims, from the untutored to the most learned, are far more likely to come to the Quran as it was originally intended by its composer, whether that was God or Muhammad, namely, as a listener; and we, generally and mistakenly, as readers.

For the literary text- and reader-oriented critic, or simply put, for its readers, the Quran presents a number of near-insuperable difficulties. First, readers are accustomed to dealing with texts as something written, and so it is perfectly natural that they approach the Quran as they do all books, as readers. But the Quran is not primarily a book in the usual sense of that word, that is, something written or printed. There is a book in our hands, to be sure, but the Quran is a book principally in the sense of Scripture, a Book written by God to which humans should pay heed. That is the theology of the Quran. On a more worldly level, it is the record of a literary performance—a devalued notion in the Muslim calculus; it is a "recitation," to use its own self-descriptive word, that has, on the face of it, undergone the same kind of literary transformations that were earlier worked on the oral tradition in the Bible and the New Testament. Both of those Scriptures issued in their final transmission stage—in the case of the Bible this may have occurred at about the same time as the Quran—as genuine literary texts that had been compiled and edited and, in effect, written.

The Cultural Environment

The Muslim tradition insists, counterintuitively and in the face of everything else we know, or think we know, about the environment in which the Quran appeared, that the Prophet's revelations were *written down* by some of Muhammad's own contemporaries. That tradition is the product of a quite urban and quite literate society of a different time and a different place so it is perhaps natural to have thought so, but it must be asked who would be writing in early seventh-century Mecca and why? For commerce? In the early seventh century, Mecca's only visible business was a modest local trade with the Bedouin, and it would hardly have required writing skills of any type. But scribes also normally occur in both municipal—they keep the city's records—and religious contexts. Mecca's political institutions were rudimentary, to say the least, and were based principally on tribal relationships that had, and have, little need of archives. Also, Mecca's religious myths had all disappeared, perhaps long before Muhammad's own lifetime, so not only would there have been no need of religious scribes; as far as we are aware, there would have been nothing for them to do if they had existed.

If the New Testament came into existence in an environment with a relatively high degree of literacy, the same is not true of the Quran. Literacy was more widespread in the seventh century than it had been in the first, but not everywhere and hardly so in either Mecca or Medina, one an isolated shrine settlement, a village by any standards, and the other an oasis date palm plantation. There are no traces, literary or archaeological, of writing in those parts, and certainly not in Arabic; indeed, the Arabs were still struggling with its script a century or more after Muhammad's death. There was a formal literature, to be sure, a poetry of boast and bravado, most of it, but none was written down as far as we can see since there was no one who knew how, and there was in fact no one to read it.

The poetry we do possess from that era—there are lingering misgivings as to its authenticity but they are not grave—was, by all accounts and our own estimates, composed orally, recited orally, and transmitted orally until the ninth or tenth century, when it was finally committed to writing. The same is essentially true of the seventh century's largest, and unique, anthology of prose-poetry, the Quran. Its components, suras and parts of suras, and perhaps even the occasional composite sura, all bear the unmistakable stamp of an oral poet at work, and the work seems to have been only marginally affected by a literary as opposed to an oral sensibility. There has been some "cutting and pasting," to be sure, and, for reasons we cannot fathom, some very unliterary rearrangement of the suras or units of composition—what are generally called, in more organic works, "headings" (*capita*) or chapters.

As just remarked, the Muslim tradition made some not very convincing efforts to demonstrate that the Quran is also a *literary text* by maintaining that at least parts of it were written down in Muhammad's own lifetime. Some few have even maintained that Muhammad himself may have put some of it into writing, a possibility contradicted by all the evidence we have for writing at that time and that place. It is even contradicted by another element of the Muslim tradition itself, namely, that the caliph Uthman was prompted to produce his standard edition circa 650 by the death in battle of many of those who had memorized the Quran. Thus, there was a concern for variations in the *oral* text and not a written one. We can only agree: the evidence is incontestable that with the Quran, the original Quran, we are in the presence of a product of an oral tradition and in an oral culture.

Writing and the Quran

If we examine the consequences of this conclusion, we can understand better, even granting Muhammad his divine source and inspiration, both the "composition" of the Quran and the early stages of its transmission. Muhammad is called *ummi* in the Quran (7:157–158), a word the Muslim commentators insisted meant "illiterate." There are those who disagree about the meaning of the Arabic word but none on the fact of the Prophet's illiteracy. Muslims underline Muhammad's inability to read (and hence to borrow from anyone else's Scripture), but he was equally incapable of writing, as were most of his contemporaries in that remote Arabian outpost. Unmistakably the Meccans knew about writing—the Quran is filled with terms related to that skill and it even calls itself a "book," "something written," though in none of these instances is there evidence that either Muhammad or his audience could have read out the contents of those "things written."

If an oral tradition and a literary tradition stand at opposite ends of a spectrum, or rather, as is clear from the redaction of the Bible, a continuum that alters only very gradually, there are good reasons for putting the Quran very close to the purely oral end of the scale. One is its own view of writing, and in particular, of writing in the form of a Book. For literate people, writing serves primarily for the recording and presentation of information, whereas in chiefly oral societies, writing, or better, the written object, has magical properties and powers; it is a symbol, an icon. That is the normal regard of "the Book" in the Quran, which is, in the first instance, its heavenly prototype, the "Mother of the Book" (13:39; 43:4) or the "Well-Guarded Tablet" (3:7), which, like the "Tablets of the Law" in Exodus (31:18; 32:16), was presumably written by the "finger of the Lord." The Book is also then, by extension, the oral "recitation" that was "sent down" from the "Mother of the Book" to constitute the "Book" that was the still-oral Quran (10:37).

The oral society's profound regard for the power of writing is signaled by the fact that even modern and quite literate Islamic societies continue to share the Quran's view of writing as possessing a power in itself. While some of the overwhelming prominence of Arabic calligraphy on exterior and interior walls—where it is often illegible by reason of its position or elaborate patterning—is doubtless due to the Islamic prohibition against images, it may owe even more to the Quran's own "oral" attitudes toward writing and their transmission and transformation in a society that has itself long remained oral in its culture. Arabic calligraphy, with the Quran at its heart, is undoubtedly aesthetically decorative but it is also, and no less certainly, sacramental.

Writing in Arabia

Part of the evidence for making a judgment about ancient literacy are the remains of writing and writing materials. In the case of Israelite literacy, it was the discovery of dated writing samples of various types on materials ranging from papyrus to the more expensive parchment, from baked clay seals that had once been attached to written documents (since disappeared), to ceramic ostraca, the "scratch paper of the Near Eastern world," to monumental inscriptions on stone.

Wooden tablets coated with stucco (Egypt) or wax (Anatolia, Syria, and Mesopotamia) are preserved and well-known writing surfaces in the ancient Middle East, and they may have been the prototypes—again like the Sacred Books of the Jews and the Christians, possibly seen but never read by the Meccans—for the Quran's "Well-Guarded Tablet" (3:7). There are no traces of such materials in Arabia, however; indeed, none have been found from ancient Israel, though they were the most common writing material for scribes, which Israel certainly did possess, and are mentioned in the Bible (Isa. 30:8; Hab. 2:2), and in considerably more concrete terms than in the Quran.

All we do have from pre-Islamic tribal Arabia, however, is a linguist's casebook of graffiti in a variety of long since disappeared tribal tongues, the scratched yelps and sighs of bored or frightened Bedouin on the steppe. There was certainly writing in the sedentary culture of South Arabia around Muhammad's time, as we know from the inscriptions on stone found there, though there is no trace of a "literature." But the largely Christian and Jewish Yemen, which then used a language far more closely related to its sister Ethiopic across the Red Sea than to its Semitic cousin, Quranic Arabic, was in political chaos and economic and social decline in Muhammad's day. For his part, the Prophet and his audience spoke Arabic, not South Arabian, and when the Quran came to be written down, it was not in some derivative of the script of the Yemen but in one that was developing in the north, on the borders of Syria.

A few pre-Islamic stone inscriptions in the language and the script that would become Arabic have been found, all from the sedentary, largely Christian, and partially Arabized environment along the edge of the Syrian steppe. The closest to Mecca, though still a month's camel journey away, is a sixth-century inscription from Umm al-Jimal, a Christian city just inside Jordan's border with Syria. But there is no evidence that this script, the one in which the Quran would eventually be transcribed, had penetrated the Arabian Hijaz or had come to Mecca in its midst, a town impervious to Christianity, which was the chief carrier of literacy in the Middle East in late antiquity, and, so it appears, to writing itself. The oldest Arabic inscription in Arabia was found at Taif, which is near Mecca, but it was put there by Syrians half a century after the death of Muhammad.

It has been remarked that the Greeks in their golden age had no word for either "literate" or "illiterate," and that *grammatikos*, the "lettered" person who could read, appeared only in the fourth century BCE. Arabic too lacked such terms. The already noted *ummi*, the Quranic word applied to Muhammad that is often translated "illiterate," means rather "pagan," hence, derivatively, one without a Scripture. Pre-Islamic poetry is aware of both books and writing, but never mentions a writer. So too the Quran, which knows books, and the pen and different writing materials, refers to no one who possesses the ability either to write or to read, save perhaps the recording angels (50:17–18) and, we must assume, God was capable reading their work, though even angelic writing, if it used the earliest Arabic writing system, without diacritical marks, punctuation, or capitals, may have taxed even divine omniscience.

So if the Quran came into existence as a written document—and when it did, it would have been "one of the earliest, if not the earliest, large scale attempt to reproduce graphically the oral language of poetry," as Michael Zwettler, who has canvassed the repertoire of Arab oral poetry, has said— it was not written by Muhammad. There is no indication that he or any of his contemporaries at either Mecca or Medina had the skills or the means to write the Quran. A written Quran would have had to be produced much later, when there were skills to match the task, in eighth- or ninth-century Baghdad, for example, as some modern Western scholars think in fact it was. And by whom? There could be no saying, of course, since the work was being passed off as the work of Muhammad, a seventh-century prophet of Mecca.

Oral Poetry and the Quran

By every index, internal and external, the Quran did not begin its life as a written document, and we must leave off "reading" the Quran and attempt to approach it for what it is: a poem or, perhaps better, a series of poems produced out of a thoroughly oral culture where writing was known (and revered) but rarely used and even more rarely read. For us a poem is a literary piece, something composed on paper or, if it is composed in the poet's head, it is soon committed to paper and edited and refined there. For oral societies a poem is a master genre, a way of recording and transmitting important events or received wisdom. It is made deliberately memorable by its use of rhythm and rhyme. As Eric Havelock, a prominent student of the Greek oral tradition, put it, "a poem is more memorizable than a paragraph of prose and a song is more memorizable than a poem." The Quran is both, at least in its Meccan suras, a poem and a song, and it was intended to be memorized.

If, then, we are to think of the Quran, the Meccan suras certainly, and discernibly the Medina suras as well, as likely the work of an oral poet, it is both proper and useful to view it against its more general type, though allowances must be made for the many variations across different cultures. The most prominent feature of the poetical product of an oral culture is its use of formulas, stock phrases that recur and serve metrically to fill out a line or a rhyme. But they have other functions as well. Formulas and repetitions or returns are the periods and capital letters of the oral composer: they mark beginnings and endings and so help to organize the composition. They are also the composer's italics and bold type. They emphasize and draw attention to important points and themes. Besides verbal formulas, there are stock images and topoi the composer may draw on to assist in the composition process.

The oral compositional technique itself has been described by Walter Ong in his study of oral literature as "additive rather than subordinative, aggregative rather than analytic, and redundant or 'copious' in its unfolding." The poet's thought, Ong continues, is expressed "in heavily rhythmic, balanced patterns, in repetitions and antitheses, in alliteration and assonance, in epithetic and formulaic expressions and standard thematic settings." In a purely formal sense, the Meccan suras of the Quran show all the indices of oral poetry—insistent assonance, if not always rhyme, a strongly emphasized rhythmic movement, recurrent or formulaic phrases, and frequent enjambment or end-stopped lines. More, the putative *Sitz im Leben* of these pieces, early seventh-century Mecca, corresponds with the social and cultural circumstances where such poetry has occurred, a very early transitional stage where writing may have been known but few had the skill to execute it or to read its mysterious runes.

On the witness of their own contents, the objective of the Meccan suras was a change in worship from polytheism to strict monotheism, and the method chosen for its achievement was preaching. The Meccan suras constituted a message for the society as a whole (with both a carrot and a stick prominently displayed in it) and delivered to a public audience. But this particular preaching was neither spoken nor read; it was "recited," that is, cantillated in a manner and form that immediately identified the performer to his audience as either a *kahin,* a "seer," or a *sha'ir,* a "poet." The Quranic recitations had, at any rate, an identifiable style sensibly removed from ordinary speech and ordinary language and ordinary behavior. And there must also have been gestures: as has been pointed out, many of the dramatic presentations of the Judgment—37:50–56 and 50:20–26, for example—would be unintelligible without identifying gestures or perhaps changes in vocal register.

Finally, there is the matter of the language of the Quran. Though the Book proudly identifies itself as *arabi,* "Arabic," no one is quite sure what that means. In a burst of hometown pride, the early Muslims imagined it must be a dialect of the Quraysh, the paramount tribe of Mecca, but that seems incorrect. The *arabiyya* of the Quran seems rather to have been a species of "artspeech," the common possession of the poetical guilds of the Arabs and the ordinary medium of their poetry. But it seems to have been transformed, quite possibly by Muhammad himself: when compared to pre-Islamic poetry, the speech of the Quran has been boldly broadened both semantically and lexicographically to express a whole range of new religious and moral images and ideas.

Muhammad, Poet and Performer

Let us turn now to the Prophet and his "performance." Everything we know about poets and poetry in an oral society like Mecca's in the Prophet's day—and Islamic culture for long afterward—indicates that the "recitation"/ performance was rarely completely improvised, that the poet, who was a skilled professional, devoted time and pains to crafting his work in private before performing it in public. We may even have been given an oblique glance of Muhammad at work (with God!) in sura 73 (1–8, with a later insertion at 3–4). But what the poet finally did perform in public was not entirely what he had composed in private: oral poetry of all types gives indications of responding to audience reaction as it unfolded so that the recited work was, in the end, the product of both preparation and "live" reaction-improvisation, even, we must believe, when the content embodied the Words of God.

The Quran shows an ongoing awareness of audience reaction. There are, as we have seen, on-the-spot explanations—"What will make you understand?"—that are obviously cued by audience reaction (101:9–11), or in these instances, perhaps a lack of it. There are direct answers to both questions and criticisms (2:135, etc.). And there was, finally, the charge that the "revelations" were somewhat too improvised, that Muhammad was in effect making it up as he went along, with one eye steadily fixed on the main chance. Not all of these responses had necessarily to occur in the original performance, however, since these performances were certainly and, in the case of the Quran, necessarily, repeated, and there was an opportunity for the poet, or the prophet, to make adjustments.

Was Muhammad such a poet-prophet? Did he compose and perform in this way? Medieval and modern distinctions between the style of the poet and the seer, and between them and the Quran are somewhat beside the point. Muhammad's audience knew far more about such things than we, and they certainly thought he filled the bill; and, moreover, they had their own theories of how he worked. It took no great sophistication to recognize him as a poet: what was proceeding from his lips was poetry by any standard: short-lined rhymed verses, chanted not spoken, and with high emotive content. His performance behavior too—"Oh you, wrapped in a cloak!" (74:1–7)—about which we are not very well instructed, may likewise have identified him as a poet. His listeners drew the appropriate conclusion, that these were "old stories" (25:4) and that he must have gotten his poetry from someone else, and even that what he was "reciting" had been "recited" or "passed on"—this is not the same word as that referring to the Quran—to him (25:5–6).

What was behind these accusations? The borrowing cannot likely refer to the *content* of the suras, which, as we have seen, was familiar to his listeners, though they may have wondered where *he* got it. Far more plausible is that, though Muhammad was playing, or better, performing, the poet, *they* knew that he had never been trained as such, that he was not a member of the guild. Poets were both born and, at the same time, made in Arabia, and if his fellow Meccans were willing to concede "inspiration" to Muhammad, that he was "jinn-possessed" (37:36), they knew he was not trained in the craft of poetry. Poets were known and admired or feared in that society; they were celebrities, and Muhammad ibn Abdullah, an orphan now in trade, who "eats and walks in the suqs" (25:7), was not. Baffled by what they were seeing and hearing, they accused Muhammad of professional imposture.

We are as baffled as they. We do not know where this minor merchant of Mecca learned to make poetry. For the Muslim tradition there was no issue here and so it offered no explanation; both the content and the diction of the Quran, its language, style, and very tropes, were from God. Hence, the Muslims quite correctly concluded, the Quran itself is a miracle and so is literally and literarily inimitable. Muhammad (or God speaking through him) claimed as much in response to his critics: let them try to produce suras like it! (2:23, etc.). And, if a miracle is an event with no natural causes, then the Quran is indeed a miracle. There was no sensible way by which an untrained Meccan—the question of Muhammad's illiteracy is irrelevant; most oral poets, and certainly the best, have been illiterate—could have produced such sophisticated verse as we find in the Quran.

The Bible in the Quran

If we can find the traits of oral poetry in many of the suras of the Quran, we must pause at Father Ong's last characteristic of the genre, the poet's use of "standard thematic settings." This is in effect what Muhammad's critics may have been accusing him of when they referred to his use of "old stories" (25:4). Muhammad denied the charge, and we must agree: the themes of his "recitation" are nothing like the stereotypes that appear in contemporary poets. One of the chief thematic settings of the Quran is in fact a Biblical one of prophets and prophecy: Adam and Abraham, Noah and Moses, David and Solomon, among many others, march back and forth across the suras, carrying with them their values and their vocabulary. And judging from the audience response as reflected in the Quran itself, the Biblical themes were comprehensible, if not always entirely familiar, to the Meccans who were hearing about those matters, and apparently not for the first time.

Biblical stories and personages must have been intelligible, or at very least familiar, to the Prophet's audience because these accounts all unfold *allusively* rather than with the kind of explanatory detail that would normally accompany strange or novel stories. In the Quran there are no "You ask who Abraham was? Abraham was . . ." The audience apparently *knew* who Abraham was, and Isaac and Ishmael and Jacob too. But there occurs occasionally its Quranic equivalent of "Stop me if you don't understand": "What will make you understand what X is?" The Quran sometimes interrupts itself, followed by an explanation—but always of words, not of persons or events. And the vocabulary of much of the Quran that pertains to ethical or religious matters—which are often words borrowed from the Syriac or Ethiopic tongues of the neighboring Christian cultures—is, as remarked, totally unrelated to that of the preserved pre-Islamic poets. The wonder is not that there are explanations of these apparently new coinages but that there are so few.

Where did this information come from, save from God? We may allow, *per cortesia*, the Muslim explanation that the Prophet received his Biblical (and evangelical) information from God, but where, then, did his apparently pagan audience receive an understanding that matched his own? The pre-Islamic poets may have had, as some maintain, some notion of Biblical *ideas*, but they certainly knew nothing of the Biblical *stories* with which Muhammad and his audience were seemingly familiar. As for the Quran itself, if it was in its origins, and to some extent remains, an oral poem, the Muslim Scripture has a backstory that is to some extent literary. It draws on and makes explicit reference to two documents, the Torah and the Gospel, that had reached fully literary (written) form long before Muhammad's day. But Muhammad's access to them was not literary. There were no Arabic versions of either the Bible or the Gospels available until long after the Prophet, even if he could have read them, which he could not.

Nor was anyone reading them to him. In this instance, we know better than his audience (25:5). Even a cursory look at the Bible and Gospel material mentioned in the Quran reveals that its author had not been exposed directly or indirectly to those texts of Scripture but rather in some fashion or another—we simply do not have enough information to say how—to what the Jews called haggadic midrashim, retellings of the contents of Scripture, often embellished with extraneous details for the enlightenment, edification, or entertainment of the audience. We now possess literary versions of such Biblical midrashim dating from the seventh or eighth century, but we can be assured that this popular storytelling form existed also, and perhaps originally, in an oral medium. We have no literary midrashim from Arabia in that era, but there were Jews in both South Arabia and the oases that stretch out in a chain northward from Medina, and it seems more than likely that their acquaintance with Scripture, and so Muhammad's own grasp, was oral-midrashic rather than literary-textual. What we have in extensive segments of the Quran are nothing less than the scattered members of a seventh-century haggadic midrash.

The same is true of the Gospel material in the Muslim Scripture. The Quran's stories of Jesus and Mary, again, allusively told or referred to, find their immediate parallels in the apocryphal Gospels and not in the canonical texts. We know less about the Apocrypha, and of the Eastern Christian popular literature on Jesus generally, than we do about the midrashim, which were rather carefully preserved by the rabbis in what were Jewish religio-cultural communities under Islam. And as in some of the Quran's Biblical stories, where Ezra (Uzayr), for example, is said to have been worshiped by some Jews as the Son of God (9:30), the accounts of Jesus there have some distinctly marginal as well as legendary elements vis-à-vis the Great Church's beliefs. In the Quran Jesus is said not to have died on the cross, but "there was a similarity to him" (4:156–159), a substitute victim according to most Quranic commentators. The way Muslims read the Quran, Jesus, the human prophet, is now on high with God (3:55) and will return to suffer his mortal death at the End-Time.

The Mantic Seer

Muhammad, then, struck his Meccan audiences as a jinn-possessed or jinn-inspired poet or perhaps a mantic *kahin* or seer, and the impression is reinforced by what seem to be early Muslim traditions about the Prophet. They relate that Muhammad told his wife Khadija apropos of his revelations, "I see light and hear a voice. I fear I am becoming a *kahin*." The accounts make Muhammad out so fearful of a demonic experience that he contemplated suicide! Nor was this the end of it. Muhammad's experience of having an angel kneel on his chest until he should recite exactly duplicates that of a contemporary poet. Hasan ibn Thabit said it was no angel, however, but a female demon who forced the poetry out of him.

The seer (*kahin*) and the poet (*sha'ir*) both provided access to what the Arabs called *al-ghayb*, the unseen world, in our terms perhaps the supernatural. Each was a familiar of the jinn, the *daimones* or *genii* of the Arabian spirit world, and both were, on occasion, jinn-struck (*majnun*) or, as we might say, inspired or possessed, though the flavor of the Arabic is closer to the latter. To the poet the jinn gave the skill to tell the tribal tales of bravery in war or sorrow in love; the poet was the memory and panegyrist of the tribe, the "archive of the Arabs," as he has been called. The kahin had somewhat more practical skills. His special knowledge made him a tribal counselor and arbitrator in matters great and small. Both were known from their speech, the rhymed prose (*saj'*) of the seer and the more poetically elaborate ode (*qasida*) of the poet.

How persistently this identification clung to Muhammad is illustrated with perfect clarity by the fact that in 622 CE, after twelve years of "reciting" his message on the streets and at the markets of Mecca, and when the Meccan authorities were making efforts to assassinate him, Muhammad migrated—his famous *hijra* or hegira—to the oasis of Medina at the invitation of the people there. They were in the grip of a civil war and they thought that this Meccan, whom we would regard at this stage as simply a troublesome and troublemaking God-crier, was the one to solve their political and social problems. It is almost as if Herod Antipas were to persuade Pilate to hand Jesus over to him so he might make him his grand vizier in Galilee. The invitation to Medina is odd, however, only if we are persuaded, as the Muslim tradition would persuade us, that there is no conceivable way that Muhammad could be confused with a kahin, though, as Michael Zwettler has pointed out, the kahin charge, unlike the poet accusation, is never refuted in the Quran. The phrase "Envoy of God" may have had one sound in the Prophet's ears, but it assuredly had quite another in the Medinans'. They spelled "prophet" with a "k".

The Oral Performance

Oral poetry is by definition spoken or, more accurately, chanted or sung, what the Quran calls "recited." The reciter may in fact be the author-composer himself or else, like the Jewish Tannaim, simply one of the "reciters" who repeat the compositions of others. But whether performed by a composer or a *rawi*, the Arabic "repeater," who is also known, in the case of the Quran, as a *qari*, or "reciter," there is one feature of the performed oral text that is important in this context: each recitation or performance will be different from the previous one. No less than the original composer, the performer/reciter is a creator: he reacts to his audience either between performances, when appropriate adjustments are made in the light of the last audience reaction, or during the performance itself as an immediate reaction to the listeners' acceptance or rejection, their understanding or bewilderment, of what they are hearing. The same is equally true of the reciter of another's work, the singer of someone else's song. According to Alfred Lord, transmission is always composition. There is always latitude for changes, though obviously less than for the original composer, and there is also the reciter's own manner of memorization: his "memory palace" may have in it some very different furniture of his own making.

The oral poetry in the Bible is still discernible in places even though it has passed through one or more scribal editings, and so we may be able to get a glimpse of the Prophet from the work of another, much earlier member of that company. In chapter 36 of his book, Jeremiah dictates his pronouncements to his scribe Baruch—as we have seen, it is not at all likely that Muhammad had such an amanuensis—and when Baruch's written transcriptions were destroyed by the irate Israelite king, Jeremiah simply redictated them, all of them, "back to the time of King Josiah," and, we are told, from memory. They were, after all, his compositions; he had composed them in his mind, memorized them, and could perform, or reperform, them as the occasion warranted, though everything we know about oral performance tells us that no retelling was quite like another.

We should probably see Muhammad somewhat in that same oral-prophetic light. The Muslim prophet pronounced as inspiration or opportunity—as his enemies charged—presented itself. And then he "recited" his pronouncements anew for those who had not heard or had not understood; or perhaps when he had simply changed his mind: twenty-two years is a long prophetic career. So, just as some Galileans heard the Beatitudes more than once and the Apostles likely many times, the Meccans doubtless heard the suras of the Quran a number of times, and what we have in our hands, as with the book of Jeremiah, is the written, and hence edited, record of a series of single performances. Though not entirely. There may be in the Quran traces of earlier, or simply other, performances of a sura in the doublets that occur there—in sura 19 (1–3), for example, and sura 3 (35–38), though they may represent no more than a formulaic theme, a kind of miniature set piece that could be used as the occasion suggested.

But while oral performances of the same composition tend to vary from one telling to another, the oral Quran may have become more fixed than most. Its repetition was not simply for comprehension or entertainment. Both the Prophet and his converts believed that what was coming forth as a "recitation" were God's own words and, like the Jews and Christians, they used this "Scripture," this Heavenly Book sent down but not yet written down by mortal hands, as liturgical prayer. Muhammad repeated his suras often enough for his followers to have them by heart, an act that helped stabilize what would otherwise have been a considerably more variable text.

A Change in Style

In our bondage to a written text, we must constantly remind ourselves that there is no "original" here. The original of the Quran is the recitation or performance Muhammad chose to have his followers memorize, and is very unlikely to have been its first utterance; and then, the finished suras either Muhammad or someone else had edited. In neither instance was there any concern to preserve what we might think of as the original revelation, the first (and only) words to issue from the Prophet's mouth. As we have seen, that notion, though theologically a cornerstone of belief—the Quran is God's unchanging Word—defies every convention of oral poetry and performance. Our Quran, like the *Iliad*, is a finished product.

But the Quran is *not* the *Iliad*: it was regarded by the one who pronounced and by those who memorized it as the words of God. This may have determined the length of the shorter Meccan suras, which had, as we have just seen, the not inconsiderable safeguard of frequent repetition by the faithful, and carefully, in a liturgical setting, and with what we may assume was the direct supervision of the Prophet. But with the turn in Muhammad's career at Medina, the suras grew longer and more prosaic, and with the loss of the mnemonic aids represented by rhyme and assonance, they would also have become more difficult for all to retain and repeat with any degree of accuracy. Hence, it is argued, the increasing need for a more stable and fixed written text. Was, then, Muhammad editing (dictated) written text at Medina, one he could not himself read? Was it then that the shorter Meccan units began to be inserted in, or perhaps added to the end of, the dictated Medina suras.

We have enough experience of oral literature and its passage into writing, even in quite modern times, to understand that when an oral performer is performing for or in the presence of one who will commit that performance to writing, considerable changes will take place, changes that emanate from both the performer's self-consciousness (altered speed, pace, deliberateness, emphasis) and a desire to impress, and the transcriber's willingness to "improve" what he is hearing. If Muhammad was really transcribed, as the tradition tells us he was, even as he was "reciting"—in short, in performance—then those same conditions might occur. And perhaps did. We are told the story of Abdullah ibn Saʿid, one of the Prophet's amanuenses who took it upon himself to "improve" the endings of two verses, at 4:148 and the other unknown. Even more boldly, he finished a verse the Prophet was dictating (12:14), at which Muhammad was reported to have said in effect, "Keep it in. That's it exactly!"

The Writing Down of the Quran

As we have seen, stories like this of Muhammad's contemporaries writing down the Quran, even in parts, present grave difficulties for us. Though the Muslim tradition clearly asserts it, it is difficult for us, who may in fact have a more realistic portrait of seventh-century Meccan society than the scholars in ninth-century Baghdad, to imagine who in Mecca could make a written transcription of the suras. As we shall see, the most the primitive Arabian writing systems of that day would have allowed would have been some crude annotations, some single words perhaps, on the themes of the revelation.

But the Quran itself cautions another look. We note a marked change in the suras after we have arranged them in something approximating their chronological order. The revelations delivered at Medina are quite different from the earlier Meccan ones. The high emotion, richly affective images, the rhymes and powerful rhythms of the Meccan poetry have all yielded at Medina to something that is not only longer but far more didactic and prosaic. The high poetic style of the Meccan suras disappears, along with their insistent rhymes and assonances. The oaths, the bold imagery, and the intense fervor of the early poems—we may even call them songs, as we have seen—have yielded to a flatter diction and a lower and more level emotional pitch.

The change is generally explained by the Prophet's preaching at Medina to a new audience of believers who needed the more commonplace instruction and encouragement in the new faith rather than urgent exhortations to leave off their idolatry and worship God alone. The change of audience, and so of purpose, from Mecca to Medina is true and important, but is it not equally plausible to think that Muhammad may have found a scribe at Medina? The Medina suras do indeed show some of the signs of a *dictated* text, in circumstances perhaps where the Prophet could no longer *recite* in the earlier bardic style but now had to *pronounce*, and slowly and clearly enough for an unskilled scribe to catch and record it. It is the same man preaching the same message—there were not two Muhammads—but where he once "recited," he now dictates.

This is a hypothesis based mostly on stylistic criteria; more specifically, it is a construct to explain a noticeable change in styles within the same collection, and it is supported in part by the Muslim tradition that parts of the Quran were written down in the Prophet's lifetime, though without suggesting that such took place only at Medina. Nor is there any reference to such a dictation in the Quran itself. It is a plausible explanation of the change in style—the study of early Islam floats on a raft of such surmises, whether medieval Muslim or modern non-Muslim—but the dictation hypothesis also has an adamantine implausibility built into it: the profound unlikelihood of a scribe or scribes being available at Medina.

We are sometimes referred to the Jews of Medina—there were apparently none living at Mecca—to explain the possibility of scribes there. The Medina Jews were said by the Muslim tradition to have had a "book"—we must think it was The Book—which Muhammad saw (read?) and accused the Jews of distorting. Such a discussion may well have taken place, but if it did, it had to do with the "Book," Scripture, not a Hebrew book neither the local Jews nor Muhammad could read. And if there were "rabbis" at Medina, as is also sometimes said, the normal assumption would be that they were literate. But there is no contemporary trace of such anywhere outside the Yemen and no trace of anything they might have read in either Hebrew or Arabic. It is easier to believe there was an actual Jewish book at Medina than that there was anyone there to read it.

Our surmise about the process of Quranic transcription may be correct, that our present Quran gives indication in its stylistic variation of the transfer of an oral text into written form, but the identification of the time and the place—Medina in the lifetime of the Prophet—is almost certainly wrong. We have just seen how unlikely it was that there should be in Medina in Muhammad's day a scribe skilled enough to have taken down the suras as dictation. The integration of the oral and memorized Meccan suras into a written text of the later revelations, which have now been divided, quite artificially or mechanically, into suras like the earlier ones, might well have taken place later, possibly under Uthman circa 650, if we give any credence to the traditions about his written "recension," though here too the presence of skilled scribes is highly problematic.

Let us pose the question squarely. The Quran was, we can be assured, an oral composition, orally delivered—"recited," as the Quran says; "performed," as it has been said here in emphasizing the Prophet's role as an oral poet—but the Quran we possess is and has long been a written document. When, and why, and assuredly how did that transformation take place? But before we attempt to answer these questions, we must entertain far more radical possibilities. If, as we have already seen, literate authors are quite capable of producing in their writing effects thought to be characteristic of the oral tradition, then the Quran may well have been written from the beginning, composed in writing out of earlier, and oral, material.

Other Possibilities

If the "repeaters" or "reciters," the *rawis* and the *qaris*, of our Arabic sources were professionals engaged in the transmission of oral texts, or, as they more likely understood it, their reperformance, the written text is the province of quite another expert, the scribe (*katib*). Many of these latter were not mere copyists, though in an age before mechanical reproduction, there is no such thing as a "mere" copy. What concerns us here, however, is the head of the file of scribes, those experts who transformed the oral "text" of the Quran into a written one. That scribal "moment" occurs twice in the reported traditions on the production of the Quran. It is said to have occurred first, as has already been discussed, when Muhammad "recited"/dictated the Quran and some of the believers, Zayd ibn Thabit mentioned chief among them, allegedly copied the suras down as they heard them on whatever material lay at hand.

The second reported occasion for this primal scribal activity is twenty or more years later—Zayd is once again involved—when the caliph Uthman was preparing his "standard edition." First, he ordered collected the existing "codices" (*mushafs*). The Arabic word suggests not random leaves but something already assembled, and the tradition tells us that there were such, more or less complete, but certainly not identical copies of the Quran in use in various Arab centers. In addition, he also had transcribed whatever could be retrieved from the "hearts" of the believers, those memorized portions of different parts of the full "Recitation." Collection was followed by collation. All these now written pieces had now to be compared—some of this may have gone on at the earlier transcriptions—and complex editorial decisions made to produce, in written form, a single version of the Quran. This became by the caliph's decree, the "standard," or better, the "official" version of the Muslim Scripture since Uthman ordered that all other copies were to be collected and destroyed and this text used in their place.

As evidence from the Bible has already suggested, though the original composition may be a product of the composer and his oral culture, in our instance Muhammad, the scribe too—the transcriber of the oral text, a figure culturally closer to ourselves than is the oral Prophet—plays an important role in shaping the final written product. As late as Qumran in the second and first centuries BCE, far down the road from the origins of the Biblical texts being reproduced there, and distant too from their first being committed to writing, we still find a great deal of "textual plurality" when it comes to Exodus or Numbers, for example, or Samuel or Jeremiah. It is not simply a matter of some textual variants but of different *editions* of the same text, and this in an era when there had long been a priestly-scribal class among the Jews who were, from all we know, the guardians of the Biblical texts.

Whether the Quran was first written down under Uthman or at an even later date, both scenarios carry the alleged dictation of suras into writing away from Muhammad's Medina; they remove the process from Muhammad's own mouth and put it into the ink-stained hands of editor-scribes like the *sofers* who worked on the written text of the Bible in the Second Temple and following centuries. On this hypothesis, it was these katibs who would have composed the Medina suras out of remembered Muhammad material in something approximating the Prophet's diction and style. How approximately we may judge by laying out two other examples of the Prophet's preserved utterances side by side, the Meccan suras and the Prophetic hadith, and it must be remembered that there were hundreds of thousands of them in circulation in the mid-ninth century. Though the Meccan suras and the hadith are very different in style and diction, Muslims accepted both as authentically from the Prophet, and in the eyes of Islamic law, they stand on a par with the Quran. The Medina suras seem to stand somewhere between the two, not as poetical as the Meccan strophes and not as "flattened" as the hadith; they would be, quite simply, scribal artifacts.

Though we do not know precisely how the first Muslim scribes of the Quran worked—nor, indeed, when or where—there is some instruction in the work of other scribes plying their skills in a transitional era between an oral and a written culture. First it should be remarked that the sound system of a language, its pronunciation, is generally far more complex and sophisticated than the system of symbols developed, or borrowed or imposed, to transcribe it, namely, its script. This is particularly so in the early stages of the passage from an oral to a written culture when the writing system is still being fashioned. This was certainly true of Arabic, whose sounds overwhelmed the few symbols of the script in use in the seventh and eighth centuries, which was the very prototype of a *scriptio defectiva*. Just as it is impossible to believe that the Sumerians and the Egyptians spoke as simply as their cuneiform and hieroglyphic scripts portray them, just so, *modo reverso*, it is impossible to imagine the chanted Quran being "transcribed" by the "scribes" of either Muhammad or Uthman into the meager scratchings of early Arabic script, which, among its other shortcomings, had no way of recording vowels and only a very limited supply of consonantal signs. At that stage of its development the Arabic script was a crude instrument indeed and hardly adequate for making notes, much less taking them down from dictation: there must be writing before there is speed writing.

Eric Havelock, who has thought about the same problem with respect to the Homeric poems, asks how the transfer could be effected from an oral to a written text with a still imperfect recording technique. By writing it down "in bits and pieces," he suggests, with the results used, in the first instance, "as promptings to a reciter how to start or, for that matter, how to stop." This might indeed have been the case with the Quran as well, that the defective Arabic writing system could produce only a prompt text to help in memorization or recitation and not, as is the case with us, a text to consult. No one was "looking it up" in the textual Quran for a very long time after the Prophet, and many Muslims still do not do so today.

One consequence of this is to urge postponement of the transcription of the Quran to later than Muhammad, and later even than Uthman, where Muslim tradition places it, to wait, in effect, until the writing hand catches up with the cantillating tongue. But there is another, equally important conclusion, or perhaps a warning. To the degree that the hand and its symbols are not adequate to the tongue, the scribe has to make choices from among the available symbols to transcribe what he is hearing. His choice may be ambiguous—the next "reader" may interpret the same symbol differently—or it may be incorrect, but in either case a distortion will have been introduced into the written text. The distortion will become enlarged and enhanced as the script grows more refined—points to sort out the ambiguous consonant signs, marks to signal the correct vowels to go along with them—when further scribal choices will be made. Even our mechanical recordings and transcriptions of oral communication are not without errors and have to be doctored; how much more likely are the misreadings/miswritings when the performance must pass through the ear of a single scribe and out his pen into a *scriptio valde defectiva*.

For the performer, whether the composer or later rawi/qari, absolute accuracy is not a great concern, nor indeed was it for his audience. Accuracy is the bugbear of a literary text society, of aficionados of the written word, and we may therefore conclude that the Jews' and Muslims' apparent concern for "fixing" their primary oral texts, the Mishnah and the Quran, was the product of an increasingly literate society's anxiety over the variable quality of an oral text that led to a decision to set it down, and so "fix" it, in writing. And this is precisely what one later and wildly anachronistic Muslim tradition asserts: the Prophet himself was concerned about variations in the oral Quran and that was the reason Muhammad ordered his "secretaries" to get it down in writing, and then, we are told, he personally collated their copies!

Both the Jewish and Muslim traditions offer that same reason when they attempt to explain this important and sometimes dubious change—writing always has its opponents in transitional societies—from an oral text to a written one. But if an increasingly literate society is an accurate description of the Palestinian rabbis who presided over the writing down of the Mishnah in the third Christian century, it is not of Uthman and his circle of putative literary editors at Medina in the mid-seventh century, which is another reason to doubt that the writing down of the Quran took place at that time or in that place.

The liturgical repetition of the Quran during Muhammad's lifetime and under his supervision must have begun to iron out some of the differences in the various versions of the recitation that people had heard, but there is little wonder that there should still be differences in the memorized body of them twenty years or more after his death. Some of those differences arose, as has already been suggested, by the memorizers' presence at different "performances" of the same sura. But some too are due to the vagaries of human memory: absolute accuracy cannot be achieved even in written texts much less in orally transmitted ones.

Uthman or Later?

The standard account of Uthman's "recension" of the Quran is improbable on many counts, but they can probably be reduced to two heads. The first, we have seen, is the lack in the Medina of 650 CE of scribes skilled and experienced enough to have performed such a complex task of transcribing, collating, and producing a single "critical" version of the Quran. There were scribes in the conquered territories, but by 650 the Muslims had barely put down sandals in Egypt, Syria, and Iraq, and there is no trace of any such guest scribes in Medina.

Then, the story continues, these same Medina scribes made copies of this Uthmanic *textus receptus ne varietur*—what were (erroneously) thought to be one or other of these "copies" were long a feature of privileged libraries across the Islamic world—which were sent to Muslim centers, mostly in Iraq. But there is no reason to think that in 650 the caliph's reach was so broad or his grip so firm that he was able to achieve such an end. Nor could any of his caliphal successors down to 1928 have likely produced a written text capable of driving out oral versions of the same work. Indeed, we know as a fact that in the ninth century and beyond there were still current a great many variant "readings" (*qira'at*), that is, different ways of vocalizing the texts in recitation. Early and late, accuracy and standardization were an issue only in oral "performance"; written copies were, and are, prized not for their accuracy but for their fine penmanship.

Students of oral cultures have pointed out that in an oral tradition there is little impulse or motive from within for committing oral performances to writing, that often that transfer is undertaken by someone well outside the oral tradition, a habitué of the literary culture like the Jewish scribes of Second Temple times. The Bible, complemented by remarks in the Gospels and with the addition of the considerable material evidence from Qumran, gives us a detailed picture of the scribe in the increasingly literate Palestine of the fifth to the first century BCE. They were members of a highly specialized profession. The scribe was not merely a copyist but an editor and somewhat more.

Searching for such skills and motives in an Islamic milieu, we must go far beyond Muhammad's or even Uthman's Medina. If the Levite has his analogue in the Arab rawi, who was an oral transmitter, though even he may have had an editorial function, the Hebrew scribe (*sofer*) finds his counterpart in the katib, the secretary of the paper-ridden bureaus of government in late eighth- and mid- to late ninth-century Baghdad. There were skilled and professional scribes in Baghdad and books and eventually booksellers, and it was there that we witness the appearance of all the major forms of Arabic literature, including all the traditions regarding the Quran! It was then too, in a number of Iraqi centers, that the great body of pre-Islamic poetry began to be transcribed from its hitherto oral transmission. Further, with its large and vocal Christian and Jewish communities, there was also present in Baghdad an apologetic motive for converting Islam's oral Quran into a written Book on the familiar Scriptural model.

Uthman's "edition," we are told, produced a fully written-out text of the Quran. We are now in the presence of a Scriptural "Book" in the literal sense. The reason, according to the received Muslim tradition, was either the dying off of Quranic reciters and the consequent fear of a disintegration of the authentic text, or, what concerns us here, the divergences in and the disagreements over the circulating "texts," with no indication whether they were oral or written. If written, there would have had to have been divergences in the consonantal text; nothing Uthman could have produced would have solved differences in vocalization since there was not yet available the diacritical apparatus that would have made a vocalized text possible. Even the written copies of pre-Islamic poetry, which had been transmitted orally by professional "carriers" (*rawis*) and not committed to writing until the ninth or tenth century, display variant readings, many of which are due to the still imperfect writing system.

"Standard" is not a univocal term as it applies to Arabic. Arabic, like Hebrew, has two quite distinct sets of notations to denote consonants and vowels. The consonants are the skeleton of the two languages, the baseline along which the various vocalic modulations are inscribed. The written form of these languages has essentially been a system of signifying that consonantal foundation, while the speaker "vocalizing" the text supplied the other, the "voice sounds" or vowels that provide the music for the consonantal words. In that linguistic setting, "standard" means in the first instance a consonantal text, which is how both the Hebrew-speaking Jews and the Arabic-speaking Muslims understood it. But God "spoke" to humanity, with consonants and vowels alike, with both words and music, and fixing the proper/authentic vocalization of the consonantal text was also a grave and ongoing concern to both groups. Jews and Muslims each developed similar systems of annotating the baseline consonantal text through various diacritical marks and symbols. The rabbis came to agreement on just how the Hebrew consonantal text should be pronounced, vowels, emphases, pauses all, and noted it down on the text page. This is, as we have seen, the masoretic text. The Muslims more simply agreed to disagree on the possible readings (*qira'at*) of "Uthman's" consonantal text.

Everything that follows confirms the unlikeliness of the existence of a fixed text of the Quran any time in the seventh or eighth century. The first time any part of the Quran appears in writing is in a dated (690 CE) inscription on the inside of the Dome of the Rock in Jerusalem, and the texts there do not always agree with what is in our Quran. In 1972 in a mosque in Sanaʿa in the Yemen, there was uncovered a cache of previously unknown Quran manuscripts that have proven to be the oldest yet known, from before 750 CE. They are still under study, but preliminary reports say they differ from our "standard" text not only in their readings but in the order of the suras as well. And finally, the debate over readings (*qira'at*), or, How to Recite the Quran, was still going on in the tenth century when Ibn Mujahid (d. 936), a Baghdadi scholar, signaled seven basic versions that were acceptable. The word is perhaps too mild; with the government's backing he had one recalcitrant flogged into compliance. Even more revealingly, Ibn Mujahid declared that the Uthmanic consonantal text was now obligatory, this two and a half centuries after Uthman himself was supposed to have made the same declaration.

The reason why there was a debate, and why there are still variant ways of reciting the Quran—though they have now been winnowed down to two—is that Islamic society was in the tenth century and for a long time afterward a society with one foot in the culture of writing and the other still in the oral culture of the Prophet and his successors. Variety concerns the first but not the latter, and Ibn Mujahid was clearly attempting to extend the literal culture's notion of invariability and standardization into the still fundamentally oral culture of the Quranic reciters. And with only partial success: flogging or not, there were seven ways of reciting the eternal Quran.

In Sum

We are now in a position to trace the idealized steps in the evolution of Scripture, and the scenario applies equally well to both the Jewish and the Muslim traditions. First, there is a Book in heaven. It is authoritative because it is written by God Himself. At some point God *speaks* the contents of the Heavenly Book to His prophet—in Israel God gives as well a written copy or summary to Moses—to be recited to His Chosen People. This occurs in the preliterate or oral stage of the society, when communication and memory are primarily or uniquely through the spoken word. But as writing becomes more common, the Revelation is committed to writing out of a fear, common to oral societies in transition, that the original oral version will be lost or become "inaccurate." Thus, the recited Torah/Quran becomes the written Torah/Quran. The Book was written down, then copied, and finally printed, and both the Bible and the Quran now circulate widely in societies where both the oral and the literary cultures still exist side by side. Yet the oral quality of the Revelation never quite disappears; the Book continues to be recited even though written copies are available.

Since the evolution of the Bible took place over an extended period of time, we are able to trace the stages of its development from a heavenly to a recited to a written Book in the text itself. Yet the primary composition of the Quran took place in a mere twenty-two years. There is still present in it the notion of a Heavenly Book, but for the rest, the context is still entirely oral-traditional. The Bible becomes a written text during the course of its own evolution; the Quran, we think, only afterward, and we cannot be certain how much later. And the Quran clings more tenaciously to its orality: the *hafiz*, the Quran memorizer who has the whole text by heart, is a revered and still common figure in Islamic society.

Chapter 6

The Book in Mortal Hands

ॐ(ᛒ)ॐ

"W riting" and "book" are the most closely attached qualifiers of revelation as that act of divine communication was understood by the three monotheistic communities. Generally speaking, it is in the form of a direct verbal communication that originates with God and is directed to mortals; only afterward is it committed to writing. Discourse in the other direction, prayer, where the creature attempts to address the Creator, invariably takes the form not of writing, however, but of speech. In prayer the writings are prompts; the petitions, praise, and thanksgiving must be addressed verbally to God and, in formal, liturgical prayer, audibly as well.

The Word Made Flesh:
Books and Bookmaking in the Ancient World

Writing and books, though closely related, are not, of course, identical. Writing is an act, in the ancient world the act of sovereigns and of closed guilds, powerful and arcane, at whose mysterious public traces societies that were still largely illiterate could only wonder. The book, the thing written upon or a collection of writing, is a product, which in the end shares the aura of the portentous marks on it. The "thing written upon" seems to be the original understanding expressed by the Hebrew word *sefer*. In the Bible the term is used for everything from personal documents and letters to the formal object, the collection of writing that we might regard as a book, while its cognate *sofer* is "one who writes," the scribe.

Scrolls and Books

The Israelites' book was in fact a scroll, a length of writing sheets, each joined, top and bottom to the next, and the whole might be as long as thirty to thirty-five feet. To take a New Testament example, the Gospel of Luke, or the Acts of the Apostles, would completely fill a thirty-foot roll. The parchment or papyrus length was spooled on two rollers and the writing ran at right angles from the spool. Thus the *sefer*, which in this form was called a *megillat sefer*, or "roll document," could be unrolled from beginning to end as it was being recited aloud—what would have been recognized as "reading"—or scanned, as Jesus is described doing with an Isaiah scroll in the synagogue at Capernaum (Luke 4:16–20). While the Septuagint changed the emphasis from the form to the material—it translated *megillat sefer* as *chartion bibliou*, "papyrus book"—the Latin translation, and the Roman tradition of books, returned to the Hebrew way of looking at it: the thing written was a *volumen*, a "roll" or even, more closely to the Hebrew, a *volumen libri*, a rolled document.

The ancients, including the ancient Israelites and the younger but still primitive pre-Islamic Arabs, wrote upon what they could, whether they found it or made it. They scratched and scribbled on stone, chiseled or incised it, at times with great elegance; they wrote with a stylus on wax-coated wooden tablets and then erased them, and with chalk on slates that could be sponged; they wrote with burnt sticks on flat surfaces or with pointed sticks in sand; and they wrote, most formally and permanently, with ink on prepared surfaces of papyrus or parchment. The first is a plant that grows in profusion in Egypt. When it is laid down in layers at right angles and rolled, it first oozes and then hardens into a surface that will hold ink but not absorb it to the point of unintelligibility. The papyrus is then cut into sheets that are glued together to form a roll.

Parchment required a more complex preparation and so was more expensive. The animal skins had to be depilated, cured, stretched, dried, and then cut to size before being sewn end to end to form a scroll or volumen. Somewhat oddly, parchment seems to have been the more common writing material in Palestine—Qumran provides a clear example—possibly because animals were readily available, from the Temple sacrifices, for example, where sheep and cattle were flayed and sacrificed in great numbers, whereas the papyrus had to be imported. Papyrus came to centers around the Mediterranean from Egypt via the Lebanon port of Byblos, whence *biblos* or *biblion*, writing material; in short, a "book."

There was no great regularity in the production of the scrolls in Mediterranean societies, including the Jewish one. The texts were copied in columns but there were no prescriptions regarding the length of a line or the number of lines in a column. Nor was anything numbered, neither lines, nor verses, nor columns. If you were looking for something, you found it by looking. There is no reason to think that the Torah scrolls preserved in the Second Temple looked any different from their counterparts in Alexandria or Athens or Rome. Nor is there—their apparent (and marginal) preference for parchment aside—any reason to think that in the matter of books and writing the Jews were very different from their Mediterranean contemporaries. What differences existed were of degree, not kind.

On the uncertain evidence available, the Jews, who formed a compact, homogenous, and cleric-dominated society in post-Exilic times, seem to have been more literate than others and so probably possessed more highly developed scribal skills and manufactured more, if not necessarily better, books than their somewhat less literate but often more prosperous neighbors. And their books were scrolls, like the others', while their scratch notes and scrap drafts were committed to ostraca, the bits of broken pottery that constituted the chief nonbiodegradable trash of antiquity, or to the already mentioned wax-covered tablets.

In the first century of the Common Era, coincident with Christianity but perhaps not coincidental to it, a new writing medium came into use. As already noted, it was common to practice writing or to compose drafts on wax-coated wooden tablets that could easily be erased. The tablets were hinged at one side to provide a flexible diptych. The arrangement was called a *codex*. The technique began to be transferred from tablets to common parchment sheets that were normally sewn top and bottom to form the volumina but were now tied along the long side to form a lighter, more portable, and certainly more leaved codex than the hinged tablet variety. The modern form of the book had arrived.

The Romans began to use these new codices chiefly for convenient note taking—the codex was quite literally a pocket book—while "real" books were still produced in the form of the bulkier and unwieldy volumen. No examples of such notebooks occur in purely Greek environments, and when Paul refers to them in the first century, he significantly uses a Latin loanword, *membrane* or "skin," rather than the Greek *diphthera*. "Please bring me," he writes to Timothy, "the cloak I left behind at Troas and also the books (*biblia*) and especially the notes (*membranas*)" (2 Tim. 4:13).

Searching the Scriptures

We cannot be sure what was in those particular notebooks, but one early use to which the Christians may have put the new codex parchment notebooks was collections of Biblical texts thought to be messianic and that Jesus demonstrably fulfilled. The resurrection, or rather, the witnessing of the resurrected Jesus, was the miracle adduced by Christians for their faith in Jesus, and it was useful with Jew and pagan alike. But the original "proof" of Jesus' messianic claims was unmistakably his fulfillment of specific Biblical prophecies. That case is made in each of the Gospels, most notably in Matthew, and it is used by Jesus himself, who announces it almost programmatically: "You search the Scriptures because you think that in them you have eternal life, and it is they that testify on my behalf" (John 5:39).

We are also shown Jesus actually using the argument. We first hear of it in his appearance in the Capernaum synagogue, when he reads the Isaiah scroll and announces that "Today this Scripture has been fulfilled in your hearing" (Luke 4:21). And it appears again, now somewhat more elaborately, after his death and reappearance to two of his followers on the road to Emmaus. On this occasion, "beginning with Moses and all the prophets, he interpreted to them the things about himself in all the Scriptures" (Luke 24:27).

As Jesus remarked, his fellow Jews were "searching the Scriptures" before his own followers took up that task. Some of the mechanics of that search became visible with the discovery of the Dead Sea Scrolls. The long scroll of the book of Isaiah found in Cave 1 at Qumran, which differs remarkably from the masoretic text and which it antedates by a millennium, has a number of scribal "X"s marking certain consequential passages, and for exegetical rather than textual purposes. That the Qumran community was interested in searching the Scriptures for messianic purposes is made particularly clear by the discovery in Cave 4 of part of the so-called Florilegium. The scroll is exactly that, an anthology of brief Biblical texts—the preserved fragment has verses from 2 Samuel, Psalms, Ezekiel, Isaiah, and

Daniel, all of which were the favorite reading of the Christians—but it is somewhat more besides: the texts are also explained in the sense, chiefly eschatological, that the Qumran community understood them.

Whatever else the Essenes of Qumran may have been with respect to Christianity, they certainly appear to be the exegetical-literary context in which the Jesus movement appeared. The early Christian messianists likewise "searched the Scriptures" and, as their Lord had instructed them, found their fulfillment in Jesus of Nazareth. Peter's very first preaching cites both Joel (2:28–32) and David (Ps. 16:8–11) in support of Jesus' Messiahship (Acts 2:14–36), and he later remarks, "All the prophets, as many as have spoken, from Samuel and those after him, have predicted these days" (Acts 3:24). In those same dawning days of the Jesus movement, even before the conversion of Paul, we are shown the Apostle Philip on the Gaza road explaining to the royal Ethiopian eunuch—"Do you understand what you are reading?" he asks him—the true meaning of a "Suffering Servant" passage in Isaiah (53:7–8).

The practice of arguing from Scripture continued as the movement, now known as Christianity, spread around the Mediterranean (Acts 17:11; 18:28), in the 50s and well before our canonical Gospels were written, and perhaps even before there were any written accounts of Jesus' life. If, as seems likely, those earliest Christians followed the same convenient practice used at Qumran and collected the appropriate Biblical texts in writing, we would have in such anthologies the earliest examples of a "Christian literature," and since the texts in question would be intended not only for Christian "assemblies" (*ekklesiai*) but for itinerant Christian missionaries, we may have discovered what was in those handy parchment notebooks that Paul left behind him at Troas.

There are important historical consequences to such a scenario. The Scripture "case" for Jesus, that based on his fulfillment of prophetic passages collected from the Bible, is completed not by Jesus' teachings but by the events and circumstances of his life. This is confirmed by the first public statement of the argument, that made by Peter in Jerusalem less than two months after Jesus' execution. "Jesus of Nazareth, a man attested to you by God with deeds of power, wonders and signs that God did through him, as you yourselves know," he asserted (Acts 2:22). And the chief of these, he concluded, "This Jesus God raised up, and of this all of us are witnesses" (2:32). Thus Peter's and the others' kerygmatic summary account of the "Good News" was a capsule narrative of Jesus' life laid upon Biblical prophecies, which is a fair description of Mark, and not a recitation of Jesus' sayings, which is an equally fair description of Q.

From Notebooks to Books

Paul's codex *membranai* had inscribed on their pages, we surmise, an early version of the "Good News," a collection of Biblical proof texts like the Qumran Florilegium and the later Christian examples called "Testimonies," supplemented with annotations of the actual "proofs," the events of Jesus' life. What changed, over a relatively short time, were the proportions of the argument. As the movement spread out of a Jewish, and so a Biblical, environment, away from Jews of Judea and Galilee, and passed first into a Jewish Diaspora unfamiliar with Jesus and then, increasingly, among Gentiles who knew nothing of Jesus and cared nothing for messiahs, the argument had to elide from Scripture to biography, from prophecy fulfilled to Risen Lord, from Messiah to Savior. Our Gospels seem to come from that transitional period, when the Jewish background is both assumed and explained, where the Scripture is present but not paramount, where there is a "mission to the Gentiles" and the Jews are visibly being cast as the "other," and where the Messianic Age is embodied not in the cosmos but increasingly in the Church.

And as the content of the Euangelion or "Good News" changed, so too did the content of those parchment notebooks. Where Paul's *membranai* might have recorded selected and biographically annotated Biblical texts, the Christian codices of the second half of the first century contained the new, accommodated version of the Gospel, an account of Jesus' life with the apposite Scriptural texts inserted. The eyewitness validation is still present, though now nearly a generation and many miles removed from its source; Peter's original appeal to his Jerusalem audience's witness, "as you yourselves know," is no longer possible, or necessary. The new handbooks are no longer vade mecums for preachers or messianic crib notes to Scripture; they are full-fledged, albeit now literary, and freestanding, testimonials to Christ.

There is no direct evidence for these surmises. We do not have Paul's *membranai* nor the notebooks of any other first-century Christian with either Biblical texts or a proto-Gospel inscribed on them. But there is evidence of a different sort. There are abundant papyrological remains from Egypt—the Chester Beatty papyri, the Bodmer collection in Vienna, the Rylands Library St. John, and the so-called Egerton Gospels—that show that the Gospels already existed as papyrus books in the mid-second century. And while contemporary secular papyri were still being published almost exclusively on the traditional rolls, the Christian books were precisely that, codices made up of parchment or, naturally in Egypt, papyrus pages bound at one edge. And they were not notebooks; they were substantial books, though in Greek literary circles the newfangled codex—there was not even a Greek word for this Western and Latin innovation—was not regarded as a genuine book until perhaps the mid-third century.

The Latins knew about those novel "books," however. We are told by the Roman historian Suetonius (ca. 70–140) that Julius Caesar was the first to circulate his letters "in the form of a journal," in contrast to the earlier practice of officials who had submitted their reports "written on a scroll." Even earlier, the Roman poet Martial, who was writing at about the same time the Gospels were being composed (ca. 84–86 CE), was unashamedly pushing new codex editions of his works, "to keep you company wherever you may be," to be "your companions on a journey. . . . Leave the bookcases (*scrinia*) to the important people; me you can now hold in one hand."

But despite Martial's heavy-handed endorsement—he included the name and address of his publisher in his poetical blurb—the new format was not immediately embraced by the Latin- or Greek-reading public. Like the earlier modern argument for and against paperback books, codices might be adequate for notebooks, but they would not do for serious literature or for library copies. They looked cheap and insubstantial compared to the traditional scrolls—except to the Christians. There is no entirely satisfactory explanation of this absolute embrace of the codex instead of the traditional roll, what has been described as not so much a preference as an addiction. The codex book was easier and cheaper to produce than the volumen—by one estimate the codex format reduced the cost of papyrus by 44 percent and the total production cost of a codex over a scroll by 26 percent. The codex could hold more content than the roll and was easier to handle, to consult, and, if need be, to conceal. But others who looked for the same advantages, like Jewish preachers or itinerant pagan scholars, stayed with the scroll.

The Christians Adopt the Codex

Some signs point to where the codex was in fact best known, to Martial's Rome, and more specifically to the Roman congregation of Christians, where, according to Papias, Peter's "reminiscences" of Jesus were transformed by Mark into a Gospel. The reminiscences, intended for private circulation in the community, may have been preserved in notebook form, though on *membranai* or parchment leaves rather than on the Egyptian-favored papyrus, and were then carried over in the same form into the extended Gospel version.

The Christians probably had few qualms about using the novel and somewhat "popular" form of the codex for publishing their Gospels in the first century since they did not as yet think they were reading or writing Scripture. In the first century "Scripture" (*he graphe*) was still solely and exclusively Tanak, the Jewish Bible. It is somewhat startling, then, to discover that the Christians did not pause even at that latter, where there was firm Jewish precedent for transcribing the Bible only on scrolls, and that at least by the middle of the second century, possibly earlier, Christians were writing out copies of what was already being referred to at the end of the second century, without explanation, as the "Old Testament" in exactly the same new codex format. It is one of the many signs of the growing and almost defiant independence of the new movement from its Jewish matrix.

Besides the obvious convenience in handling and ease in carrying about, the codex offered certain other advantages to the Christian enterprise. Its flexible length allowed for the collection or combination of a number of works, the four Gospels, for example, or the letters of Paul, into a comprehensive edition. And it suggested even broader collections, all the Jesus documents into a "New Testament" or, even more ambitiously, a whole new view of Scripture or the Bible that included both an "Old" and a "New Testament," terms current in Christian circles by the end of the second or beginning of the third century.

The technology of the codex, if it did not create these bold new theological notions, enabled the Christians to give them a material form, to be able to say "*This* is the New Testament," *tolle, lege*, or "These two Testaments, the Old and the New, constitute genuine Scripture." The Jewish Scripture was simply "the Books" (*biblia*), a collection of twenty-six scrolls; the new Christian Bible was an idea contained within the covers of a single book.

With their promotion of the Old Testament in tandem with the New, the Christians accomplished two objectives. In the face of obstinate and radical opposition, they extended and enlarged the original argument that the authenticity of Jesus the Christ or Messiah rested on his fulfillment of Biblical prophecies. They advanced as well their growing conviction that their own writings were also Scripture, a New Christian Testament fit to be placed next to the Old Jewish Testament. The case is eloquently if silently made by the fact that the earliest preserved manuscripts to include the *entire* New Testament—the Codex Sinaiticus and Vaticanus of the fourth century and the Codex Alexandrinus and Codex Ephaemi Rescriptus of the fifth—are all *complete* Christian Bibles, that is, codex books that contained both the Old and New Testaments.

Not many of those early Christian Bibles were bound as a single book, however. Far more typically, they were published as a set of four volumes, which could of course be purchased separately. From what we learn from the preserved early manuscripts, the four canonical Gospels constituted one volume, far and away the bestseller of the collection. A second volume included both the Acts of the Apostles and their letters. Paul's letters alone made up a third volume and the Revelation of John was the fourth.

Toward a Standard Edition?

It was the purpose of the emperor Diocletian (r. 284–305), the author and instigator of the last general persecution of Christians in the Roman Empire, to destroy all copies of the Christians' Scriptures, which at that time included both the Old and the New Testament. His edict to this end was published in 303 and all across the Eastern Empire churches were razed and the Scriptures consigned to the flames. There was one notable escapee, however, the single most important Christian library in the Mediterranean, that of the Christian school in Caesarea in Palestine. It was the foundation of a rich Christian named Pamphilus, who was responsible for the collection—which included a great many of Origen's works, among them a copy of his multicolumned comparative text of Scripture, the Hexapla. Pamphilus was not only a founder and benefactor; he also worked in the library, together with his friend and fellow scholar Eusebius. The two men compared and corrected, quite in the manner of Origen, the various versions of Scripture, and their work is still remembered in the colophons appended to much later manuscripts that could still boast that they were originally copied from "a very ancient copy edited by the hand of the holy martyr Pamphilus."

Pamphilus was indeed a martyr. He died in the persecution in 310 but the library survived and so too did Eusebius, who became bishop of Caesarea and then friend and biographer of Constantine and the first historian of the universal Church. As Eusebius tells the story in his *Life of Constantine*, the now Christian emperor undertook to supply the churches he planned for his new capital with sumptuous copies of the Scripture. In 330 Eusebius was commissioned to prepare, at the emperor's expense, fifty copies of the Scripture for distribution to the churches. At the emperor's own command, the copies were to be "written on well-prepared parchment by copyists most skilled in the art of accurate and beautiful writing (*kalligraphoi*). The copies should be very legible and easily portable in order that they may be used." When finished, the copies were to be sent off to Constantinople "by threes and fours." The latter expression is difficult. In three- or four-volume sets? Or, as seems more likely, three or four copies at a time, as they were finished?

Some have thought, or wished, that the great Sinaiticus and Vaticanus codices are surviving examples of this "Eusebian edition" of the Bible, but that is far from certain; nor is it even known which of the available Greek texts Eusebius had had copied. Origen's Hexapla, which was available to him, gave Eusebius a wide choice. What seems to have been the case, however, is that in the interest of speed, Eusebius had had copied whatever was available for any given book of the Bible. The Council of Nicea may have laid down a dogmatic statement of what all Christians must perforce believe, but there is no sign that either the emperor or his bishop gave thought to creating a single standard version of Scripture. So the texts that went out to churches were, as far as concerns the books of the Old Testament, now the Septuagint version, now one or other of Origen's corrected editions from the Hebrew or from the later Jewish translations.

Even before Constantine and Eusebius began their enterprise, which had as its stated objective supplying Scriptural exemplars to Christian churches and not the creation or imposition of a standard text, the papyrus fragments of Christian Scriptures that have survived from the second to the fourth century—the overwhelming majority of them from codices—show no great uniformity in their versions of the text. Though fundamentally the texts are identical—no omissions or additions of a substantial nature among them—there are many different readings on minor matters, scribal errors, for example. In short, already in the second and third centuries the Christian text of Scripture was fixed but far from standardized in the details.

Origen had attempted to improve the Christian copies of the Septuagint version of the Old Testament by comparing it with the current Hebrew text and with a number of later Jewish translations into Greek that aimed at being more faithful to the Hebrew original. The result was the Hexapla, which, if it did not put forth a fresh and accurate version of the Septuagint—it was apparently never a question of starting afresh with the Hebrew—it did make the Hebrew Tanak available to Christian scholars and provided a direction and the means to a more accurate Old Testament. But Origen made no similar systematic effort with regard to the New Testament. That task was left to the scholars at Caesarea he had inspired, Pamphilus and Eusebius.

⠶⠶   *Note: A Comparative New Testament.*

One of the fundamental instruments of New Testament research is a synoptic edition of the Gospels whereby the texts of the canonical Gospels are published in columns side by side to illustrate the similarities and differences among them, and, if their dependence can be established, how the later, Matthew and Luke, for example, modified the earlier, Mark. The method, if not the intent, has ancient antecedents. Eusebius, the text editor who at the turn into the 300s had trained at the famous library in Caesarea in Palestine, had in mind just such a synoptic view of the Gospels.

In a letter written to a contemporary, he described how a certain Ammonius of Alexandria had attempted it by taking Matthew as his base text and arranging the parallels in the other three next to the continuous text of Matthew. This broke up the narrative line of the other Gospels, however, and Eusebius thought he had a better way. The better way was the Canons. He first numbered consecutively all the pericopes or sections of the four Gospels: 355 in Matthew, 233 in Mark, 342 in Luke, and 232 in John. Then, in a series of columns, he noted the parallels by number. The first noted, by number, the parallels shared by all four Gospels; the second the parallels in Matthew, Mark, and Luke; the third in Matthew, Luke, and John; and so on through column nine. The tenth noted the numbers of the pericopes that were unique to a single Gospel.

Finally, in the Gospel text itself, Eusebius added an annotation as to which column or columns any given passage might be found in.

The Canons was a useful device, if not for New Testament critics, then certainly for preachers and Gospel commentators, and Eusebius' tables long continued to be reproduced in both manuscript and printed copies of the New Testament for long afterward.

As we already have had occasion to note, the words in Greek, Latin, Hebrew, and Arabic that are usually translated as "book"—*biblos, sefer,* and all their relatives—normally indicate "something written," without much regard for the form of the product (roll or codex or simply a sheet) or the writing surface (papyrus or parchment). Eventually the ancients knew and recognized a book in our sense of the word, multiple written sheets bound together at the edge. The Latins, as we have seen, called it a codex and the Greeks, eventually, a *somation,* literally, a "small body." Greek and Latin books, which are the prototypes for the embodiment of both the Christian and the Muslim Scriptures—the Jews clung tenaciously to the traditional scroll/volumen for their *Sefer Torah*—generally followed a standard form. They began with a title, which was repeated at the end, where it was followed by the number of lines and columns in that text—a consumer protection device! The practice of counting lines was already current in the profane literature of antiquity, prose as well as poetry, and was carried over by the Christians not only into their copies of Scripture but into their other religious works. The writing itself was in two, three, or four columns that ran parallel to the rollers, each normally two or three inches wide, though eventually the columns yielded to a full single page of script.

The extant codex manuscripts of the fourth and fifth centuries show us what a Christian edition of Scripture looked like, but it is also possible to get behind the product and understand some of the techniques and labor—and thinking—that lay behind the Alexandrinus, the Vaticanus, and the Sinaiticus. A great many of the early manuscripts bear a colophon, a kind of scribal "postscript" that supplies details on its making. We are led in many instances back to the same school and library at Caesarea where Pamphilus and Eusebius were following in the footsteps of Origen a half century earlier and preparing carefully collated texts of both the Old and New Testaments, which then became the base of many later editions of the Christian Scripture.

The Shape of the Page: Chapter and Verse

The modern reader of an English Bible or a New Testament or even a translation of the less familiar Quran is accustomed to finding the text parceled out into a variety of units. There are the distinctive books designated by title in the Bible and the New Testament, though not in the Quran. The Jewish and Christian Scriptures are further divided into chapters with a number throughout; the similar-appearing units called suras in the Quran bear both names and numbers. Deeper into all these texts are ever smaller numbered units called verses, which subdivide each chapter or sura. At the front is usually a "table of contents" in the form of a separate list of the books or the suras within, and at the end sometimes an "index," a topical list arranged alphabetically with each item located by reference to book, chapter (or sura), and verse.

Many of the divisions of Scripture are to assist in memorization or recitation. But some of them, certainly the books and certainly the suras, were parts of the original composition, the pieces out of which the finished Scripture was made, while others, the chapters and verses, were later aids to the study and understanding of the Book. Understanding too is one of the goals of Scripture recitation, as we shall see. This is a "clear" or "manifest" Book, the Quran testifies of itself, and one of the functions of the signs and symbols in manuscripts of all the Scriptures is to assist the reader's comprehension of the Word of God. These manuscript aids were the fruits of a long tradition of Scripture study, much of which unfolded in the specialized institutions all three religious communities eventually developed to that end: the mosque or cathedral school, the yeshiva, the madrasa, the university. And it was in these latter settings that the Sacred Page was constrained even more exigently to yield up its meaning.

Dividing the Text

As the very words of God, Scripture is not only an inexhaustible encyclopedia of religious knowledge; it also provides life's surest form of guidance, grounds all laws, and validates and prohibits public and private behavior. Scripture explains the past and foretells the future. As such, it is of the utmost importance for all believers, and most especially the experts who were and are its primary interpreters, to understand the text and explain it to others. For centuries they have been sifting the text dialectically, comparing and contrasting its parts, reconciling, harmonizing, puzzling.

To perform this exacting task requires, it is clear, an extraordinary command of the entire text, the kind that is possible only if the text has been memorized from start to finish. In the oral culture of the Jews and Muslims such a task does not seem terribly difficult. But where literacy prevails and oral texts are replaced by written ones, a different problem emerges and different solutions have to be devised. The chapter and verse divisions of Scripture are those solutions and the table of contents and the index, their happy consequences.

Numbered divisions into chapters and verses are only the final, almost mechanical, solution to the problem of finding and identifying the parts, even the smallest verse units, of Scripture. Before they were introduced, however, the Hebrew scribes had already begun transforming the vocal values of the *qere*, the recited text, into the *ketib*, the written text. The recitative pause became a manuscript space; a vocal emphasis was expressed by a change in the letter size, shape, or shading, or even a change in height. On the Qumran manuscript evidence, markers were spread through the written text that, if they did not exactly mark divisions, as they do in later manuscripts, enabled the (new) reader to find and then to understand what he was reading. The Qumran divisions of the Scriptural texts, the *parashah*s, which are separated by an empty space or empty lines, are longer than the later verse divisions, and they were used, like the later markers in Quran manuscripts, to facilitate memorization or even to make it easier for the user (who was likely to have been another scribe) to find a place in the text. It is possible that they mark recitation units, though there is no evidence for such a liturgical use of Scripture at Qumran at that time.

After Qumran our next written evidence for Biblical text division does not occur until the tenth century, when the preserved Aleppo Codex, copied and annotated in Palestine sometime about 930 CE by the leading masorete of the day, Aaron ben Asher, shows us the Scripture in full annotated flower. By the time Ben Asher was working, the recited Scripture was fully established in synagogues: the Babylonian Talmud of three centuries earlier already laid down regulations governing it. We have already seen that the Torah was divided into fifty-four parashahs to distribute its reading across an annual cycle of Sabbaths, but that liturgical-recitational division is accompanied in the masoretic texts by a different one whereby the text is divided into sense pericopes of two types. The larger one, which always begins on a new line and is preceded by a blank line, is called "open" (*petiha*) and marked with a "p" in the text; the other, which is more like a sentence than a paragraph, is called "closed" (*setuma*) and is preceded by a blank space and marked by an "s."

As was the case at Qumran, it is impossible to discern the exact use of the open and closed section divisions. They do not correspond to the recitational cycle of parashahs. They may have been intended to assist the reader in discovery, a typographical way of opening and spreading the text so it could be scanned more easily. Nor can we readily sort out the criteria for breaking up the text in this manner. The open division seems to correspond to what we mean by a paragraph and represents a new theme or idea, while the shorter closed division appears to be its subdivision. That is, in all its vagueness, a guess. The scribal sectioning has aptly been called "impressionistic." But whatever lay behind them, the masoretic divisions do not correspond to the later "chapters" of Scripture. These latter first appeared in the Christian Scripture, as we shall see, in the thirteenth century and were thence incorporated into Hebrew Bibles.

Still another, even smaller division came into play, another import from the oral into the written tradition. This is the division into the smallest sense unit, the line or verse. Poetical texts in both the Hebrew and Greek versions of the Bible were early on transcribed stichometrically, or by the verse-line (*stichos*). We are also aware of these line and verse divisions from the regulations regarding the Aramaic translation that accompanied the Hebrew Torah reading in the synagogue, which was to be done, the rabbis insisted, line by line or verse by verse, which means that such units were known and recognized in the text.

This last division of the Torah—and only later the other parts of Scripture—into its smallest sense units began very early on—we are not surprised to hear it attributed to Moses—as a function of reading or reciting the text intelligently, so that both the reader and the listener might follow and understand the sense. For a long time these divisions must have been passed down orally in the recitation tradition but eventually they found their way into manuscripts—though none in the *Sefer Torah*, where it is explicitly forbidden—and were signaled by an accent and a colon at the end of each verse. The verses were not, however, identical from text to text since neither the oral nor the written texts where they occurred were yet identical. The numbering of these units, and all the attached benefits, required a fixed and stable text and, we may add, scribal experts with writing-weakened memories.

Marking the Text

Though the New Testament conceptually flowed from the Old, the Christian Scripture belongs to a Greek manuscript tradition rather than to a Hebrew one. It was customary in Greek prose texts to divide the body of the writing into "headings" (*kephalaia*) or chapters, each numbered, with or without a title (*titlos*). The two oldest complete Christian manuscripts of the New Testament, the Codex Vaticanus of the fourth century and the fifth-century Codex Alexandrinus, are both divided into chapters, though in neither case does a book begin with chapter 1 since the classical tradition always regarded the opening lines as a form of prologue. Nor are the chapters identical in the two codices. The book of Acts in the Codex Vaticanus has in fact two different chapter systems, one added by a later hand, running concurrently in its margins. The chapters are numbered throughout the whole collection of Paul's letters.

The New Testament chapters originated with the scribes of the manuscripts, but a later hand divided and numbered the Old Testament text in part or in full. But here too there is no single system of dividing and numbering the text. These chapter divisions were obviously devised, and were probably used, for cross-referencing—Christianity is founded on cross-references between Old and New Testaments—but only for the single-user with his individually marked text. Jerome could not write to Augustine and tell him to look at John 16:22.

The New Testament also carried with it traces of the academic apparatus of the Hellenic tradition in which its scribes, and many of its readers, had been trained. The chapters were often given explanatory titles like "Concerning the Marriage at Cana," and a list of these titles at the head of the book supplied a convenient table of contents. Ancient books likewise had by way of preface what is called in Greek a *hypothesis* and in Latin its *argumentum*, a brief statement of the book's contents. Eventually the Old Testament books had them as well, and then another feature of ancient bookmaking, a *bios* or biography of the author. Illuminated manuscripts went one step further and presented a portrait of the evangelist, usually in the initial capital letter of his book, and in the Old Testament the likeness of Moses and of Ezra were often included.

The chief Christian additions to the repertoire of reader's aids included in the manuscript were the already mentioned Eusebian Canons. Eusebius had given consecutive numbers to what he understood to be the pericopes or units within each Gospel and then constructed out of those numbers a series of ingenious tables that enabled the reader quickly to find, and so compare, passages in the four canonical Gospels. Copies of Jerome's Latin Vulgate often had the Eusebian Canons at their head, with the Eusebian pericope numbers in the margins of the Gospels, but they seem not to have used the Greek system of kephalaia and titloi.

The Western system of chapters was introduced into the text around 1205 by Stephen Langton, then a professor at Paris and later archbishop of Canterbury, for the benefit of his university students who were studying Scripture. He introduced numbered chapters into all the books of the Vulgate and the system took and became, and remains, standard—so standard in fact that it was introduced by the Jews into their Hebrew manuscripts in 1330 and thence into Hebrew printed texts. By 1400 the system of capitulation was beginning to drive out the old Byzantine kephalaia from the Greek manuscript tradition as well.

The standardized chapter numbers thus enabled authors to make citations more exact, and authors (and editors) began subdividing the pages within a chapter by a sequence of letters, A through G, in the margins, a system still used in classical texts. The final and momentous step in the process of providing a searchable Old and New Testament was taken when the Parisian printer Robert Estienne (aka Stephanus, Stevens) printed in 1551 a Greek and Latin concordance of Scripture with the Greek text in the center, the Vulgate on the inside margin, and Erasmus' translation of the Greek on the outside. For all three Estienne kept, as was now customary, Langton's numbered chapters throughout, but he added for the Old Testament the rabbinic verse divisions, now numbered, and for the New Testament, what appear to be his own set of numbered verses, famously contrived while riding on horseback from Paris to Lyons. It quickly became the standard system, first of all the printed editions of the Vulgate, then of all the translated versions of the Christian Scriptures into the European vernaculars.

Suras and Ayas

An English translation of the Quran looks invitingly like a New Testament, with 114 chapterlike suras and numbered verses within them. Yet there are no "books" in the Quran, and no author's name appears either on the title page or on the individual suras. Again, the editor-designed chapters of the Old and New Testaments are roughly the same length; the author-edited suras vary greatly, from the 286 verses of sura 2 to the four, five, and six verses of the last three suras. The suras are in fact named, not numbered, in the Muslim tradition; the numbers attached to them are late non-Muslim additions. It is the writing tradition that favors numbers. Muslim scholars cite the suras by name, not number, and, like their rabbinic counterparts, they cite the actual text of the verse to which they refer, not its number.

Like the word "Quran" itself, sura is another of the Quran's self-descriptive terms and, again like Quran, may be an Arabic borrowing of a Syriac technical turn meaning "Scripture" or "Scriptural readings," either by Muhammad himself or in the days before Islam. The nine occurrences of the word in the Quran seem to point, albeit somewhat ambiguously, in the same direction. A sura has been "sent down" (9:64, 86, 124, 127, etc.), that is, revealed, and when the authenticity of Muhammad's own "recitations" were questioned, the Prophet famously challenged the skeptics to "produce a sura like it" (2:23; 10:38), or even "ten suras like it" (11:13). A sura, then, appears both etymologically and contextually to refer to a unit or units of revelation.

A later generation of Muslims, perhaps the very first, and perhaps under Muhammad's own direction, used the word in a related but more concrete and specific sense. The 114 units into which the Quran is divided are now individually called suras, each with its own descriptive name. These are, on the face of it, literary units in the sense that they are the divisions of the unitary text line before us. But the text before us also professes to be composed of revelations. Are these also (and primarily) divisions of the revelation? Is each sura a discrete revelation? The Quran does not say so, and the internal evidence of emendation and interpolation strongly suggests that such was not the case.

We conclude, then, that the sura is an editorial unit, with Quranic origins, to be sure, but essentially the result of a decision about an already revealed text. That decision does not appear to have divided what once were single revelational moments, but the evidence is unmistakable that revelational moments were combined into a single sura-unit. The Gospels show the same editorial point of view at work. Matthew, for example, organizes Jesus' teaching into five great swatches (chapters 5–7, 10, 13, 18:24–25), each introduced by the most nominal of narratives—which the Quran lacks—to suggest that all the following were delivered on a single occasion (13:3–52).

We cannot tell when the sura divisions were introduced or who gave them their present names, which we know were not the only ones in circulation. This ignorance extends to many other areas of the text simply because there is no textual history of the Quran, no early manuscript tradition substantial enough to allow us to trace the evolution of the text. As we have often had occasion to note, the history of the Quran is chiefly, and very defectively, written from later literary texts about the Quran. And even these traditions are uncertain about many things, on how or why the names were attached to the suras or why twenty-nine of the suras open with a series of "mysterious letters," or what those letters mean.

The word *aya* appears very often in the Quran, and with the unmistakable meaning of "sign," or, more precisely, a "wonderful" or "miraculous" sign. Its semantic range in the Quran extends from natural signs of God's power to the more restricted sense of "miracles," and more precisely still, to the miracles that appear in conjunction with the work of a prophet and confirm his authenticity and authority. Such was the case with Moses (43:46), and with Jesus (3:49), among others, and such was also demanded of Muhammad (6:37, etc.). Though at first the Prophet refused to comply with the demand, eventually the Quran itself was adduced as just such a "sign" because it came from God and was recited by Muhammad (45:6). And though it never quite reaches this exact meaning, there are occasions in the Quran when *aya* very nearly means "portion," what we would call a "verse" of the Scripture (2:106; 16:101).

Some of the ayas of the present Quran are transparently verse units since they follow a recognizable rhyme scheme, but elsewhere, particularly in the Medina suras, the verse divisions are more arbitrary and indeed they vary in early manuscripts. But whatever their origins, and however they got there, the two Quranic terms *sura* and *aya* have come to mean what they do not quite mean in the Quran itself, namely, a chapter and a verse of the "Recitation."

There are, then, any manner or means of dividing the multiseamed garment called Scripture. Some are author-inspired, like the preservation of the identity of the single books that make up the Jewish Bible and the Christians' New Testament. Some of these books may have had single authors, like the Gospel of Mark, or may be some edited form of disparate pieces of earlier, and anonymous, material, like the book of Genesis. But in both cases the communities that regulated such matters judged it appropriate to keep Genesis and Mark as separate books within the larger canon. Other divisions are obviously editorial, like the marking off of recitation or memorization portions in the Torah and the Quran, and indeed the suras of the Quran may belong in this category, as defined liturgical units composed perhaps by Muhammad himself out of his own revelations to assist his followers in the liturgical repetition of the Word of God.

Still other divisions signal their intent in a different fashion. The separation of the text into chapters or other units identified by names points to a searching device, a way of opening the content of the text to the reader's glance, much in the way illustrations were once used in Christian manuscripts. Units like chapters or verses identified by number also betray a searching intent, but they indicate that a means of citation is also in place.

These increasingly sophisticated means of opening the text to recitation, memory, and study, which reached their sophisticated apogee in the Latin West in the twelfth to the sixteenth century, make possible a flood of scholarly material tied to the new identification systems within the text. Alphabetizing on one hand and numbering with Arabic numerals rather than the awkward letter systems or the equally cumbersome Roman numerals, on the other, provided the technological oil that made the newly devised identification systems operate smoothly and effectively. The results are evident in the concordances and indexes to Scripture that were in widespread use in university circles on the very eve of the age of printing.

All these advances in searching and citing Scriptural passages rested on a fixed written text with standardized divisions within it, and the deliberate insistence on the oral tradition in Scripture among the Jews, who were otherwise as text-literate as their Christian counterparts in the West, and the continued predominance of the oral tradition among the Muslims generally, made such devices impossible. While the new European universities were bursting with textual study, the Jewish yeshiva and the Muslim madrasa remained bastions of an oral tradition of transmission and study without the benefit of standard numbering and so too without the benefit of the efficient searching and citation tools developed in the Latin West.

All the divisions just described are marked in the text by symbols or signs or, somewhat more occasionally, by descriptive editorial names. But at their side were other, more intensive methods of explaining or clarifying the text, methods that originated in the Hellenistic schools and found their way quickly, in the first instance, into Christian circles. These explanations could take the form of a freestanding commentary in which the text of Scripture—or of any other text being commented on—could be cited piecemeal in the commentary as lemmata. Or, to reverse the procedure, the commentary might be inserted, line by line, into the Scriptural text as a gloss. Scripture, once it was produced as text, was subjected to both treatments. Exegetical glosses appear in the margins of the Bible, the New Testament, and the Quran, then between the lines, and finally, like an enveloping parasite, completely surrounding the Scriptural text, which is sometimes confined to a cramped box at the center of the page, while commentary spreads ever more luxuriantly around it. For many centuries it was difficult to read Scripture without those master explainers, Rashi (d. 1105), the prodigious rabbi of Troyes, the Arabized Persian Tabari (d. 923), or the Franciscan master Nicholas of Lyra (d. 1349) peering over the reader's shoulder, which was, of course, precisely the intent.

We will not here give ear to these other voices that begin to rise from the Sacred Page since they summon us away from the Word of God to a different issue, that of the harmony of Scripture and exegesis. Once Scripture has become a document, other, very human voices can be heard mingling with the Word, and if we detected anonymous human echoes in Scripture before, these new exegetical choristers reveal their identity boldly. God has always had human company; now they had simply moved into His Scriptural temple.

The Sacramental Text

The Quran operates within Islam on a number of different levels. It is, to begin with, the eternal and uncreated Heavenly Book, the Quran's "Well-Guarded Tablet" (28:20) on which God's Word is inscribed. It is then the

Quran, the "Recitation" pronounced privately but audibly by God—the Muslim theologians professed not to know how—and then repeated publicly, and identically, by Muhammad in the historical circumstances of Mecca and Medina between 610 and 632 CE. And finally, the Quran is Muhammad's "recitation" committed, inerrantly, we must believe, both to memory and to writing, and that during the Prophet's own lifetime, we are told.

Muhammad's original replication of the original recitation of the "Mother of the Book" that had been "sent down" to him in the "night of power" in the month of Ramadan was guaranteed by its source, God Himself, in the manner that all prophetic messages from on high find their validation. It is only in the next generation of replication, the remembering and recording of the message by humans without the cachet of prophetic infallibility, that problems arise. Doubts about the Prophet, and indeed about all prophets, may be credited, and dismissed, as sheer unbelief, but charges against his scribal successors, his copyists, translators, and exegetes, are likely to be worryingly concrete and demonstrable. Such charges have certainly arisen among groups who share the same revelational premises and who possess a competing Scripture of their own. Beginning with Muhammad himself, Muslims have accused the Jews and Christians, for example, of deliberately tampering with the revelations given them by their prophets. Jews accuse Christians of getting the Bible wrong in translation. Jews and Samaritans argue about who has the authentic Pentateuch, and Sunnis and Shiites about an edited Quran; Catholics and Protestants quarrel about their respective translations of the New Testament.

There have been two ways of meeting such charges of inauthenticity. The irrefutable one is to invoke the Holy Spirit—who has been far more active in this regard among Christians than among Jews or Muslims—who has vouchsafed the accuracy of the Scripture, and even its translations, the Septuagint (the Jews once concurred here, but no longer) and the Vulgate. The other is the more proactive tactic of taking steps actually to guarantee the accuracy of the product of prophecy. Both Jews and Muslims have gone to great lengths to ensure the accuracy of chirographic copies of the Bible and the Quran, and early in the Middle Ages the masoretic editors, who appear far more obsessive in the matter than any imaginable critic, had adopted every conceivable strategy to protect the integrity of both the written (*ketib*) and the recited (*qere*) text of the Bible.

And since the Reformation Christians have adopted the text-critical methods of their secular colleagues if not to preserve the "authentic" Word of God, then at least to join the "Quest for the Historical Scripture."

These are the transactions of polemic. More powerful by far than the display of mere authenticity of the Copy of Scripture, the Word Made Flesh, is its transfiguration into a sacred object. This is accomplished in several ways, through its enshrinement, for example, the physical framing of the object by a setting that indicates its sacral character; through the development of a liturgy or ceremonial accompanying its display; and, related to that last, through the setting out of an etiquette governing its public or private use.

Sefer Torah: *Torahs and Their Arks*

From first to last, in heaven or on earth, whether on Sinai or at its foot, whether inscribed by God's finger or Moses' pen, or both, the Torah was understood to be a written document. In the first instance, it was the Ten Commandments inscribed on tablets of stone that the Israelites kept in their close possession. More broadly, it was the document referred to as the Torah, the Pentateuch or Five Books of Moses, in which the Commandments were embedded. And finally, it referred to the Bible as a whole, the Book par excellence, formally and permanently bounded or canonized.

God's will was presented to the Israelites not as speech but in the form of writing. Or so it was understood. It does not mean, of course, that the Israelites had a book, or anything like it, until much later, when their own technology permitted them to manufacture such. Books were always easier to imagine in heaven than to produce on earth. And even when made, it was for a long time an object written upon rather than an object read. In the oral culture of early Israel—as in the parallel oral culture of early Islam—something written was both powerful and mysterious; it was not the medium of communication as it usually is for us, but rather the expression of a higher will. It was not necessary to be able to read to get the message of the Book. The medium was indeed the message.

We can observe this understanding of the written object unfold in the story of the Israelites and the Covenant. Initially, God had communicated His Covenant, which elsewhere in the Middle Eastern societies was a written document, in oral form: God spoke and Abraham listened. But when it was time to set down the binding terms of the Covenant on Sinai, God gave them to Moses here below in a written form, inscribed, as we have seen, by God Himself on two tablets of stone (Exod. 24; 32:15–16; 34:27–28). Moses also received detailed oral instruction, which he then passed on, orally, to the people. But the Israelites continued to carry the written tablets—a second set; Moses had improvidentially smashed the first in anger and God was constrained to make a duplicate—throughout their wanderings across the wilderness of Sinai. They were deposited—enshrined, we would say—within a gold-plated chest (40:20), over which the Presence of the Lord was seated (25:21–22) to protect and validate the contents.

This was no mere carrying case. As the history of the Ark of the Covenant unfolds piecemeal across the Pentateuch, we understand that we are in the presence of what is, to our categorical eyes, a sacred hybrid. It was, to begin with, a not unfamiliar Middle Eastern throne atop which the Lord—in the unique Israelite case the invisible presence of God, what a later generation of Jews called the *shekinah*—was worshiped and whence He issued His decrees in oracular form (Exod. 25:22; cf. Num. 7:89; Lev. 16:2). But the Ark was at the same time a chest that enshrined the Covenant in its summary form on the two Tablets of the Law written by God's own hand (Exod. 40:18; Deut. 10:5) and which were its sole contents (1 Kings 8:9). And later, in an era when Israelites could write and it was thought that Moses had written down what was delivered to him on Sinai, the book version of the Law, Moses' written work, was placed not in the Ark but at its side (Deut. 30 1:24–26).

The throne-shrine, which was generally and rather precisely called the Ark of the Covenant, was a potent combination indeed. It was transported by the Israelites across Sinai, shielded deep within its own tent during the halts, carried by hand during the marches. Once in Canaan, the Ark found a more or less permanent resting place in a tent in Shilo (Josh. 18:1), though it continued to be carried into battle (6:6–21), just as the pre-Islamic Arabs did their portable shrines, the Muslims the Quran, and the Crusader Christians the relics of the true Cross. The Ark was a formidable Israelite totem: when captured by the Philistines in battle, its mere presence in their midst caused havoc until it was returned to the Israelites (1 Sam. 5–6).

Once David had conquered the Jebusite city of Jerusalem and made it into the capital of his kingdom, it was a logical step to bring the Ark, the most visible token of Israel's identity, into that city. An event in the joyful transfer must have erased any doubts that the Israelites were in the presence of a *sacrum*: when a man reached out to support the apparently toppling Ark, he was struck dead for his well-intentioned temerity (2 Sam. 6:6–7). It was the same deadly penalty promised to any Israelite who dared approach the slopes of Sinai (Exod. 19:12). And once again, the Ark was housed in a tent.

For the rest of its known history, the Ark would reside in David's city of Jerusalem—but not in a tent. Though perhaps David's plan, it was his son and successor Solomon who constructed the grandiose Jerusalem "house" for the Lord—not quite as grandiose as his own house nearby (1 Kings 7:1–13)—a housing, in fact, for the Ark of the Covenant, which was installed deep within its interior in a remote Holy of Holies shielded from all possibility of contamination (1 Kings 8:1–9). And here it rested, though it may still have continued to be carried abroad in battle or in celebration since there is a later note in 2 Chronicles (35:3) in which King Josiah gives orders that "you no longer need carry it [the Ark] on your shoulders." And there the matter ended in darkness. The last Biblical reference to the Ark is in Jeremiah (3:16), where it is prophesied that in the coming New Age the Israelites will no longer speak at the Ark of the Covenant, a remark generally understood to mean that the Ark had been carried off in the general Babylonian looting of the Temple (2 Kings 24:13).

The Ark did not, however, fade from Jewish consciousness as Jeremiah had predicted. There was in fact in circulation in the second century BCE a rumor—likely little more than that, though it fathered a substantial body of legend—that Jeremiah himself had removed the Ark from the Temple before the looters arrived and hidden it in a sealed cave in a place "which will be unknown until God gathers the congregation of the people and receives them in mercy" (2 Macc. 2:4–8). More than rumor, images of the Ark survived in Jewish imagination. Figurative art did not often flourish among the Jews—as we shall see, the interpretation of the Second Commandment, though often labile, generally flowed against it—but when it did appear, the Ark of the Covenant was an important feature. The Ark appears prominently in the panels depicting Bible history in the third-century synagogue from the Euphrates town of Dura Europus and in various fourth- to sixth-century synagogues across the Land of Israel.

These are all illustrations in and around ancient synagogues. We can detect a more symbolic transfer of both the concept and the imagery of the Ark from the Temple to synagogue in the appearance of the term "Holy Ark" (*aron ha-qodesh*), one of the Biblical expressions for the Ark of the Covenant, in connection with the privileged place within the synagogue where were enshrined not the long-disappeared Tablets of the Law but their written surrogate in post-Temple times, the *Sefer Torah*, the "Torah Book."

The term *sefer* occurs throughout the Bible, and like many of its analogues in the same semantic field, it is probably better understood as "something written" or "written document" than simply a book. The rabbis of Talmudic times thought there was a master copy of the Torah kept in the Second Temple of the post-Exilic period. They may have been correct. The Ark of the Covenant with its Tablets of the Law had been kept there in the First Temple, though there is no mention of it in the rebuilt Second, and since we know the priests were the guardians and interpreters of Torah, it makes sense that *the* Torah should be in their possession and should be kept in the Temple. No mention of it is made in the description of the destruction of the Second Temple, nor any in the years that followed. But there were Torahs kept in shrines in synagogues for as far back as our patchy evidence reaches, and the almost interchangeable portrayal of Torah Arks and Torah shrines strongly suggests a continuity of practice.

The rabbis stressed the continuity of the Temple services with those of the synagogue, and the portrayal of the Torah Ark, sometimes flanked by twin menorahs, as well as its name, the "Holy Ark," points in the same direction. In some of its depictions the Torah Ark also bears a distinct and pointed resemblance to a contemporary Temple structure. That was clearly what one was intended to *think*. But there was a functional side as well, and the Torah was being stored within the synagogue in a chest depicted in the preserved art as closely resembling the kind of double-doored cabinet the Romans used for storing their volumina or scrolls. And on certain occasions it was wheeled (as it is portrayed in the fourth-century [?] synagogue at Capernaum) or otherwise carried into the public domain for a public ceremony.

The practice in synagogues seems to have fluctuated. The Torah Ark was either a (portable) chest (*tevah*) kept in the synagogue proper or in an adjoining room whence it was carried for services, or else it was stored in a

special niche built as an architectural feature into the wall of the synagogue, and eventually into the wall toward Jerusalem, so that the worshipers stood facing both the Torah and the Holy City. And where early
synagogues show evidence of Torah niches, they also show signs of a
bimah, a raised platform standing in front of it. Both niche and bimah became a standard feature of the synagogue.

The medieval synagogue that emerged out of its ancient prototypes was
not terribly different from the earlier versions save in its generally more
modest scale. Christian and then Muslim sovereignty in the lands where
most Jews lived straitened the communities in fact and by prescription.
Within, the central room was still dominated by the Torah Scroll, whether
within its (portable) chest or enshrined in a curtained wall niche, which,
like the Muslims' *mihrab*, the niche that marked the direction of prayer,
became the focus of attention and the chief object of architectural refinement in the synagogue. But there was competition. In the ancient synagogue the bimah stood before the Torah Ark. It was a platform of no great
height but of some sacred importance since from it certain priestly blessings were pronounced and solemn oaths sworn. It was natural, then, that
the Torah should also be read from that place. In certain places and certain
circumstances, the bimah became a lectern or reading desk on which the
Sefer Torah rested.

But *bimah* had a secular ancestry as well. The Greco-Roman *bema* was a
speaker's platform, a more modest cousin to the rostrum. In the restrictive
world of Christian and Muslim sovereignty the synagogue became more
than ever a community center, and the social and political functions of the
bimah reasserted themselves. There were secular concerns that dictated
the size and shape and placement of the bimah in the evolving synagogue.
In the end the bimah suffered the same ambiguity as the Christian pulpit,
which itself occasionally served as both elevated rostrum and lectern. Not
so the Muslims' *minbar*, which was, from the Prophet's day to this, nothing more or less than a pulpit.

What the Ark of the Covenant once represented in the Jerusalem Temple the *Sefer Torah* now bore upon itself in the synagogue. The synagogue
Torah Scroll was surrounded by convention and ceremonial at almost
every step of its creation and use. In a world where papyrus had replaced
parchment and paper had replaced both, the *Sefer Torah* was to be copied,
in the most conservative manner imaginable, only on the skins of kosher

animals, by hand, and only by using a reed pen (later relaxed to include a quill). The scribe, then as now, must vocalize each word as if transcribing an oral recitation, and, at the same time, with a nod to the literary tradition, he is forbidden to copy from memory! The Torah Scroll is a pure consonantal text, without vocalization or any of the elaborate masoretic apparatus fashioned by the rabbis to make certain it was recited correctly. There is no punctuation and no verse divisions. There are, however, tradition-dictated breaks in the text that are signaled only by spaces left in the line. There are prescribed numbers of words per line, prescribed numbers of lines per page. Nothing is left to choice or to chance.

The highly sacramental quality of the making of a Torah scroll is carried through in its appearance and use. It is draped with a richly decorated mantle; the staves upon which it is rolled are capped with crowns. No one may touch the taboo text itself; it is handled under cloth, the reader's place is kept by a silver "hand." The text is carried to and from its place of enshrinement with great ceremony, while the congregation stands in respect and those who can, kiss the mantle in which it is draped.

The great liturgical celebration of the Torah is called precisely that, *Simhat Torah* or "Rejoicing of the Torah." It falls on the twenty-second or twenty-third day of the lunar month Tishri, on the first or second day after Sukkoth (customs vary for what is a late medieval entry in the Jewish liturgical calendar) and marks the completion of the annual recitation cycle of the Torah. During the celebration the *Sefer Torah* is carried joyously in seven circuits around the bimah of the synagogue. The "circuits" are borrowed from Sukkoth, when, according to the Mishnah (Sukkoth 4:5), those celebrating the feast in Jerusalem made daily procession around the altar of the Temple and then, on the seventh day of Sukkoth, made seven circuits. The custom survived the destruction of the Temple, and we are told of Jews in the tenth century making the Sukkoth circuits around the Mount of Olives. Here the circuits ritual has been incorporated into the synagogue not only in connection with Sukkoth but now with the new Torah celebration that followed.

The Jews are far more ceremonial in their treatment of the Torah than the Muslims, who have, as we shall see, a Quranic etiquette but not quite a liturgy. The difference arises from the Jews' deliberate linking of their post-Temple liturgical practices, particularly in what pertained to the synagogue, to the liturgy of the ceremonial Temple. The Torah, like the

Tablets of the Law before it, is housed in an ark, a container that is at the same time both a shrine and a *temenos*, a sacred enclosure, and is carried in procession round the bimah, the surrogate altar of the synagogue, in imitation of Israelite processions around the great altar in the long-destroyed Jerusalem Temple. This practice is echoed in the Muslims'—and, indeed, the pre-Islamic—liturgical circumambulation of the Kaʿba, "God's House" in Mecca.

The tradition of a careful copying of Scripture extended in the scribal culture of Judaism far beyond the *Sefer Torah* specifically destined for use in the synagogue liturgy. All the surviving copies of Hebrew Scriptural manuscripts show a remarkable consistency—far more than is evident in contemporary copies of the Latin Vulgate—that testifies to an equally re-markable carefulness on the part of the scribes who produced them. The *Sefer Torah* continued to be copied by hand, of course, but Europe entered into the age of printing with Gutenberg's Latin Bible in the 1450s. The first printed Hebrew text appeared at Soncino, in northern Italy, in 1488, with reprintings in 1491 and 1492. By then there were Christian scholars who could also read Hebrew, and though the Soncino texts were prepared by and for Jews, it was not long before they began to be used by Christians for ends both scholarly and polemical.

Washing Their Hands of the Christians

In the High Middle Ages, and with increased vigor in the Renaissance, Christians were rejoining a Jewish Scriptural tradition they had left many centuries before. The separation of Jesus' followers from their fellow Jews was a painful process that began with Paul, or perhaps with those anony-mous Christians who asked Paul's advice and so prompted his letters to the Galatians and the Romans, and proceeded by steps we cannot chart with certainty through the first three centuries of the Christian era. We hear a good deal about it from Christian writers whose tone becomes more strident and more polemical as the decades, and then the centuries, pass. The Jews, who found themselves in an increasingly Christian world, were understandably more circumspect on the parting of the ways. But here and there we can hear the fabric being torn, though guardedly, and sometimes in surprising places.

The rise of the Pharisees, with their emphasis on the extension of ritual purity, placed the question of the sanctity of Scripture in a new context in the last centuries BCE and the first of the Common Era. The discussion that arose illustrates the ambivalent nature of what we normally translate in a Jewish context as "ritually impure" and which should more likely be rendered "taboo." All sacred objects were taboo, and contact with them made an individual taboo as well, or as the rabbinic lawyers prefer to put it, "rendered the hands unclean." Scripture was obviously such an object, and handling it of course "rendered the hands unclean" in the sense that they had to undergo ritual washing before the ordinary business of life could continue.

This is the context in which the rabbis of the Mishnah and Talmud discussed what precisely was Scripture and what was not, or to put it in the terms in which they phrased it, which works precisely "rendered the hands unclean." First there were the nagging questions of detail beloved of lawyers—the rabbi is often in the details—whether, for instance, the spaces in a Torah scroll were taboo to the touch. What if the letters had been erased? Or partially erased? Once those matters were settled—we are now in the midst of a treatise of the Mishnah called, helpfully, "Hands"— the rabbis passed on to the larger question of which books constitute Scripture and which do not, still from the point of view of the transmission of ritual impurity or the taboo state.

The immediate controversy that provokes the discussion in "Hands" has to do with two works in the third, very problematic division of the Bible called "the Writings." All the Holy Scriptures render the hands unclean, the text begins, and, what is pertinent here, both the Song of Songs and Ecclesiastes render the hands unclean, though there is some disagreement about the latter.

The discussion in "Hands" later returns to the question of Scriptural translation in this same ritualistic context. Do the few Aramaic passages in Scripture, like Ezra 4:8–7:18 and Daniel 2:4–6:28, enjoy the same sanctity as those in Hebrew? Do they too render the hands unclean? They do, as it turns out, but subsequent *translations* of the Bible do not share that same holiness. So Aramaic Ezra and Daniel are genuine Scripture but not so targums, the Aramaic translations of Scripture.

We can see over the next hill: what of the Christians' so-called Scriptures? "Hands" edges toward the issue, but the text is uncertain at a critical point. There is more enlightenment elsewhere in the Mishnah, in the tractate "Sabbath," for example, where Scripture raises problems in a different

context. May one, the Mishnah asks, violate the stringent regulations surrounding the Sabbath to enter a burning building to save a copy of Scripture? It is the kind of question the rabbis were fond of asking to test the
precise boundaries of the Sabbath rest. The answer is easy: "All sacred
books may be saved from burning on the Sabbath." More than that, one
may dash into the blaze to save the case of a *Sefer Torah* and even a phylac-
tery container, the small box containing written fragments of Scripture
that was tied across the forehead and onto the left arm in obedience to
God's command to the Israelites to bind His commandments "on their
arms and as a pendant on their foreheads" (Deut. 6:8).

There is no mention of the Christian Scriptures here, but in a similar
place in the Tosefta, a kind of supplement to the Mishnah, the issue is met
head-on, and in a somewhat startling way. "We do not save from a fire (on
the Sabbath) the Gospels and the books of the Minim. Rather, they are
burned in their place, they and their Tetragrammata [that is, God's name
in them]." We are obviously in an era when the followers of Jesus were still
worshiping side by side with their fellow Jews, and their books, "the
Gospels and the books of the Minim," could be found inside Jewish places
of worship. The anonymous opinion just quoted would let them burn, but
immediately another authority is cited who had qualms and preferred to
cut out references to the divine name before burning (or letting burn?) the
Christians' books.

The issue must soon have become moot, however, as the Christians and
Jews soon mutually went their separate ways, each taking their sacred
books with them.

A Matter of Etiquette: The Book in Our Hands

Islam possesses a master concept that has little parallel in either Judaism
or Christianity. It is *adab,* a typically diaphanous Arabic term with a broad
semantic range. The notion is Arab and secular, not one of the many loan
terms or concepts taken over, often via Syriac, from the seventh-century
Jewish or Christian environment in Arabia and domesticated in Islam
through the Quran. Adab was local and native. In its broadest and most
fully evolved sense it means not behavior but a way of behaving; indeed, a
proper or appropriate way of behaving, an etiquette. It readily covers the
English "manners," the French *politesse,* and the Italian *cortesia.* It means,
in that relentlessly urban society of medieval Islam, both urbanity and ci-

vility. And since it can be transmitted and taught, adab also passes as "education" or "culture." At the outset adab was a conservative term in a tribal society: the appropriate behavior was the traditional behavior, and *adab* stood at not too great a remove from *sunna*, "customary behavior." And as it did with sunna, the "sending down" of the Quran affected a revolution in adab. Tribal etiquette no longer sufficed; in Islam only a Muhammad adab would do.

That personal adab of the Prophet was handed down to future generations of Muslims through the great body of hadith or Prophetic reports testifying to the sayings and doings of Muhammad. Very many of those sayings have to do with what the Jews call *halakha*: they provide prescriptive guidance in moral matters and as such have been built into the foundations of Islamic law. But a great many more are simply the Prophet's "tabletalk," or perhaps better, his "pillowtalk," since the majority of them come down to us on the testimony of his wife Aisha. In them, and in the many anecdotes passed on through the hadith, Islam received a rich and detailed portrait of the Prophet's adab. Moses delivered just the Law to the Jews, but Jesus and Muhammad offered a model life to the believers. The sketch of Jesus' lifestyle in the Gospels is limited by the brevity of Jesus' public life, the evangelists' staying carefully on message, and, in the end, the believer's understanding that Jesus was, after all, the Son of God. Muhammad's humanity was visible to all, however, and more, he was in the public eye for twenty-two years in the most varied of circumstances. The reports on Muhammad, whether of dubious authenticity, are nonetheless full and plentiful—full enough, in any event, to provide the believer with a life-scaled and complex model of Muslim adab.

One result of this profusion of information about the personal adab of the Prophet is that Islamic behavior has, in addition to an internal moral code and prescriptive regulations regarding behavior, a sense of a particular lifestyle not immediately present in either Judaism or Christianity. Both of these latter prefer epigone models, a Francis of Assisi—whose own appropriation of the Jesus adab proved unsustainable—or one of the Eastern European *rebbes* who stand behind the Hasidic movement. The Muslim lifestyle is psychologically reinforced, doubtless, by the residual Arabism that rests at the bottom of Muslim identity, but the pervasiveness of the Prophetic adab is real enough and apparent in the relentlessly male Muslim society. It is visible in everything from dress and dining to the manner of prayer, particularly the Friday community prayer that is so obviously a common exercise performed in the most exquisite unison and at the same time an unmistakably individual, almost solipsistic, communion with the divine.

The Muslims are well aware of the role of adab in their lives, and the subject has generated a literature that has attempted to describe and transmit it in its various forms, whether it referred to a rather specialized culture, where the "Adab of the Scribe" or "What Makes an Educated Person" became a fashionable literary enterprise, or as it pertained to the more general notion of adab as "etiquette" or "appropriate behavior" and, precisely here, the etiquette of dealing with the Quran.

Muslim treatment of the Quran falls under two larger categories of concern. The first is the proper liturgical recitation of the Quran (*qira*). The other has to do with the "handling" of the physical copy of the Quran, the *mushaf* or codex. Jewish prescriptions about the Torah copy are chiefly about the *Sefer Torah*, the ceremonial copy or copies reserved for the synagogue liturgy. Muslims addressed a much broader spectrum of concerns regarding a text that was in very wide circulation throughout the society. Both Jews and Muslims approached the question of handling the physical Scripture from the same perspective, however. As we have just heard from the rabbis of the Mishnah, and as Muslim writing on the subject makes equally clear, the copy no less than the original was a sacred object and therefore was surrounded and protected by the same safeguards as any sacramental object or action—the Scripture copy is the object equivalent of the act of prayer.

At the heart of each community's security system lay a fear of contamination of the sacred not simply by the profane but by a far more deadly and virulent threat, the impure. That fear led to the construction of a system of baffles and barriers in both Jewish and Muslim law and is represented most graphically by the *cordon sanitaire* constituted by the limited access courts of the Jerusalem Temple. That system of impurities and their remedy, which is described in great detail in the Pentateuch and is the subject of special treatments in both the Mishnah, as we have just seen, and the Talmud, has left only the faintest trace elements in Christianity—in the now disused custom of the "churching" of women after childbirth, for example—but is in full vigor in Islam. It stipulates, first, that certain acts and conditions incur a state of impurity in the believer, which then prevents that believer from performing sacralized acts or coming in contact with sacralized objects, unless and until that believer undergoes a purification ritual, usually some form of washing.

The impurity principle is already set out in the Quran (5:6), where the defiling acts mentioned there are the use of the latrine and sexual intercourse, the inhibited act is ritual prayer, and the purification ritual is described as the washing of the face, the hands up to the elbow, and the feet up to the ankle—what later came to be known as the "minor ablution." In another place it is remarked that touching the Quran is permitted only to the "pure" or the "purified" (*mutahharun*).

The latter verses are interesting: "This is indeed a noble Quran, in a book that is hidden, and none touch it save the pure" (56:77–79). The reference here to a "hidden book" seems to point us toward the Heavenly Book, that "Well-Guarded Tablet" (85:21–22) or "Mother of the Book" that is with God (43:4). To read it otherwise, that the reference is to a material Quran, is to suggest that there was a written copy in existence even at Mecca—sura 56 is early Meccan in the standard dating. We have already seen how improbable that is, but Muslim legal exegesis read it exactly so and the verses served as one of the cornerstones on which a Quranic etiquette was constructed.

Given the clarity of the Quranic requirements for "purity" (*tahara*; the Quran uses the same word as the Hebrew for this important concept) in connection with liturgical prayer and handling the Quran—and later extended it to the ritual circumambulation of the Ka'ba—there was little debate or discussion of the principle among Islam's lawyers; what remained, as always, was to work out the modalities of ritual purity and impurity, the topic with which most Muslim legal handbooks begin. What precisely caused ritual impurity and what removed it? Contact with (or emission of) feces, blood, semen; touching of pork or carcasses were what the Torah called the "fathers of impurity" and the consequent condition might be either a major impurity (*janaba*), which required a full and uninterrupted washing of the body (*ghusl*), or a minor condition of impurity (*hadath*), requiring only the already described washing of the face, hands, and feet. In either event, in the presence of a major or a minor impurity, the Muslim must purify himself before handling the Quran in any fashion.

✥ **Note: Sex and the Sefer:**

The same principle operated in Judaism: the emission of bodily flu-
ids, like semen, created a condition of ritual impurity and rendered contact with the sacred forbidden. The emission did not take its moral
weight from intent and so even the emission of semen during legitimate
marital intercourse, for example, set up a tension between that act and a
sacred or taboo object like the Torah. The rabbis laid it down that marital intercourse should not take place in view of a *Sefer Torah*, though it is
not clear whether this was to protect the gaze of the couple or of the
Torah. Either the latter should be removed to another room or a five-
foot-high opaque partition erected between Book and bed. Other copies
of Scripture, handwritten or printed copies of the Bible, fall into a different class, as do phylacteries and copies of the Mishnah and Talmud that
happen to be in the marriage chamber: they must be placed inside a *double* container. If there is a mezuzah in the room—a small container with
Scriptural verses inside and attached to doorjambs—it should be covered with a double drape.

Since the Quran had spoken on the subject, and with a growing understanding of the Jewish precedents, it was predictable that there would soon
be Prophetic reports circulating on the manner of handling the Quran
and that this would become a subject of interest to medieval Islam's vol-
unteer army of legal experts. Two of the most eminent, whose works
found a wide popular circulation—they were intended for the layman
rather than the specialist—were almost exact contemporaries. One was
the native Syrian Yahya ibn Sharaf al-Nawawi (d. 1277), the author of "The
Clarification of the Etiquette of Dealing with the Quran," and the other
was a Spaniard who spent most of his career in Cairo, Muhammad ibn
Ahmad al-Qurtubi (d. 1272), who wrote "The Collection of Legal Enact-
ments on the Quran."

Al-Qurtubi formally sets out the principle: it is forbidden, taboo
(*haram*), for anyone to touch the Quran, or any part of it, while in a state
of even minor impurity, a condition that did not prevent the handling of
other books of a religious nature. Al-Nawawi concurred, though there
were other legal considerations of the type beloved by casuists. What of
someone touching the Quran with a stick? Or with the sleeve draped over

the hand? Of somewhat more pragmatic consideration is the issue of Quranic verses on other commonplace artifacts. What if they are cited in a law book, for example, or incised on coins, as was commonly done, or embroidered on clothing? Al-Nawawi considers it permissible in those cases for someone in a minor state of impurity to handle the object in question, though he does note that some have voiced the opposite opinion. He has some hesitation, however, on the matter if the book in question is a collection of Prophetic reports with only incidental Quran citations since the hadith seem to share something of the sacramental nature of the Quran itself. And what of Quran commentaries? Al-Nawawi here resorts to some common sense: if there is more Quran than commentary in it, the book is taboo; if not, it may be handled.

On the matter of buying and selling copies of the Quran, opinion seems to have been divided, but sales to non-Muslims were forbidden, whether the non-Muslim lived within Muslim territory or not. And in a hadith that is obviously a later fabrication, Muhammad is said to have explicitly forbidden travel with a Quran among the nonbelievers. The only question with regard to such sales was whether they were valid, in other words, whether the seller had to return the money.

Contrary to the book titles, it is al-Qurtubi, "the Cordovan," who shows the greater interest in the actual etiquette of handling the Quran. Some of his advice has to do with deportment during what might be called nonprofessional recitation, that one should brush the teeth and refresh the mouth before beginning, sit up straight, and dress properly. Entire suras should be recited, not just parts. Individual recitation in private is preferable to that in public since there is less chance of interruption in the former. Finally, the Quran should not be sung, certainly not in the tremolo favored by the Christians or the plaintive tones of their monks.

Other prescriptions have to do with the physical treatment of the mushaf. It should not be placed on the floor but on the lap or on a stand. The copy should not be left open, nor should other books be stacked on it: the mushaf should always be on top. It should not be used as a pillow and should be handed, not thrown, to another; nor should it be miniaturized in any way. Verses of the Quran were frequently inscribed on amulets and worn on the body, which creates a problem, warns al-Qurtubi, and the wearers of such amulets should take care that they are covered or encased when entering a latrine. Al-Qurtubi also says that the Quran should not be written on the floor, which of course makes sense, nor on walls, "as is done in some new mosques," a warning that obviously availed naught: the Quran is a signal feature of Islamic calligraphy. Indeed, the earliest testimony we possess to a Quranic text is just such an inscription high up in the Dome of the Rock in Jerusalem.

Chapter 7

In Other Words

☙❧

Though the sacred stuff of all three religious communities had its origins in oral tradition, the notion of a written Book runs deep into the vitals of each religion. It is the Book—for Christians, the Jewish Book as well as their own—that has given them their identity and their authenticity. And, importantly, that selfsame Book has in large measure created them as "religions" in the modern sense of the word, a set of beliefs and practices rather than simply a way of life, and what is more, a set of beliefs and practices that could be offered to or imposed on others.

Religious assimilation was not unknown in the world into which first the Jews and then the Christians were born. A conquered people might be constrained to accept the worship of the gods of their conquerors, or the conquerors might even accept, as the Romans did, the cults of their subjects if attractive or useful. But neither the conquerors nor the conquered were inclined to give up their own religious beliefs and practices or to force others to do so unless the "foreign" cults were thought to be politically subversive or socially destructive.

Conversion is quite different from assimilation, however. Conversion in its proper sense, the voluntary exchange of one set of accounts—the "foundation story"—and cult practices for another, is a function of a conviction of truth and a characteristic of monotheism. The monotheists' is a universe of boundaries, with a dark chasm between their own sharply defined and brightly lit world and that of the unchrismed and unshriven Others. Both Christians and Muslims, though they resisted assimilation, actively sought to draw others across that damning divide, as did the Jews as well once they had become a Diaspora community. Indeed, once they were in a position to do so, the Christians *required* conversion, at times by proscribing paganism, as in the early Byzantine Empire, at times by coercing baptism, as in Spain and the New World in early Renaissance times.

Scripture was an essential part of the conversion process. The converts had not only to worship the One True God to the exclusion of all others; they had also to accept the Word, the Book in the form of the book (Torah, New Testament, Quran) in which it was authoritatively preached; and they had to accept the control of the literate clerics (rabbis, priests, and *ulama* or mullahs) who could "read" and interpret it.

Other religious communities had "stories" of national identity or "myths" that "explained" the gods and their workings. These were tales told across the generations; the monotheists preserved the Word, God's unchanging and unchangeable charge to humankind, in the form of a literary work. Even the core of the Israelite Book, which is also a story of national identity, was broadened by their prophets, and by the Jews' own experience, into a universal Word. That ambiguity still exists—the tension between a national identity and a universal Word, urged in one closed and ethnic direction by the Jews' own painful experiences with the religious "other," and in the open, universal direction by the Christians' own universalizing of the notion of a Chosen People.

Amid the tension between the tribal/local and the universal lay the urgent issue of language and, deep within that, the more vital question of the conditioning of the Word of God. There are human fingerprints all over the Scripture, its delivery, its shaping, and its transmission. And the sounds that reach the ears of the faithful are not those that God murmured to Adam in Eden but one or other of the babble of tongues first heard at the base of a tower in Babylon.

The Loss of God's Tongue

The Bible is well aware that humankind speaks diverse tongues, and Genesis 11, immediately before the appearance of Abraham on the Biblical stage, presents a brief but colorful account of how the diversity, and the mutual unintelligibility, came about. God addressed Adam and Eve and the first couple understood; indeed, Adam was allowed to use his new speech—we are not told what that first language of humankind was—to name all the animals of Creation (2:19). Sometime after Noah and the devastating Flood, we are told the moral tale of Noah's descendants' ill-advised attempt to build a tower to reach God's own abode. The Lord was not pleased: "Come, let Us go down and confuse their language so that they will not understand what they say to one another" (11:7). The result was a "babble," a confusion of tongues, and a dispersal of the human race across the face of the earth.

One of those languages, or language sets, fell to the descendants of Shem (10:31), among whom is numbered, in the tenth generation, Abraham (11:26). We are not told what the Shem-itic languages were—it rested with the encyclopedic scholars of the nineteenth century to sort out what was then and thereafter called the "Semitic" language family—but Abraham's story was later told by one of *his* descendants, Moses, in Hebrew, and so we must assume that when God first addressed Abraham (12:1), it was in that same post-Babel language. We are not sure what it was called then—Isaiah (19:15) refers it as "the language of Canaan"—since its current name, after the quite specific people who spoke it, the *Habiru* or "Hebrews," does not occur until the prologue of Ben Sirah/Ecclesiasticus (ca. 132 BCE), and then in Greek!

Historians may prefer to see Yahweh—or Allah—as a local or tribal god who grew to universal status over the centuries. But not so His worshipers, for whom He was from the outset the creator and preserver of the universe and the guardian and judge of all who lived within it. This universal God nonetheless chose to speak to His creatures of salvation in the very provincial tongues of the *Habiru* (or the Canaanites) and of the seventh-century Arabians. Even Jesus, the Son of God and Redeemer of humankind, addressed the world not in ecumenical Greek or the rising tide of Roman Latin but in Palestinian Aramaic. The appropriateness of God's linguistic choices were of no concern as long as the language of address was the same as that used and understood by the audience. But whereas the former was unchanging, the latter was not, and Aramaic-speaking Jews and Greek-speaking Christians and Persian-speaking Muslims had to find, or be given, paths of access to salvation other than the Very Words of God.

It seems likely that it was the rise of Christianity that provoked the related issues of the language of Scripture and the role of humans in its production. We know that some Jews, perhaps most Jews, lost their Hebrew in the course of their dispersal across the Middle East, whether in the deportation to Babylonia that they called the Exile or in their later and longer "broadcast" (*diaspora*) across the Mediterranean basin in search of fortune or, more simply, breathing room. The earlier dispersion seems to have taught the Israelite exiles to speak the proudly named Imperial Aramaic, Hebrew's far more successful linguistic cousin, and from the seventh century onward the lingua franca of the Middle East. Even before the Exile, however, Israelite leaders conducted their diplomatic negotiations in that language (2 Kings 18:26), and after they returned, even ordinary people spoke it. Religious texts, parts of what would later be called Scripture, were composed in Aramaic—Jeremiah 10:11 and Ezra 4:8–16; 7:12–26 (citing Aramaic documents); Daniel 2:4–7:28—and interestingly provoked no protest or even comment.

The texts are but mute testimony to a more public and pressing reality: literate Jews in increasing numbers could no longer read the Hebrew Scriptures, and their illiterate coreligionists could no longer understand when these were read to them. The social reality is dramatically presented in the book of Nehemiah. After the return from the Exile the priest-scribe Ezra brought forth the "book of the Law of Moses" before the people assembled in a square in Jerusalem. His assistants "read from the book, from the Law of God, with interpretation. They gave the sense so that the people understood the reading" (8:8).

Targums and Methurgemans

There the matter, or rather, there our evidence rests. We do know that the literate Jews of the Diaspora read and wrote Aramaic and then, after 300 BCE, chiefly Greek; that the languages of Palestine were Aramaic, Greek, and then, after the first century BCE, Latin. There are no apparent changes in the Temple liturgy, whose oral components are in any event mysterious to us from beginning to end. Evidence for synagogue practice is scanty until the second century CE, but it seems to have reflected linguistic-cultural differences. There were in Jerusalem at least congregations of "Hebrews," that is, Aramaic-speaking Jews distinct from those of the Greek-speaking "Hellenes" who, whether or not there was a Hebrew prologue, heard the Scriptures read and expounded in the languages with which they were familiar.

Jesus, we are told, habitually taught in the synagogue on the Sabbath. Luke lets us look in on the scene. "He stood up to read and the scroll of the prophet Isaiah was handed to him." The setting and circumstances suggest that it was the Hebrew text he was about to read. Jesus unrolls the scroll and "finds" the place he is looking for in Isaiah 61:1–2. He reads it and then sits down and explains it is in Aramaic to the wondering—and disbelieving—Nazareth congregation: "Today the Scripture has been fulfilled in your hearing" (Luke 4:16–21). We are not told, because Luke either did not know or did not care, if Jesus' reading of Isaiah was accompanied by someone else's translation—in later rabbinic legislation the translator had to be someone other than the reader—into Aramaic, but we can be sure that in other synagogue places and other circumstances that was generally the case.

Our first written evidence for an Aramaic translation of Scripture dates, in the preserved copy, almost exactly from the lifetime of Jesus, though its original may have been a century older. From our perspective an Aramaic translation, generally called simply a *targum* or "translation," was originally a running translation-paraphrase, perhaps line by line, of an incomprehensible text, the oral equivalent of what was once the schoolboy's best friend, the interlinear "trot." But when we look at its earliest literary counterpart, the substantial parts of targum of the book of Job and fragments of similar Aramaic treatments of the Pentateuch that have turned up at Qumran, we can only conclude that there were written Aramaic translations of the Bible in circulation in Palestine in the first century BCE. To what end? The preserved parts of these early targums were literal enough to suggest a utilitarian function for the benefit of those at Qumran, or wherever those targums were written, whose Hebrew was failing or nonexistent and not, as was the case later, to make some doctrinal or legal point.

But if the Qumran targums' purpose was functional, it was not likely liturgical. Later oral translation was the rule rather than the exception and the rabbis were quite specific that in the synagogue service the Aramaic translation should be provided line by line for the Torah—up to three lines might be read and translated for the Prophets—that the translation must *not* be read from a written text, and, finally, that the translator (*methurgeman*) must be someone different from the Hebrew reader. If the methurgeman took too many liberties with the text, those of the synagogue congregation familiar with the Hebrew should correct him then and there. Some of these stipulations are doubtless due to the lingering suspicion of writing in a still very oral-attuned society, but a good deal are obviously prompted by a fear that the Aramaic scroll might usurp the canonical status of the Hebrew: the Torah was Hebrew and nothing else.

Despite its tradition-heavy anchor in the oral tradition that presided over the birth of the Aramaic version of Scripture, its literary expression, which is already visible at Qumran, continued to develop in post-Temple, Aramaic-speaking Palestine. It moved away from the fairly literalistic renderings of the Qumran targum for Job to a more interpretive reading of the Hebrew (or the Greek!) text of Scripture, to harmonize discordant passages, for example, or to sharpen the legal prescriptions elicited from the text. There may have been debates over the propriety of the whole targum phenomenon—the period from the stilling of the voice of the historian Josephus (d. ca. 95 CE) to the opening discourses in the Mishnah (ca. 200 CE) is still a historiographic dark age—but when the lights go up again there are in Palestine two officially sanctioned targums. One is a fairly literal translation of the Torah credited to a certain Onkelos, though there are suspicions that this targum is nothing more than an Aramaic version of the Greek retranslation of the Pentateuch by Aquila, whose name got garbled into "Onkelos" in the process.

There are other targums extant, a number in fragments but at least two complete targums to the Pentateuch, one called Neofiti I and the other Pseudo-Jonathan. Like much of the other literature of the early rabbinic period, both probably originated in Palestine and underwent extensive revision at the hands of the increasingly influential Jewish community in Babylonia. There are also Aramaic versions of the package called "The Five Scrolls" (Song of Songs, Ruth, Lamentations, Ecclesiastes, and Esther), all read on special feast days in the emerging synagogue culture.

From the Pentateuchal targums in particular we can begin to read the intentions of these now more literary and so more deliberate translators. Their objective was not merely to translate but to explain or clarify, by paraphrase, for example; to edify, as when the Scriptures' more obvious anthropomorphisms are softened; and to teach, more specifically to reinforce Pharisaic/rabbinic doctrines. Indeed, in the centuries just before and after the turn into the Common Era, the targums may well have been the most prominent form of interpretation of the Bible, and the reading they gave to Biblical texts, to prophetic texts in particular, may well stand behind the way Jesus' followers understood those same passages.

⊰⟨⊱ *Note: A Christian Aramaic Bible.*

As a living language Aramaic underwent its own evolution, not only of forms and syntax but of script as well. The eastern or Mesopotamian dialect of Aramaic developed a distinctive, more cursive script, and that form of the language, known as Syriac, became the chief literary vehicle for Christians living outside the eastern orbit of Hellenism. The Jews continued to use Western Aramaic with its block Hebrew script.

As early as the first or second century CE an Eastern Aramaic or Syriac version of the Bible was circulating. It is not entirely clear whether it was done by Jews or Christians, but its primary reliance on the Hebrew original rather than a Greek version—unlike the Septuagint-based Syro-Hexapla (see below)—suggests the former, perhaps Jewish converts to Christianity. The earliest manuscripts of this Syriac version of the Bible, known as the Peshitta or "Simple Version," date from the fifth and sixth centuries. It has undergone few revisions—the Pentateuch at least is quite literal—and has remained the standard Old Testament text for Eastern Syrian Christians to this day.

Scripture for the Hellenized: The Septuagint

Many Jews still cannot read the Hebrew Bible, and though they read and hear their Scripture in a modern vernacular, they, like contemporary Christians, are constantly exposed to another ancient version, the Greek. We have already encountered the word "Tanak," the rabbinic Hebrew-based acronym for the Bible. The rabbis also preferred to call the individual books by their Hebrew opening phrases, just as Catholics later did the Latin papal encyclicals, and Muslims, in a much more general fashion, the suras of the Quran. Thus the initial Hebrew word of the first Biblical book, *Bereshit,* "In the beginning," also becomes its name. What is familiar to the rabbis and to some other Jews is not, however, the common name of that book for most readers, Jewish, Christian, and others. For them the book's name is Genesis, followed not by a book called *Sefer ve'eleh shamot,* or simply *Shamot,* but by Exodus and all the rest, which, from the tongue-twisting Deuteronomy to the curious Ecclesiastes, all bear upon their souls the stamp of the Greek language, as do Pentateuch ("The Five Pieces") and Bible (*Biblia,* "books") themselves. The reason is not mysterious. The Bible came into the European languages under Christian auspices, and the Christian Bible, or the Old Testament, as they call it, was, in its "original" language, the Greek Septuagint.

It would not be surprising if the Jews of the Mediterranean Diaspora, where a learned scribal culture would naturally be far thinner on the ground, lost their Hebrew even more quickly than those in Palestine. And without remorse. On all the evidence, the Diaspora synagogues dispensed with the reading of the Hebrew text: the Scriptures were read, and prayed, entirely in Greek, the Greek of the version called the Septuagint or "The Seventy." And from there hangs a tale both ingenious and moralistic.

The story appears first in a document of the second century BCE titled the "Letter of Aristeas," which professes to describe how the Jewish Scriptures came into Greek. In this telling the Greco-Egyptian ruler of Egypt, Ptolemy II Philadelphus (r. 285–246), expressed an interest in the sacred books of the Jews, and at his solicitation, the high priest Eliezar sent from Jerusalem to Alexandria an accurate Hebrew text and seventy-two senior scholars—the number is sometimes given as seventy, hence the *Septuagint*, a paradoxically Latin name for the Greek version—six each from the twelve tribes of Israel. They translated the Pentateuch as a kind of collaborative effort that was finished, it is said, in seventy-two days. The letter goes to some lengths to underline the wisdom and moral integrity of the translators and so to underline, for the benefit of the Jews using it, the reliability of the Greek translation of the Torah that they had in their hands.

The Christians, whose Bible was invariably the Septuagint version, improved the story in two general ways. To move the emphasis from underlining to boldface, the Christians' retelling, of the second century CE, put the translators in separate cubicles where they produced, independently and, obviously, miraculously, perfectly identical Greek versions of the Hebrew Pentateuch—a similar form of that turn of events already occurs in the retelling by the Alexandrian Jew Philo (ca. 20 BCE–50 CE). More circumstantially, they extended the story to cover the Greek translation of the *entire* Bible, all translated under Ptolemy II. Philadelphus and all under the inspiration and infallible guidance of the Holy Spirit.

Elements of the Aristeas story may indeed be true. The Pentateuch may well have been translated from Hebrew into Greek in the third century BCE, possibly, though somewhat improbably, through the intervention of the Pharaoh, since the Hebrew-less Jews of Egypt needed Greek Scripture for their own prayer and study. The rest of the story of the translators is patently apologetic. The Greek translation of the Pentateuch is sufficiently homogeneous in vocabulary and style strongly to suggest that it was translated at a single point and perhaps even by a single hand. But not so the rest of the Greek Bible. The task of the translators that resulted in the so-called Septuagint seems to have stretched over two centuries and, more importantly, included, like the library at Qumran, a wider range of books than what the rabbis eventually regarded as "Bible." The Septuagint did not include "apocryphal" books; it was the rabbis who created the Apocrypha by excluding them from *their* Bible.

The Septuagint thus became the Bible of the Greek-speaking Jews of the Mediterranean, for Philo in Alexandria, for Josephus in Rome, and for Paul in Tarsus in Cilicia. It was the Scripture not only of Paul but of all those who believed that Jesus was the promised Messiah—promised, that is, in that same Greek text they and their fellow Jews were hearing and reading in the synagogue. By the second century, however, Jews were beginning to have their Christian-provoked doubts about the Septuagint, whose text was critically different in places from what the rabbis, who were increasingly being drawn into Biblical dispute with the Christians, told them was in the Hebrew Tanak. The "virgin"—*parthenos* in the Septuagint—who was to bear a son in Isaiah 7:14, a text beloved of the Christians, was in fact a "young girl" in the Hebrew. In the rabbis' eyes *parthenos* was a blatant mistranslation of the Hebrew; it should have been rendered *neanis*!

And soon it was. The Jewish solution to the failings of the Septuagint, and the advantage to which they were being put by the Christians, was a new Greek translation. Two new Jewish versions appeared in the second century CE, one by a convert named Theodotion, which was more a revision of the Septuagint toward literalness rather than a fresh translation; and the other by the Jewish proselyte Aquila, who also stayed close to the Hebrew and seems to have been particularly careful to avoid Greek expressions that had passed from the Septuagint into the Christian vernacular. Neither translation is particularly well known to us, though they were familiar to the Christian Biblical scholars Origen and Jerome, and Origen included both in his Hexapla version of the Old Testament. Ironically, Theodotion's translation of the book of Daniel eventually found its way into the Christians' Old Testament, dislodging the original Septuagint ver-

sion of that book. Slightly later there was a third attempt at a Greek version, this time by a certain Symmachus, a Palestinian Jew, whose translation was known and consulted by Christians and was also included by
Origen in his comparative edition of the Greek Bible. There are three additional Greek translations in that portmanteau work by Origen, all of
them anonymous. One was reportedly found in Epirus in Greece, another
discovered sealed in a jar in Jericho sometime around 210–220 CE, and a
third about whose provenance nothing whatsoever is known.

Origen: Multitasking the Bible

By the second century, the drawing apart of Judaism and Christianity began
to create serious Scriptural problems for the latter. Though many Jews were
incapable of reading Hebrew and had to rely chiefly on Greek translations,
the Hebrew Tanak was still recited aloud in the synagogue and the rabbis remained faithful to the Hebrew text, which, as we have seen, they were then
in the process of refining and fixing as the "masoretic text." The Christians
had no such linguistic compass to give them their Biblical bearings. The
Septuagint had been their "Bible" from the beginning: it was their road map
to the Messiah, the foundation of both their morality and their piety, and,
most importantly here, the text upon which, then as now, every dispute with
the Jews began and ended. And the Septuagint, whose manuscripts differed
among themselves, was also different from the Hebrew Bible of the Jews not
only in its readings but in terms of what was in it and what was not.

For most Christians these discrepancies made little difference, but for
Christians who knew Hebrew or the Jewish tradition, or who were engaged in argument with Jews, the differences between the Septuagint and
the Hebrew Tanak were troubling. One such was the Alexandrian scholar
Origen (ca. 185–254), an academic prodigy of the university there. He acknowledged the textual primacy of the Hebrew and understood the defects of the Septuagint. The Jews attempted to remedy those latter, as we
have seen, by successive new translations by Aquila, Theodotion, and Symmachus, but that may have been no longer possible for the Christians, for
whom the Septuagint had always been their *primary* text and in which by
Origen's day they had too profound a theological and psychological investment to be able to simply jettison it and start over as the Jews had.

Origen proposed to improve the Septuagint with the same text-critical methods that had been honed to a sharp edge at Alexandria over the course of nearly five centuries. He took as his base a text of the Septuagint in common use, and where it departed from the reading of most of the other Greek manuscripts he had available, he corrected his copy to the common reading and so created a kind of consensus text. But that was merely the beginning. He also compared his text to the Hebrew Bible, and where the Greek had verses not in the Hebrew, he did not remove them but signaled them with a kind of dash sign, the "obel" of the Greek textual critics. And, more boldly, Origen inserted in his Greek text—though marked with an asterisk—a version of the verses present in the Hebrew but missing in the Septuagint.

This then was Origen's "edition" of the Septuagint and thus, in effect, of the Christians' Old Testament. It must have been a great success since Jerome remarks in the next century that Origen's Septuagint, with all its obels and asterisks, was the only Bible to be found in the libraries of the Greek East. But Origen pressed on. He next produced an edition in which the Septuagint text had reproduced in columns next to it the Greek translations of Aquila, Symmachus, and Theodotion. Not content with this, he went further and contrived the massive project already referred to and called "The Sixfold" (*Hexapla*). He arranged the Bible across the page in six columns, first the Hebrew text in Hebrew characters, then the Hebrew transcribed into Greek characters, followed by the translations of Aquila, Symmachus, the Septuagint, and Theodotion. We now possess only fragments of this work—its most substantial remnant is some parts of the Psalms that have survived in manuscript—but it seems that copyists soon ceased copying the first column, and when Christian preachers cited the Hebrew of the Bible, it was generally from Origen's second column, the Hebrew phonetically transcribed into Greek characters.

৯৬৩   *Note: A Syriac Origen.*

The work called the Syro-Hexapla is a Syriac translation of Origen's "emended" text of the Septuagint, with obels and asterisks intact and with many marginal annotations of a doctrinal character. The translation was done in 616–617 by the skilled professional translator of Greek into Syriac, Paul of Tella.

From Old Latin to the Vulgate

The Letter of Aristeas casts a bright if misleading light on the translation of the Bible from Hebrew into Greek for the benefit of the Hellenized Jews of the Mediterranean Diaspora. But the somewhat later passage of the Bible into the Roman Empire's official Latin tongue is shrouded in darkness. It seems safe to conclude that the Latin-speaking Jews of the empire read and prayed the Scripture in that language. Our evidence centers on Carthage, the chief urban center of Roman North Africa. Here Christian authors like Tertullian (d. ca. 225) and Cyprian (d. 258), the bishop of Carthage, were quoting various passages in Latin from the Old Testament that we must assume were in general circulation and that, absent any counterindication, were originally made by Jews for Jews. The Biblical quotes in Latin show by their variety that there was no standard Latin version for the Jews or Christians and, more interestingly, they derived not from the Hebrew but from the doubtless far more familiar Greek Septuagint.

This reconstructed Jewish past of the Latin Bible was soon overshadowed by the Christians' use and considerable revision of the same Latin texts of the Bible. The texts are called generally the Old Latin versions of the Old Testament, and they eventually show up, as expected, in a wide range of provenances—Spain, Gaul, Italy—in the Roman, and now Christian, Western Empire. Liturgically, they functioned in much the same fashion as the earliest Aramaic targums. So at least we conclude from the preserved evidence of the "Old Latin" versions of the New Testament, those Latin translations of the Gospels prepared for reading in church by at least the second century, again possibly in North Africa since Christians at Rome—to whom Paul could write in Greek in the late 50s—remained comfortable with Greek for a longer time. Some of the pre-Vulgate Latin manuscripts have Latin translations interlined with the Greek original, or else the Greek and the Latin is arranged in parallel columns, and with the lines broken into units of varying length to assist in the public reading.

There is substantial manuscript evidence for these Christian or Christianized Old Latin versions, and later Jerome, who was in a position to know, remarked that there seemed to be almost as many versions as there were manuscripts. Augustine (d. 430) had his own explanation: every

Latin Christian with even a smattering of Greek felt qualified to try his hand at a translation of the Gospels. It may not have been quite that bad, but the condition of the Latin New Testament was chaotic enough for Pope Damasus (r. 366–384), himself a Latin speaker from Spain, to commission the brightest Latin star in the papal employ to prepare a new and more accurate Latin translation of the Gospels.

That star was the Dalmatian provincial Jerome, who had studied at Rome with Donatus, the premier Latinist of his day—and the grammar tutor of all of medieval Europe—and was then, in 382, aged about forty, a secretary in the papal household. He had already traveled in the Middle East, where he polished what was probably his native Greek and had begun to study Hebrew. So Jerome set himself to the papal commission using whatever Greek manuscripts were available in Rome. Some of them must have been of very recent origin since they contained—and Jerome integrated into his own versions—the Canons, the tabular method of comparing parallel texts in the four Gospels contrived by the somewhat older Greek Church historian and Biblical scholar Eusebius of Caesarea (ca. 260–340).

When Damasus died in 384 Jerome went on to other things and so it took him only two years to complete the Latin translation of the Gospels and then to produce a new Latin version of the Psalter, the Biblical book of Psalms and the Church's chief liturgical text then and for very long thereafter. It survives under the name of the "Roman Psalter." Jerome headed back to the Greek East, first to study in Constantinople and Antioch, and then in 386 in Bethlehem, where he remained until his death in 420. His life in the East was one of asceticism—he lived in a monastery of his own founding in Bethlehem and guided another nearby community for women—and scholarship. He had been collecting Greek manuscripts for years and at Caesarea he acquired the gem of his collection, the copy of Origen's Hexapla.

Jerome was a prolific and varied author, but of concern here is his work on Scripture. He wrote a number of commentaries on Biblical books whose interest for us is in the prologues that describe his work, and views, on translating. He clearly learned as he went along. His now sophisticated knowledge of Greek, his collection of Greek manuscripts, and perhaps the example of Origen himself prompted him in the mid-380s to translate the Bible afresh with particular attention to the Old Testament. We do not know how far he got, but the clearest example of this stage in his work is his Septuagint-based revision of the Latin Psalms, complete with the diacritical signs borrowed from Origen's Hexapla, and now preserved in the "Gallican Psalter" that was for a time in wide use among Christians in Late Roman Gaul. He also continued revising his Latin New Testament, though we cannot follow all the details.

We can see where Jerome was heading, particularly with the Old Testament. If the Septuagint enabled him to improve the Old Latin versions, would not the Hebrew, as Origen too had thought, give him the most authentic—Jerome used the phrase *Hebraica veritas*—rendition of the Bible? Jerome had begun the study of Hebrew on his first stay in the East, and now he had access—for a fee—to skilled Jewish Hebraists, one of whom worked with him on the notoriously difficult Job and another on Chronicles. Another gave him regular lessons in the evening in Bethlehem. Again, we do not know how far this Hebrew-Latin project proceeded. In addition to Job and Chronicles, we know he translated Tobit and Judith. And once again the Psalter, so we have three versions of the Psalms from Jerome, this last based on the Hebrew. We do not of course have the Hebrew manuscripts Jerome worked from—nor the Greek ones, for that matter—but they seem to have differed little from what was later codified as the masoretic text.

By chance or by accident, the so-called Vulgate was neither from a single hand nor from a single source. Jerome's own work on the Gospels was mixed with that of earlier translators—the anonymous figures behind the "Old Latin" New Testament—and of later editors who finished or revised what Jerome had started. The Old Testament rested in large part on the Septuagint as represented in a very varied manuscript tradition, some of it mediated through Origen's Hexapla, and with elements derived directly from the Hebrew or, perhaps more accurately, from the Septuagint corrected from the Hebrew. Jerome's well-intentioned scholarly and refined revision did not easily displace the tradition-sanctioned Old Latin New Testament, which had found a firm anchor in the liturgy of the Western churches, and the Old Testament had its own moorings in the Septuagint, which was immune to correction by reason of its own miraculously attested authenticity—so the Letter of Aristeas and the Church Fathers—and it did not help that Augustine, who knew no Hebrew, was opposed to the innovation.

Hebraica Veritas and the Latin West

Jerome did not introduce Hebrew into Christian Bible studies—the honor belongs to Origen, who showed Christians that there was something Scriptural beyond, and indeed, before, the Septuagint. It was Jerome, however, the Eastern expatriate Latinist, who, with the considerable help of Augustine, called that fact to the attention of the monolingual Latin-reading and -writing Church of the West. His ongoing study of both the Old Latin translations of the Old Testament and of the Septuagint version on which they were based brought Jerome the growing conviction that, if not the true Scripture, then the truth of Scripture—what he called, in a broader context, the *Hebraica veritas*—lay in the Hebrew original.

By the fourth century it was apparent to all that, where it concerned the Old Testament, Christians would have to read Scripture in a translation. Jerome was concerned that it should be as philologically and contextually accurate as possible; others, that it should be as faithful to the Christian tradition as possible, and for them that tradition was represented by the supernaturally authenticated and validated Septuagint. That was the conviction of Augustine (354–430), who, though he knew not much Greek and almost no Hebrew, felt more comfortable with a Septuagint-based translation of the Old Testament and told Jerome so in their correspondence. But while he did not really approve of a Hebraized Vulgate, Augustine agreed with Jerome on other related matters, that Judaizing was not a good thing for Christians, for example, and, more importantly and consequentially, that the literal sense of Scripture was supremely important to an understanding of God's Word. Both men wrote commentaries on Genesis in that vein, Augustine's *On the Literal Interpretation of Genesis*—there are two versions—and Jerome's *Hebrew Questions on Genesis*. Augustine's work was probably more influential in the end because Augustine was the more influential theologian, but Jerome obviously enjoyed an advantage when it came to literal interpretation: he had more than enough Hebrew to work with the original whereas Augustine did not.

What counted in the end was Augustine's insistence on the importance of the literal sense of the Old Testament in addition to the allegorical and typological reading of its books, and anyone who read Jerome, whose prefaces were often copied with his translations, knew that the primary locus of the literal sense was in the Hebrew. Few would dispute that proposition, but even fewer were able to act on it. Josephus's *Antiquities of the Jews* was of some help and was assiduously copied, but knowledge of Hebrew, like knowledge of Greek, grew dim in the Latin West. There were glimmers of interest in the Carolingian era when a few scholars like Theodulf, bishop of Orleans (d. 821), and Rabanus Maurus, the learned abbot of the Benedictine abbey of Fulda (d. 856), both gave indications of having consulted the Hebrew text of the Old Testament. There was even an anonymous attempt at emulating Jerome's *Hebrew Questions on Genesis*, an effort during which Jewish scholars may have been consulted.

The task of writing commentaries on the Old Testament seems not to have appealed to many in the eleventh or twelfth century, and those who did were more taken by the nascent Scholasticism of the era than by the *sensus literalis* and the relatively broad literary and philological skills and interests it required. That was the burden of the criticism leveled at the Scholastics by the Franciscan scholar Roger Bacon (ca. 1214–1294) in his *Compendium of the Study of Philosophy*. Their approach to the Old Testament was too abstract and their manner was better suited to, in fact was borrowed from, a commentary of Aristotle. Opening Scripture requires skill in the language of Scripture, Bacon insisted. And he not only diagnosed the disease—he compiled a list of glaring errors, many of them based on false etymologies—but also provided the cure: Bacon composed, or at least drafted, both a Greek and a Hebrew grammar for the benefit of those who were ignorant of those languages. One cannot understand the Scripture—or Aristotle for that matter!—without a knowledge on the languages in which they were written.

Bacon's insistence on language training echoes a similar call being issued from other monastic quarters, chiefly the Dominicans, and for somewhat different reasons. Already in 1235, the master-general of the Dominicans wrote to all the houses of the order calling for volunteers who were "prepared to learn Arabic, Hebrew, Greek or some other outlandish language," in order to convert the Muslims, Jews, and heretical Greeks to the Catholic faith. Later in that same century another Dominican, Ramon of Peñaforte, took more direct action, and under his leadership language schools for missionaries were opened on Majorca, in Murcia, Valencia, Barcelona, and Játiva in Spain, and even in Tunis. We do not know much about them save that they did not last very long and the emphasis appears to have been on Arabic, though there was a Hebrew teacher at Murcia for awhile.

The motive behind this new emphasis on intensive language learning was conversion, or that part of the conversion project that involved polemic. This was certainly in the mind of Ramon Llull (1232–1316), the energetic Majorcan layman with a lifelong plan to convert Muslims with a program of pacific argument—it would work on Jews as well—but it required serious language training, as he kept reminding the pope and anyone else who would listen. His drumbeat was apparently heard. The Church Council of Vienne (1311–1312), which Llull himself attended, decreed that there should be set up at Paris, Bologna, and Salamanca, as well as in the Papal Court, two professorial chairs each for Arabic, Hebrew, and Aramaic.

There were already at Paris men who knew Hebrew, and not simply for missionary or polemical purposes, as was intended at Vienne. The thirteenth-century commentaries on Scripture may have been in the Scholastic mold criticized by Bacon, but there also began to appear under the name of *correctoria*, "corrections," not so much to emend the Vulgate text of the Old Testament as to show where it differed from the original, and the evidence is unmistakable that at least some of their authors, some named, like the thirteenth-century Franciscans William de la Mare and Gerard of Huy, but many more anonymous, had consulted either a Hebrew text or Hebrew informants. And there were texts to read and study, like the Hebrew Psalter, with the Latin openings of each Psalm noted in the margin, that once belonged to Bury St. Edmund's; a number of Latin-Hebrew bilingual Psalters, including one remarkable specimen commissioned by Robert Grosseteste (1170–1253), bishop of Lincoln, that juxtaposes the Hebrew with the Old Latin version of the Psalms called the "Gallican" that made it into the Vulgate; Jerome's own "according to the Hebrews," which did not; and, for good measure, a new and more literal Latin version written word for word between the lines of the Hebrew.

There is other manuscript evidence that Christian scholars were not only reading Hebrew in the High Middle Ages but using it in their Bible studies. Indeed, it has been remarked more than once that in the fourteenth century it was easier to acquire knowledge of Hebrew than of Greek, and that there were more Hebrew-capable scholars working on the Bible than those who knew Greek. Greek manuscripts, Greek grammars, and instructors in that language were not easy to come by in Western Europe before the Renaissance, whereas in every large European city, and in many of the smaller ones as well, there was a living tradition of Hebrew scholarship and Hebrew instruction to which interested Christian scholars also had access. Some used it for polemical purposes, more readily to convict the Jews out of their own mouths—knowledge of the Talmud was growing as well in Christian circles—but just as many, or more, put their newly acquired version of the *Hebraica veritas* to work improving and illuminating the Christians' own understanding of the Scripture they shared with their Jewish instructors.

The most remarkable of these scholars was the French Franciscan Nicholas of Lyra or Lyre in Normandy (1270–1349), like most of the others an exegete of Scripture rather than a textual scholar—that latter breed would need two more centuries of gestation. His fifty-volume work, *The Ongoing Postillae or Brief Commentaries on the Whole Bible*, became one of Western Christendom's standard exegetical works and was studied and used by every Biblical student of note from his own day down through the Reformation. Nicholas was in a sense the incarnation of the Augustine-Jerome ideal, a scholar who regarded the literal sense of Scripture as of prime importance and turned to the *Hebraica veritas* to understand it. In his general introduction to the *Postillae* Nicholas remarks that "I intend, for making clear the literal sense, to introduce, not only the statements of the Catholic doctors, but also of the Hebrews, especially of Rabbi Solomon who, among the Hebrew doctors, has spoken most reasonably." The "Rabbi Solomon" who spoke so reasonably to Nicholas of Lyra was no less than the celebrated Rashi of Troyes (1040–1105), the paramount Jewish Torah commentator of that, and perhaps every other, day, and himself a dedicated exponent of the *sensus literalis*. Just as Jewish students generally read the Bible with Rashi peering over their shoulders—the first printed text of the Pentateuch (1475) has Rashi's Torah commentary printed in the margins and the practice quickly became standard—so it was Rashi who guided Nicholas through the original Hebrew text of the Bible and whose own work, and almost his very words, were being used at every turn in the *Postillae*.

Through the *Postillae* Rashi's encyclopedic version of the *Hebraica veritas* worked its way into the Christians' Old Testament, both text and understanding. One such Christian was Martin Luther (1483–1546), who not only used Nicholas, and so Rashi, in his German translation of the Old Testament but took the additional step that Nicholas of Lyra's enormous influence, to say nothing of Augustine's, was promoting and in his early twenties began the study of Hebrew. The means were readily at hand. Germany's premier humanist of that generation, Johannes Reuchlin (1455–1522), had published his Hebrew grammar and lexicon, *On the Rudiments of Hebrew*, in 1506, and then in 1512 he produced for the use of students an edition of some of the Psalms accompanied by a literal Latin translation. Luther studied Reuchlin, but later—a highly indicative sign of the times—he discovered and recommended the commentaries and Hebrew grammars (in Hebrew!) of the brothers Moses (d. ca. 1190) and the more famous David Kimhi (d. 1235), members of a distinguished twelfth-century family from Narbonne.

Luther, who apparently had little head and even less taste for formal grammar—"I cannot bear to be hampered by rules," he wrote—claims to have found David's *Sefer Mikhlol* or "Completion," which is still in use, most helpful, or perhaps simply more authentic since Luther seems to have relied far more substantially on Reuchlin's more comfortable Latin presentation of Hebrew. He praised Hebrew as a necessary tool but he was never an aficionado, and he despised his fellow Reformer Ulrich Zwingli for showing off by using Greek and Hebrew from his pulpit in Zurich. But he did what was needful: when he translated the Old Testament he had at his elbow the printed masoretic text published by a Jewish press in Brescia in 1494.

ᔕᕲᔰ   ***Note: Printing the Bible.***

With the appearance in Mainz sometime between 1453 and 1456 of Johann Gutenberg's complete Latin Bible reproduced with fixed metal type, we begin our passage from the age of the manuscript to that of printing. But the text continued to be the Latin Vulgate and there were more than a hundred printings of the Latin before the Greek appeared in print. There was never a question of Gutenberg's printing anything other than Jerome's translation, and likely little debate about the use of what passed at that time as the standard recension of the Vulgate, the one first prepared at Paris in the twelfth century and frequently tinkered with thereafter. Though there were earlier printings of parts of the Bible (the Psalms, with a commentary, in Bologna in 1477; the complete

Pentateuch, with vowels and accents and accompanied by the targum of Onkelos and a commentary, also at Bologna in 1482; the Former Prophets followed quickly by the Latter Prophets with an interlinear commentary, and then by the five *Megilloth,* all at Soncino and all likely in 1488; the Writings meanwhile had been printed in three volumes in Naples in 1487), the first complete printed Hebrew text of the Bible, prepared by Jews for Jewish use, appeared at Soncino, in northern Italy, in 1488. The first printing of the Septuagint Greek was not until 1518 in the so-called Aldine Bible, the work of Aldus Manutius in Venice; the New Testament in Erasmus' edition had been printed a year earlier in Basle by Johann Froben.

The Polyglot

Origen and Jerome seem to have been among the last Christian Fathers to have treated the Bible as a text as well as Scripture. Throughout the long Latin Middle Ages the Old and New Testaments represented for Christians the work of God rather than that of mortal hands and so subjects for interpretation, not objects for correction or emendation. Then, from the heart of the European Renaissance and, more consequentially, from the dawn of the age of printing came two works that turned the attention of scholars and churchmen back to the texts of which God was still unmistakably the *auctor,* but men, it now appeared with great clarity, their very fallible *scriptores.* That was the effect of the almost simultaneous appearance of the Complutensian Polyglot of Cardinal Cisneros in Spain (1514–1517) and Desiderius Erasmus' *Novum Instrumentum* in the Low Countries (1516).

Francisco Jiménez de Cisneros (1436–1517) was an extraordinary individual for any time or any place. From modest origins he began his ascent to prominence on the ascetical path of monasticism and at the height of his career became first the confessor to Queen Isabella of Castile (1492), then archbishop of Toledo and so the primate of the Church in Spain (1495), then cardinal and grand inquisitor of Spain (1507). Finally, at the death of Ferdinand in 1516, he was appointed the regent of Spain on behalf of the minor Charles I, later the Holy Roman Emperor Charles V.

Cisneros was no lover of the Muslims or their books: he is the villainous instigator in the oft-told tale of a wholesale burning of Arabic texts after the fall of Muslim Granada to Isabella and Ferdinand in 1492. The cardinal was also the instigator, financier—it was too expensive for the Crown to handle, even for a crusade—and commander-in-chief of an expeditionary force that crossed the Mediterranean and took and sacked Muslim Oran (1509), and later he was the architect of the program for the forced conversions of the conquered Muslim population of Spain (1515). And yet, paradoxically, part of his personal share of the loot from Oran was a bale of Arabic manuscripts he gave to another of his pet projects, the university of Alcalá. The university was his foundation, confirmed by a papal bull of 1499 and called, after the Latin name of the city, the Complutense. The university, and its name, and its manuscripts, were all later moved twenty miles westward to Spain's new capital of Madrid.

Cisneros' Scriptural project probably dates from his astonishingly busy years in the early 1500s. He planned what might later be regarded as a critical edition, or rather, the material for a critical edition of the Bible, both Old and New Testaments. He was in effect the paymaster and manager—and on occasion the micromanager—of a team of editors he had assembled at Alcalá, among them the preeminent philologist of Europe, and the author of the first grammar of any European vernacular, Elio Antonio de Nebrija. What he put before them was a collection of manuscripts he had borrowed—most famously from the Vatican library—or bought, the best Greek and Hebrew texts available. The first volume to be completed, the fifth of a projected six-volume set, was that of the New Testament, original Greek and Jerome's Vulgate printed side by side. The New Testament volume was printed in 1514. But the death that same year of its patron and moving spirit, Cardinal Cisneros, by then in effect the ruler of Spain in the name of Charles V, stalled the project until 1520 or 1522, when the complete six-volume set of the Complutensian Polyglot was formally published.

The Polyglot not only gave the public a printed edition of the Greek and Vulgate texts of the Bible; it used a page design more complex even than Origen's Hexapla to enable the reader not merely to read the text but to *judge* it. The layout of each page of the Polyglot Old Testament resembles that of the Talmud. Pride of place is given to the Vulgate, which is presented in a slender column in the center of the page, flanked on the left or inner margin by the Greek Septuagint text and on the right by the Hebrew.

The Greek has a literal, word-for-word Latin translation above each word. This would not do for the Hebrew, however, which runs, in the Semitic fashion, from right to left on the page and so the editors have placed over the beginning of each word of the Hebrew a letter keyed to the same letter over the Latin word in the Vulgate that most closely translates it. More, on the margin outside the Hebrew text is a running list of roots of the main words in the Hebrew. Finally, in the Pentateuch at least one finds across the bottom of the page a double column of texts. On the left, in Hebrew characters, is the "Chaldean" translation, the Aramaic targum Onkelos to the Biblical passage above, and on the right, a literal Latin translation of the targum.

Enter the Humanists

Cisneros had constructed an instrument more useful, and more danger-ous to traditional beliefs, than perhaps he knew or intended. The readers of the Complutensian Polyglot had in their hands a formidable instru-ment for both studying and emending the received texts of the Old and New Testaments. The point was clearly pedagogical and scholarly, as the sixth volumes of the work, a collection of grammars, dictionaries, and other study aids—Nebrija's influence is manifest here—attests. All the evi-dence is present to show what Jerome had done to the Greek and the He-brew, though perhaps not exactly since Jerome's manuscripts of those lat-ter were not identical to the Polyglot's. If the editors of the Polyglot were not quite ready to emend the sacrosanct Vulgate—they occasionally ad-justed the Septuagint to Jerome, however—the material lay at hand to do precisely that.

While the unbound pages of the Complutensian Polyglot awaited pub-lication in Spain, a somewhat similar enterprise was proceeding more rap-idly in northern Europe where Desiderius Erasmus was preparing nothing less than a revision of the Vulgate New Testament. Erasmus was not the first but he was certainly the most influential of the Renaissance human-ists who had turned back to the texts of classical antiquity with a new ap-petite not merely for their style but also for their language. In a world where the intelligentsia still wrote in Latin and both Church and State rested on a deep foundation of Latin—and under them, Greek—documents, the humanists found much matter for contemplation and comment. Under their gaze what had hitherto been Sacred Scripture began slowly to turn into something at once more human and more flawed, Greek and Latin *texts*.

One of the first humanists to comment publicly on the matter was the Roman polemicist, near-professional provocateur, and considerable scholar Lorenzo Valla (1407–1457)—from the relatively protected position as Latin secretary in the Neapolitan court of Alfonso V of Aragon, who ruled not only Aragon but Sardinia, Sicily, and the powerful Kingdom of Naples that ran up to the doorstep of the papal states. Alfonso V and Pope Eugenius IV were fierce rivals in power and Valla put a formidable weapon in Alfonso's hands with his 1440 "Protestation," a devastating demonstration that the document known as the "Donation of Constantine," by which the first Christian emperor was alleged to have bequeathed his temporal sovereignty over the Western Empire to the bishop of Rome, and was often invoked by the papacy to its own advantage, was a crude and blatant forgery.

The "Protestation" was simply the best known of Valla's many explosive works and he never ceased hurling grenades in the direction of the papacy, the Church generally, and the Latinity of his enemies, of whom there were many. He enthusiastically embraced the unfashionable: he preferred Epicurus to the Stoics in philosophy and the Latin style of Quintilian to that of Cicero; he attempted to take down Aristotle's sacred *Categories*, and he doubted in print that the Apostles had actually composed the "Apostles' Creed," as was piously believed by all.

In 1448 both Alfonso V and Eugenius IV were gone and the papal states were ruled by the more humanistically complaisant Nicholas V. Valla returned to his native Rome and was appointed papal secretary. In this setting, among his other labors—at the pope's request he undertook to translate Herodotus and Thucydides into Latin—he began, with the encouragement of Cardinal Bessarion, Rome's chief advocate of Hellenism, and the redoubtable Cardinal Nicolas of Cusa, what later emerged—it was not printed until 1505—as his *Adnotationes*, more formally the "Annotations on the New Testament Based on a Comparison of Manuscripts in Both Languages." The "New Testament" in question was of course Jerome's Vulgate. To attack Cicero's Latinity was one thing, and doubtless a head turner, but to criticize Saint Jerome was quite another, and in the next century, when the Church began to tighten its moorings against the Reform, the "Annotations" was placed on the *Index of Prohibited Books.*

The "Annotations" was indeed a revolutionary work, not so much for its criticisms of the Vulgate, which were rather mild, but for its method: Valla applied the approach and techniques of the new secular science of classical philology to Holy Scripture. He judged Jerome not under the light of the Holy Spirit but in comparison to the usage—when it came to language, Valla was a great believer in usage (*consuetudo*)—of writers who were the epigones of paganism. Jerome had once castigated himself for being too much the Ciceronian and too little the Christian; Valla now found him much too little the first and showed little interest in the second. But he did not change the text; he simply annotated it, noting what he detected as scribal errors in transmission and, more provocatively, where Jerome had apparently misunderstood or mistranslated the Greek. The mistakes were minor; it was the pointing to them that was new.

Desiderius Erasmus, the Dutch humanist (1469–1536), found a manuscript copy of Valla's *Adnotationes* in a Belgian monastic library in 1504 and arranged to have it printed in Paris in 1505. Erasmus was trained in the *litterae humaniores* of antiquity but he had also had a monastic and spiritual formation, and his easy mastery of Catullus and Ovid seemed constantly compromised by an attraction to the less elegant but more meaningful works of Christian Fathers like Jerome and Origen. Valla rekindled Erasmus' already considerable interest in Jerome, not Jerome the commentator but Jerome the translator of Scripture. He set to work quickly, and in the spring of 1506 he produced a new Latin version of the Gospels and the New Testament Epistles. But the great work still lay ahead. He began to plan a new edition of the Greek original, and in 1507 he described the project to the humanist-printer Aldus Manutius. It was long in the making, and not until 1516 did there appear in print with a solemn dedication to Pope Leo X—not from Aldus but from Froben in Basle—what Erasmus called the *Novum Instrumentum omne,* and what was in fact the first edition of the New Testament in the language in which it was written.

Novum Instrumentum in place of the traditional *Novum Testamentum* was Erasmus' scholarly but somewhat outlandish attempt to ruffle feathers. It did, but Erasmus judged it not worth the fuss and restored *Testamentum* in the very next (1519) of the many editions his work went through. But even more disturbing was his own Latin translation, which he had printed, instead of the Vulgate, next to his edition of the Greek and which was, whether he intended it or not—Erasmus never seems entirely innocent in these matters—a correction and a rebuke to Jerome, a saint and Father of the Church. It took more than a little courage, or gall, perhaps, to replace Jerome's already canonized *In principio erat verbum* at the opening of John's Gospel with *In principio erat sermo*. As editions passed, Erasmus dropped some of his novelties, and in that of 1527 he felt constrained to include the Vulgate along with the Greek text and his own translation.

Erasmus' edition of the Greek New Testament was, of course, only as good as the manuscripts he used. We do not know precisely which they were, certainly the ones available at Basle and very likely he had made his own notes of the Greek manuscripts he had seen in England. It seems unlikely that he had seen the Polyglot, however, since, though finished, Cisneros' edition would remain in printed but unbound pages in Spain for another fourteen years. Generally speaking, what Erasmus chiefly had access to were unedited, that is, unemended, manuscript copies of the New Testament in circulation in the Eastern Church, and none apparently older than the twelfth or thirteenth century. In the eyes of modern scholarship they are not the most reliable family of witnesses to the New Testament text, but Erasmus made do with what he had.

This first edition of the Greek New Testament was revolutionary merely as such and it was in effect canonized when in 1550 the Parisian printer Robert Estienne made it the basis of his third and so-called Royal Edition—he was the official "Printer in Greek to the King"—of the Greek New Testament, this one with a critical apparatus, that is, annotations, in this instance marginal, on variant readings in the manuscript tradition. He printed this edition again in 1551, this time with the Vulgate and Erasmus' own Latin translation of the Greek. Estienne had begun printing the Vulgate in 1528, and in 1546 had printed with it an "improved" Latin translation of the Greek. There was a clerical outcry and eventually Estienne had to relocate his press to Geneva. The same kind of outcry had greeted Erasmus' own *Novum Instrumentum*, for precisely the same reasons: they had reduced the Vulgate to a text and, on the evidence of both the manuscripts and their own retranslations, a very imperfect text.

But not only was the Vulgate translation being undermined; doubts were being cast on the Greek itself. With Estienne's edition of 1550 the

Western Church had a stable text—the *textus receptus* or "received text"—of the original Greek New Testament, and it remained such until the nineteenth century. But the message being beamed from its marginal notations was that what now rested so solidly and immutably in print was, word for word, not all that certain. At the very moment that the Reformers thought they had saved Scripture from the Church by crying *sola Scriptura,* "Scripture *alone,*" Erasmus was pointing in the other direction: it was not only *sola* that was in question; *Scriptura* itself, or at least the Greek and Latin versions that were passing through human hands, was proving to be problematic.

Translating the Untranslatable Quran

Christians were at home with the notion of translation, though not always with its results. They had been given the New Testament in what was already a form of translation—Jesus taught in Aramaic, not the koine Greek of the Gospels—and there was no apparent hesitation in bundling in with those four "translated" Gospels a series of other works, starting with Paul's letters, whose language had no connection whatsoever with Jesus' own. As for the Old Testament, the Christians inherited a translation, the Septuagint, whose purely scholarly defects were recognized first by the Jews for whom it had originally been made and then, as we have seen, belatedly by Christian scholars like Origen who had enough Hebrew to compare it to the original. They were apparent even to Jerome, whose stated purpose was a translation of a translation, to turn the Greek Septuagint into a Latin version for the benefit of his Western readers.

Western Christians had problems once again with their Latin Old Testament, and even with the Greek Septuagint that stood behind it, when in the late twelfth and thirteenth centuries they engaged with the Jews in a series of debates on the only subject that mattered, whether Jesus was in fact the Messiah, and both sides had recourse to the only evidence available and agreeable to both, namely, the Bible. Had Jesus fulfilled the Biblical prophecies regarding the Messiah? The Christians were at a grievous disadvantage when their Jewish respondents served, as they inevitably would, their Hebrew ace: you Christians have misunderstood the Bible; your translation has betrayed you! Game. Set. Match.

If the possession of a translation put the Latin Christians at a disadvantage vis-à-vis the original of the Bible, their willingness to translate Scripture was a distinct advantage in the propagation of the faith. Early on Christianity, which was a missionary religion from the outset, showed its ability to leap political borders into Sasanian Iran, Armenia, and Ethiopia, all beyond Rome's frontiers, where the New Testament was quickly and unquestioningly translated into local vernaculars. The same occurred later in Europe for the benefit of the Goths and successive waves of Slavic peoples, even where the pagans had first to be converted from orality to literacy and supplied with a Latin or Greek alphabet so that the Good News could be not only preached but inscribed on the page.

Islam was not a missionary religion. The new faith of the seventh century spread only in the wake of Muslim armies, the Prophet's in the first instance and then those of his successors. Conversion followed conquest, not as an effect but certainly in consequence of it. And though such matters are not easy to determine, the conversion of the Christian and Jewish population of the conquered territories seems to have been preceded by their Arabization; indeed, there was apparently not a majority of Muslims in the Abode of Islam from Spain to China until the mid-tenth century when most of them had long since been speaking Arabic. There was no pressing need, then, to translate the Word from God's own Arabic into Aramaic or Greek or Coptic or Berber: Arabic acculturation and Islamic conversion proceeded in tandem, certainly among the elite.

But the Arabization did not take hold everywhere equally. There remained in Iran, for example, a deep-seated and sophisticated local-Dari-Farsi culture that refused to yield in its entirety to the triumphant Arabic, and eventually emerged into literary respectability in the ninth and tenth centuries, though now written in Arabic script. Later that same literary resistance repeated itself among the Ottoman Turks, again with the Turkish vernacular written in Arabic script. And both cases had necessarily to raise the issue of a translated Quran, not as such, but rather as the more sensitive liturgical question of whether it was permissible to address God in the worshiper's rather than in His own tongue.

We can observe the issue arising out of the doubtless apocryphal story of Salman, the legendary Persian convert who was inserted into Muhammad's life to guarantee an Iranian presence there at the very beginning of Islam. He provided Muslim lawyers a convenient peg on which to hang a test case. Salman had allegedly translated part of the Quran, at least sura 1, the *Fatiha*, into Persian so that other Persian converts could use it in prayer, but only, a cautionary backnote adds, until the newcomers had learned enough Arabic to pray properly in God's revealed Words. Legal opinions were rendered on this probably hypothesized case. The majority thought the converts' action improper. The Quran could, and perhaps even should, be translated to enhance the personal piety of the Arabic illiterate, or even to further the conversion of non-Arabic speakers, though there is not much evidence the translations were made or used for that latter purpose. But the majority—and the still prevailing opinion—ruled that a Quranic translation might not be used for any liturgical purpose, nor could a translated text be invoked as the basis of a legal opinion or ruling. In short, a translated Quran is not really a Quran.

There the matter rested, somewhat inconsequentially, until modern times. The early twentieth-century disestablishment of Islam as the state religion in the Turkish Republic and the Turkification of all aspects of public life, including, most suggestively, the substitution of a Latin for an Arabic script in the writing of Turkish, seemed intended, if not to abolish Arabic, then at least to make a place for Turkish by its side in the mosques and *sharia* courts of the land. That did not occur, however, at least formally, inhibited perhaps by the closest the Muslim world had to a high court at that time: in 1936 the Grand Assembly of Ulama of the Azhar University in Cairo ruled that translations of the Quran were appreciations of the text; they were not Quran.

The issue here at least is theological. True translation was impossible in the case of the Quran because God had revealed not only the contents of the Book but also its external form: its language, tropes, style, meters, and rhymes. This problem concerned Islam's lawyers, but it was a cultural question too, and it concerned and affected many more Muslims. The Quran, as well as the personality of the Prophet and the circumstances of his life, had stamped Islam with an unmistakable Arabic cast, and this in what was intended to be, and in effect was, a universal religion. Local pride was undeniably hobbled by an Arabic Islam that rested, of course, firmly upon an Arabic Quran, and Iranian and Turkish efforts to subvert it reflect a cultural nationalism and the growing resistance to being Arabized by conversion to what was, and is, understood as the "religion of Abraham."

More potent than either the legal or the theological arguments was the fact that over the centuries more and more Muslims were not Arabic speakers and that for them the self-advertised "clear Arabic Quran" (41:3; 43:3, etc.) was in fact a closed book. That this might be a problem was understood from the outset, even by the lawyers who banned Quranic translations from prayer and legal discourse but allowed it as an aid to faith. And so the Quran was inevitably and necessarily translated, even though the effort was never officially applauded. More than four thousand translations (including duplicates) have been identified in manuscript, in fifty-eight different languages, though, not surprisingly, 90 percent of them are in either Persian or Turkish.

There were, of course, translated fragments of the Quran inserted as lemmata in works of rhetoric or, most commonly, in Quranic commentaries, like the Persian version of Tabari's celebrated *Tafsir*, which was translated into Persian in the early decades of the tenth century. More substantial are the literal word-for-word translations that were generally written interlinearly in the Quran text and generally in a smaller hand, a different color of ink, or both. There is no confusing text and translation. Another type stands closer to the Jewish targum in that it is a paraphrastic translation into another tongue, now usually written in the margins of the Quran and in a distinctive slanted script.

But neither the fragmentary translations nor the literal-minded interlinears nor the marginal paraphrases were true translations of the Quran in the sense of integral renderings that sought actually to reproduce the text in another tongue. It was this latter type that might raise scruples among the pious, though certainly not some of the earliest efforts in that direction, which were made neither by nor for Muslims. The first European translation of the Quran, and possibly its first full translation into any language, was the Latin version done in Spain by the Englishman Robert of Ketton in 1142–1143 under commission by Peter the Venerable, abbot of Cluny, as part of a program to proselytize among the Muslims of Spain. Robert's was perhaps more of a paraphrase than a translation—he incorporated fragments of Muslim exegesis in the text—but in 1209 another professional translator, Mark of Toledo, made a quite literal Latin translation at the behest of the archbishop of Toledo, Rodrigo Jiménez de Rada, who also had a plan for turning Spain's Muslims into Christians. These were team efforts and both men had Arabic-speaking Muslim assistants.

The fact of the translation of the Quran is long settled: the Book circulates freely among all the world's peoples in all the world's languages as Islam has spread far beyond the traditional borders of the Abode of Islam—to Africa, Western Europe, and North America, for example. Outside the Middle East and North Africa Arabic is going the way of Hebrew in the Second Temple period or Latin in the post-Renaissance world: it is becoming the unique preserve of a learned elite who remain, however, the guardians of the Sacred Text, its exegesis, and its legal applications. Perhaps too the issue of the propriety of translating God's Word is being eroded by the overwhelming fact of translation. But the legal and theological issues persist, tied to the transcendental Arabic of the "Mother of the Book" and God's own boast of a "clear Arabic Quran." "We have made the Quran in Arabic," God says, "so that you all may understand" (43:2).

Chapter 8

Picturing the Word

ॐ(6)ॐ

In the beginning was not the word but the picture, of which the word was merely the scion, and whose own dazzling offspring were the precocious letters of the alphabet. But there was a serpent in that graphic Eden, and the tension, estrangement, and finally open warfare between word and picture was fought most ideologically and violently on the ground of religion. The telling is mostly one-sided: only among the words do we find an account of the hostilities, but it appears that the casus belli lay not in the picture as such but in its more sinister sibling, the portrait, and, more particularly, portraits in the round of the deity, what our reports polemically call "idols."

The Rabbis and the Second Commandment

All people make some effort to portray the objects of their worship in both word and figure. Prayer is word-speech to the god and sacrifice is an act of worship likewise addressed to that deity, and it helps with both prayer and sacrifice if its object can be visualized or imagined. To that end the gods have been portrayed for human contemplation in sketch, symbol, or word for as long as memory records. But not equally by all. Among the fundamental commandments given to Moses on Sinai was "You shall not make for yourselves a sculpted image or any likeness of what is in the heavens or on the earth or in the waters under the earth" (Exod. 20:4–5), and then, in what appears to be an elaboration of that Second Commandment, "You shall not make idols of silver alongside of Me, nor shall you make idols of gold" (20:23). Still later, Deuteronomy seems to approach the same or a similar issue from a different angle. The Israelites are bade destroy all the pagan shrines and sacred sites they encounter, to "tear down their altars, smash their pillars, put their sacred posts to the fire and cut down the images of the gods" (12:1–3).

The Israelites seized the point with a sure grasp. Not only were the idols and effigies of the gods of the pagans to be abhorred; in an abundance of caution, they reckoned that their own God was not to be represented. Indeed, eventually not even His name dared be uttered, though when and why this latter custom began is uncertain. The caution was perhaps justified. Though image worship is gravely and continuously condemned in the Bible—the terrible vengeance visited upon the Israelite worshipers of the Golden Calf (Exod. 32–34) is the paradigm—the books of Kings and Chronicles are filled with lurid accounts of the later Israelites' frequent lapses into idol worship, the idols of other gods, to be sure, and their unfortunate consequences.

The final word on the folly not of idol worship but of idol making was uttered by one of the prophets the Bible calls Isaiah: "The makers of idols all work to no purpose. . . . The thing in my hand is a fraud" (Isaiah 44:1, 20). Isaiah describes at length (44:1–20), and in terms dripping with sarcasm, the banal business of "making" a god out of wood. In the course of his diatribe he puts his prophetic finger on what will later be identified as one of the root problems in the discussions of religious images. The idol maker chooses and measures his block of wood and then "gives it a human form, the beauty of a man to dwell in a shrine" (44:13). The god, all gods, were being depicted transgressively in human form. Isaiah had unerringly scented the anthropomorphism implicit in image making.

⚮   *Note: A Mocking of Idols.*

Isaiah and then, nearly a millennium later, the Muslim Ibn al-Kalbi (d. 820) in his *Book of Idols* both resort to the same mocking topos to ridicule idolatry. Isaiah's idol maker takes wood, uses some of it to cook his supper, and of the rest, "he makes a god of it and worships." As Ibn al-Kalbi tells it of the pagan Arabs of pre-Islamic Mecca, "Whenever a traveler stopped at a place or station (to spend the night), he would select for himself four stones, pick out the finest of them and adopt it as his god, and then use the remaining three as supports for his cooking pot."

Idolatry and anthropomorphism, whose somewhat embarrassing evil—
"If horses had gods, wouldn't they look like horses too?"—was taught to
the Jews in their earliest contact with the more sophisticated Hellenes, are
recurring and alternating themes in all subsequent discussions of images,
whether on sacred sites or sacred pages. Present too among the Christians
on occasion, though notably not among Jews or Muslims, was the more
familiar theme of the magical or miraculous quality—the line was mar-
velously thin between them—of pictures, or icons, as they were called in
their Christian context.

Contact with the Greeks and Romans seems to have made the Jews simultaneously more relaxed and more wary about images. Pictures both
sacred and profane, though assuredly not of the deity, make their appearance on the floors and walls of synagogues in the post-Temple era. Both
myth and *mythos* are abundantly represented, albeit in one dimension: the
synagogue floor at Beth Alpha in *Eretz Israel* has one mosaic of Apollo or
Helios driving his steeds across the Zodiac and another of Abraham about
to sacrifice Isaac, with the restraining hand of Yahweh, later sensitively
changed to a surrogate angel, making an unmistakable cameo appearance
upper stage left.

The rabbis meanwhile were a little perplexed by the custom and attempted to sort out the issues more precisely. One school thought that all
images were forbidden "because they were worshiped once a year." This is
a rather odd conclusion and it suggests that they were not talking about *all*
images to begin with. Another rabbi ventured more specificity: images
that looked like they might have been idols are forbidden. We cannot always be certain whether it was pictures (frescoes, mosaics, etc.) that were
being talked about or, as seems more likely, statues. The context suggests
that these latter caused the problem, and, even more precisely, portraits in
two or three dimensions of the deified ruler, whose cult was the most public and pervasive form of worship in the first- and second-century Roman
Empire.

Figurative mosaics and frescoes, however, were quite another matter, as
the physical evidence attests and the Palestinian Talmud confirms. In the
tractate called "Alien Cult" (*Abodah Zarah*), it is recorded that in the third
and fourth centuries Jews began to "paint on walls" and make mosaic decorations, and that the contemporary rabbis allowed them. The reason was
clearly one of intent. When the targum Pseudo-Jonathan translates the

verse in Leviticus (26:1) that says quite clearly, "You shall not . . . place figured stones in your land to worship upon," it renders it in Aramaic as "You shall not set up a figured stone in your land to bow down to it," and then immediately adds, "but a mosaic pavement of designs and forms you may set in the floor of your places of worship so long as you do not prostrate yourselves to it."

The ongoing Jewish interpretation of the Second Commandment, though later read, perhaps from the sixteenth century, in the restrictive sense of a ban on all figurative art, was far broader, and more ambiguous for long stretches of history. The prohibition on the portrayal of the God of Abraham and Isaac and Jacob was absolute and uncontested, but beyond that there was considerable latitude in the figuration of themes both secular and religious. The walls and floors of ancient synagogues testify to it, and so too, we suppose, would the books in use among the Jews.

As we shall see, there are no illustrated books preserved from antiquity—there were scribes but apparently no artists at Qumran—to enable us to extend this Jewish discussion of images into the realm of Scripture. But there are suggestions that the same people who admired the mosaics and frescoes in their synagogues could see the same scenes in books. The mid-third-century synagogue at Dura Europus on the Middle Euphrates has on its well-preserved front and side walls a crowded panorama of illustrations in fresco, some single-themed, others in series, cartoon style, on the life of Moses or Elijah or Ezekiel. This is programmatic painting, and it may very well go back to a manuscript original where the same stories were set forth, in the same cartoon manner, on a parchment to serve as a pictorial midrash. It is interesting to note that at exactly this time, and in the very same area, the prophet Mani was producing his own pioneering illustrated Scripture and the Christians too began drawing in their Book.

⊗⚭⚭   *Note: The Manichaean Scriptures.*

Mani (d. 277 CE) was a Mesopotamian ascetic and prophet of Iranian ancestry who claimed to be the "Paraclete" promised by Christianity and the successor of Zoroaster, Jesus, and the Buddha among others, and to have incorporated all previous prophecy in himself—the Quran's own characterization of Muhammad as "the Seal of the Prophets" (33:40) was first used by Mani. As a matter of fact his prophetic message and its institutionalization was a bold syncretizing of many different elements, Christianity and Zoroastrianism not the least among them. That message is contained in six writings in Aramaic, the common vernacular of that time and that place. They are now lost except in translated fragments and citation, but we know they included Mani's own "recitation," a book of songs titled "Psalms of the Bema." And in anticipation of both Muhammad and Joseph Smith, he emerged from a year of seclusion in a cave with the "Book of Painting," which he claimed had been miraculously sent down from heaven and whose unique perfection was the miraculous confirmation of his own prophethood. The paintings were not only miraculous; according to Mani himself, he was the first prophet not only to broadcast his Scripture in writing but to illustrate it as well: "My Brothers, all the Apostles who came before me," he wrote in his *Kephaleia*, "did not write down their wisdom, as I write mine, nor did they paint their wisdom in pictures, as I paint mine."

Adorning and Illustrating the Hebrew Bible

Unlike many books, religious and secular, from antiquity and the Middle Ages, all the earliest Hebrew manuscripts of the Bible are notably devoid of illustration: there are neither pictures nor illumination. Hebrew, like Arabic, has no upper case and so the often elaborately decorated capital letters that leap forth from many Latin manuscripts are nowhere to be found. Were the Jewish Bibles always so? The marked, almost stringent, conservatism of the Hebrew text tradition—there are far fewer textual variations in Hebrew manuscripts than in Greek and Latin Old Testaments—would seem to argue that from the outset images were banned from Jewish Scriptures, whatever their provenance or intended use. But note has also been taken of signs pointing in the opposite direction. The programmatic presentation of Biblical scenes on the walls of the Dura synagogue and similar scenes in early Christian manuscripts seem to suggest that the Christians were following a Jewish model and that the model not only was in fresco on walls but lay before the Christians on the parchment page. But not before the Christians had begun their own skirmish with the Second Commandment.

Did, then, the Jews too draw in their Scripture? If the Dura frescoes and the Christian manuscript parallels—where the earliest illustrated Scriptures are of the Old Testament—lead us to think that the Jews had illustrated books of some sort, a strong current of tradition asserts that those books were very likely not Scripture. As He is among the Muslims, God is *represented* for the Jews not by His image but by His Word, quite literally so since He handed over His materialized Word, the "Word made flesh," in the form of two written tablets, written by God Himself, to Moses on Sinai. And if the Ark of the Covenant was a throne upon which the presence of God was ensconced, it was also a Shrine of the Word since those same inscribed texts lay, like the Quran's own "Well-Guarded Tablets," within it. And when they disappeared in the sack of Jerusalem that preceded the Exile, their place was taken by the *Sefer Torah* enshrined, and guarded, within every Jewish synagogue. The *Sefer Torah* is the purest form of the Word; copies of the Quran are marked for convenience and beauty, but not so the *Sefer Torah*, which was and remains pristine, without markings of any kind.

This distinction between the sacramentalized *Sefer Torah* and other copies of the Bible made for reading, meditation, study, or simply display is important for our purposes. The *Sefer Torah*'s pristine state was protected by the masoretes' stringent code for their production, always on parchment, always on rolls, always without markings of any kind. But the masoretes' own instructions on this matter are preserved in the other, nonsacramental copies of Scripture where they unfold in the horizontal and vertical margins and become in fact part of the decorative scheme they had banned from the *Sefer Torah*. The scribes of medieval Hebrew Bible manuscripts often used the masoretic instructions, shrunk down to micrographic, sometimes illegible, proportions and then bent into a variety of vegetal and animal forms to adorn the text page.

Designs such as these fall into the category of decoration, and if Jews were originally reluctant to illustrate the Biblical text, which is not at all certain, they, like the Muslims, showed no hesitation in decorating the Scriptural text page. The illustrator draws a pictorial representation of what the text is saying in words; the picture is in some fashion connected to the text it is illustrating, both substantively—it reflects the meaning of the text—and typographically, in that it is placed in or by the text being illustrated. Decoration is ornamentation; its objective is to enhance the appearance of the text page, though that may not be its only function. It accomplishes its end by the addition of color, the process called "illumina-tion," or by drawing in the empty spaces on the pages.

One common technique of ornamenting the page is by framing a word, a line, a section, or even the entire page. This may be to beautify the page but, as we shall see, it may be as well part of the process of ordering the text by calling the reader's attention to a section of the text and, by varia-tions in the size and importance of the framing, to the hierarchization of its parts. What chiefly concerns us here, however, is the practice of filling in the spaces on the page, the inner and outer vertical margins and the horizontal ones at the top and bottom of the page. Scribes and artists of all three monotheistic communities have taken these spaces as their canvas and put upon them, or often quite filled them with, a great variety of mo-tifs, from dots and lines to figures, geometrical, vegetal, animal, and, com-monly in Christian Scripture and occasionally in the Jewish, but never in the Quran, human shapes and forms.

Though we know by name a number of Biblical exemplars used and cited as such by the rabbis in their preparation of the standard seventh-century "masoretic text," actual manuscript evidence for the Hebrew Bible is exceedingly thin in the interval between the second-century-BCE exam-ples discovered at Qumran and the twelfth century in Europe. Since there is a gap of nearly ten centuries between the Qumran finds and the next preserved Bibles, perhaps—it is merely a guess—the preparation of the standard masoretic text led to a wholesale, and deliberate, destruction of most of the earlier, and variant, copies.

The scarcity of early evidence may have been aggravated by the occa-sional bouts of iconoclasm, the impulse to destroy images, which surfaced among the Eastern Christians in the eighth and ninth centuries, and the abhorrence of imaging, which pulsed spasmodically through the Muslim milieu in which the Jews also lived. The Jews' own attitude seems to have hardened at those same intervals, and they too may have destroyed some of their own illustrated manuscripts.

The oldest extant post-Qumran manuscripts are the parchment rolls of parts of Genesis, Numbers, and Deuteronomy, apparently written in the East sometime before 604 and preserved in St. Petersburg. The same col-lection has a parchment codex, the oldest preserved Jewish codex, of the Prophets (with the masorah) and dated from the evidence to 916. The old-est dated Hebrew manuscript of the Bible tells us that it was copied in

Tiberias in Galilee in 895. This begins a trickle of dated manuscripts, all in codex form. There are only six from the tenth century, eight from the eleventh, and then twenty-two from the twelfth century CE.

When they do occur, Bibles in Hebrew, like their Christian "Old Testament" counterparts in Greek and Latin, are produced either as the complete text or as parts, the Torah, for example, or the Prophets or Psalms, for both public liturgical use and private study and meditation. But unlike the Christians' Scriptures, the Jewish Bibles distinguish keenly, as we have just noted, between the Torah Scroll, the *Sefer Torah* used and kept in the synagogue, and its less exalted siblings made for use in the synagogue, like the *haftarah*s, the texts of the Prophets designed for the liturgy, or copies executed for more private purposes. The *Sefer Torah* and, by tradition, the book of Esther were always copied onto a parchment scroll, the Romans' *volumen*, while most of the rest adopted the codex or book form popular throughout Mediterranean culture from the fourth century onward.

The codex, the standard book form from late antiquity through the Middle Ages and beyond, was a latecomer among the Jews. When the Mishnah and Talmud and its contemporary literature talk about written texts, they always refer to them as "scrolls." The word "codex" does not appear in Jewish texts until the early ninth century, and then the word used to describe it is a loanword from Arabic. All the evidence points to a Jewish resistance to this more economical and convenient medium of writing storage—and it must have been resistance since the codex book was nearly universally used in both the Latin and Greek Christian cultures and the Arabic Muslim one in which Jews lived. The codex was strongly associated with the Christian Scriptures, where its popularity began, and this may have affected Jewish usage, or nonusage of the form, but it is equally likely that the Jews among the Christians and the Muslims were, for all their high literacy, a tenaciously oral community and a uniquely religious one and so had little need for books for any, save ceremonial, purposes.

Generally speaking, nonsacramental Jewish manuscripts, including but not limited to the Bible, resemble in style and manner those of the surrounding culture, Latin or Greek Christian or Arab Muslim. The earliest Bible manuscripts come from the East, from the ninth and tenth centuries, and though they have minimal decoration on the text pages, there is an entire page of decoration, at the front or the back, with geometric patterns and interlaced leaves and palmettes familiar from Qurans. Headings were occasionally framed in the manner of sura titles in the Quran, and so too were colophons. The Karaites in particular, a dissident Jewish sect that rejected the authority of the rabbis and formed their own communities in the Middle East and Byzantium, seemed particularly fond of decoration, or perhaps were particularly fond of bruising rabbinic sensibilities by adorning their Bibles in the Muslim decorative style.

But the Jews were considerably bolder than their Muslim contemporaries when it came to enhancing Scripture. The Muslims' carpet pages, pages filled with patterned decoration in the manner of a carpet, remained steadfastly nonfigurative, but in the tenth century Eastern Hebrew Bibles began to show actual figures on those opening pages: menorahs, the Ark of the Covenant with the Tablets of the Law, the incense altar, and implements of the Temple, sometimes arranged schematically, sometimes randomly. Only in very rare instances do any of these pictures creep into the text and become an illustration rather than a decoration. For manuscripts with genuine illustrations rather than mere adornment, one must wait until the thirteenth century, for the first Western Bibles copied in Germany, though probably from French models.

The Sephardic manuscripts produced in Spain and Portugal both before and after the Jews there passed from Muslim to Christian sovereignty are Eastern in their general style, with carpet pages of intensely geometric or vegetal design, or some combination of both, framed headings and colophons, and, at least until the second half of the thirteenth century, minimal figurative art for either decoration or illustration. Like their Eastern counterparts, they open with full-page drawings of Temple paraphernalia, and they too use micrography, a scaled-down writing of the masoretes' notes for purposes of decoration, as tendrils curling up or between columns, or as filigree, or even bent into figures.

The later Spanish manuscripts of the Hebrew Bible were drawn into the Ashkenazi stylistic orbit of France. Although few French exemplars have survived, the style is well represented in German manuscripts. Clearly figurative art is no longer an issue, and both the micrographically represented masorah and the manuscript painter had only the slightest hesitations to portray human figures: Adam and Eve, Abraham and Isaac, Noah and the Ark, Jonah and the whale, all get their due. Where we sense the hesitation is in the occasional practice of portraying those human figures without faces or with animal heads. In the Hebrew Bibles copied in Italy, particularly in Florence, in the thirteenth to the opening of the sixteenth century, the art of the painter is on full display in the full-page illustrations that now precede many books of the Bible.

Christian Images

If Paul freed Jesus' Gentile followers from circumcision and many other obligations of the Torah, it remained for the Christian communities and individuals to decide which parts of the Bible still bound them and which not. Christian sexual ethics differed little from the Torah prescriptions, save in the matter of divorce, which Jesus had proscribed on his own authority. The dietary laws were abrogated but ambiguity about the Sabbath remained. Was Sunday, now unmistakably "the Lord's Day," the Christian Sabbath with all its elaborate prohibitions in force? And what of the prohibition of images, the Second Commandment?

Jews could and did draw a distinction between innocuous images with no religious significance and those of the deity, their own or others', which were forbidden. For Christians the matter was less simple. If the Jews could conceive of Yahweh as a spiritual "presence"(*shekinah*), the Christians had before them a fully enfleshed God-man, Jesus the Christ, whose representation they would have to deal with in due course. But first the circumstances. Christian pictorial and sculptural art was literally underground for at least two centuries, painted on the walls and carved onto sarcophagi in the subterranean graveyards known as catacombs. The single quasi-public place of Christian worship preserved from the earliest era is the mid-third-century private house used as a church at Dura Europus on the remote Euphrates frontier. The room used as the baptistery is decorated with frescoes, like the synagogue a few houses away. There we see Jesus as the Good Shepherd of the Gospel parable, a common if somewhat featureless depiction of Jesus in early Christian art; Peter walking on water and the Samaritan woman at the well, both water images from the Gospels; as well as Jonah and the whale and David and Goliath from the Old Testament. The catacombs too show that the Christians had no hesitation in using the styles, techniques, and iconography of the pagan world around them and, of course, of their Jewish neighbors down the street, to portray scenes from both Old and New Testaments, of Jesus himself, in either painting or sculpture.

The ubiquitous portraits of the deified emperor presented a different problem, however. These were sacred images, the objects of public worship. Jews were exempt from emperor worship from the outset of their contact with Rome, but the rabbis still issued grave warnings about the use or reuse of such imperial artifacts. Christians lost their Jewish exemption early on, and as the New Testament itself notes (Rev. 20:4), some believers were executed precisely on the ground that they refused to participate in the imperial cult. But then the emperor was suddenly himself a Christian, and though the imperial iconography did not much change, the Christians' attitude and images did. Eusebius, bishop of Caesarea, the emperor's biographer and the Church's preeminent historian, assured the faithful that there was no longer a sacrilege in accepting the imperial image, especially since the ruler was frequently portrayed on coins and in statuary "gazing up to heaven and holding out his hands, as if in prayer."

Eusebius had quite other thoughts about the images of Jesus that were beginning to be prominently displayed in the splendid churches of a newly liberated Christianity. In a letter to the emperor's sister, he quotes the Second Commandment on the subject and asks, "Are not such things [that is, images of Christ] banished and excluded from churches all over the world?" If there was such a ban it must have been brief and perhaps more local than Eusebius allows, and it was, in any event, overwhelmed by another manifestation of the sacralization of the material, the cult of the Church's martyrs and saints. The altars and shrines of these holy men and women were rising across the face of Christendom, East and West, and their material remains, their relics—which would have been a source of ritual impurity for Jews—were now being handled without apparent qualm or question and their portraits were publicly displayed.

Icons and Iconoclasm

Whatever the qualms about attempting to reduce the deity to a material image, qualms shared in antiquity by pagans and Christians alike, Jesus was after all a man, as the Church insisted, and so might be portrayed "in the flesh." He was certainly being so portrayed in Eusebius' day, and the bishop was constrained to resort to the familiar Biblical, and Jewish, argument. "Can it be," he wrote to the Christian sister of the now Christian emperor, "that you have forgotten that passage in which God lays down the law that no likeness can be made either of what is in heaven or what is in the earth beneath?" The appeal to the Second Commandment is predictable; what follows is not. "Are not such things banished and excluded from churches all over the world," Eusebius continues, "and is it not common knowledge that such practices are not permitted to us alone?"

Eusebius was obviously drawing a contrast between the Christians and contemporary pagans—still the overwhelming majority in that world—who filled their temples with effigies of the gods worshiped within. We know from the archaeological evidence of the catacombs and the private houses where the earliest Christians worshiped that there were figures, including figures of Jesus, upon the walls, but not perhaps formal portraits, and almost certainly not sculptured representations of the Savior. But the emergence of the churches from their private and clandestine quarters into the bright sunlight of first the favored and then the official cult of the Roman Empire worked aesthetic as well as political and social changes.

The new decorative practices of the Established Church are revealed in a letter written by the bishop Epiphanius to the emperor Theodosius late in the fourth century. An earlier generation of Christians had not painted pictures of Christ, the bishop instructs his sovereign. "Which ancient bishop ever dishonored Christ by painting him on door curtains?" Nor did they portray any of the figures of either the Old or the New Testament, Epiphanius continues, and then he gives us a rare look into the earliest churches of the fourth century, buildings that have long since disappeared under later and more grandiose structures: "Our fathers delineated nothing except the salutary sign of Christ [that is, the cross] both on their doors and everywhere else." Finally, Epiphanius recommends that all those figured tapestries be pulled down and used as shrouds for the poor, and that the frescoes appearing on church walls be whitewashed by imperial command. Eventually, some Christians did exactly that.

In 787 CE a church-wide council of bishops was convened by imperial command at Nicea, the town near Constantinople that had been the site of the first General Council of the Church. The bishops' mandate was to settle the matter not of images but of image worship, which had been agitating the Eastern Church for more than half a century. As part of their deliberations the bishops requested a background report on the events earlier

in that century that had led up to the outbreak of religious image smashing in the Byzantine Empire. The report was submitted, and according to
its account, iconoclasm, the "smashing of images," was a Jewish-inspired
plot that had taken wing because a credulous Muslim ruler had been persuaded by the self-serving advice of a Jew to ban all images and image
worship in his realm. And the anti-image virus had spread from the Abode
of Islam into the Christian Roman Empire of Byzantium.

If such a Muslim ban was in fact promulgated, whether at Jewish
prompting or not, it probably occurred sometime around 720 since soon
afterward the first outbursts of image smashing were reported in Byzantine Anatolia, the land the Muslims called "Rum." A number of bishops
there apparently succumbed to the "infection," and they in turn caught the
ear of the emperor Leo III (r. 717–741), who was himself a native of the
Syrian frontier region and, as one Byzantine historian had it, a notorious
"Saracen sympathizer." Imperial edicts against images were issued beginning in 726 CE, and there followed a wholesale and official destruction of
religious images. In the words of a contemporary witness, "Wherever there
were venerable images of Christ or the Mother of God or the saints, these
were consigned to the flames or were gouged out or smeared over."

The destruction continued under Leo's son and successor Constantine
V (r. 741–775), who in 754 convened another council of bishops to make
the prohibition of images part of the official teaching of the Church. As
the creed issued by that council put it, it was prohibited to follow the example of the "demon-worshiping Gentiles"—of which, at that point, there
were very few left—and to portray Mary, the Mother of God, or the saints.
And so, the council of 754 concluded, anyone manufacturing an icon, as
these venerated images were called, or worshiping it, or even setting it up
in a church or a private house, would be found guilty of a crime against
the empire and a blasphemy against God.

Among those who rallied to the defense of the veneration of images was
John of Damascus, the scion of a Christian family that had long served in
the Muslim civil service in Damascus. John followed another course, however; he retired to a monastery near Jerusalem where he wrote tirelessly in
defense of Christian orthodoxy. And for him that included the veneration
of images of Jesus, his mother, and the saints. He wrote a special treatise,
On the Holy Images, defending *ikonodouleia* or the appropriate Christian

veneration of icons. John argued, as did many other apologists for icons, that veneration of the image was really veneration of the prototype, not the portrait but the person or thing portrayed.

The arguments of John and others, to say nothing of powerful popular sentiment, prevailed in the end, and in 780 the empress Irene suspended the earlier iconoclast decrees. The issue of image worship was apparently settled forever in 787 CE by the seventh ecumenical council, again convened at Nicea. It rejected the policy of Leo III and the theology of his son Constantine V. It ruled that "the venerable and holy images, either in painting or mosaic, or in any other suitable materials, should be set forth in the holy churches of God." But a distinction was in order, and the council made it, carefully: "These images should be given due salutation and honorable reverence (*proskynesis*), not indeed true worship (*latreia*), which pertains to the divine nature alone; but to these, as to the figure of the precious and life-giving cross, and to the book of the Gospels and to other holy objects, incense and lights may be offered according to ancient pious custom."

But this was by no means the end of the controversy over images, neither in the Western Church, where it resurfaced during the Reformation (see below), nor even in the Eastern Church, where it first arose. There was a final brief flare-up in 815, when the emperor Leo V reinstituted the ban on images and their veneration. This time the ban lasted a bare twenty years, and in 843 a new council reversed it once and for all.

At this remove, the controversy over images seems unnecessarily long and inexplicably violent: much of the rich artistic heritage of the Eastern Church was destroyed during the two iconoclast interludes (726–780, 815–843). The argument was not about art or aesthetics, however. It was about theology and, more precisely, about sacramentalism. The icons of the Eastern Church were not mere representations; they were physical objects, most often richly framed and ornamented paintings that were frequently believed to possess miraculous powers. For the Eastern Church they were *sacramental*, a sacralization of the material world, a second and lesser, though still wonderful, incarnation of the spirit. For the theologically sophisticated, such beliefs represented superstition and primitivism; for the ordinary believer, the icons too were the Word made flesh.

The issue of Christian iconoclasm arose precisely from icons, those portraits of Jesus, his mother, and his saints that the theologians thought, or hoped, were being venerated because they represented persons worthy of veneration but that many ordinary people were convinced possessed in and of themselves an intrinsic power to change the course of nature, to heal or to harm, to cause victory or to avoid defeat. It was the portrait as object, not as representation—icons are not illustrations—that effectively lay at the root of the problem.

The Bible with Pictures

The second- and third-century "parting of the ways," as it has been called, between Judaism and Christianity gradually separated the new Christians from their Jewish origins and shook them, and indeed many Jews, loose from their cultural moorings in Second Temple Judaism. The Gentiles who now in increasing numbers accepted Christ as their savior were no longer Hellenized like many in the first generation of Jesus' followers; they were genuine Hellenes who, although embracing a new religious perspective, were still the natural heirs of a different aesthetic culture, one that was at home with figurative art and books with pictures.

The aesthetic of the new Gentile Christians was Hellenic and the visual language of their artists was the Greco-Roman one of classical antiquity. Thus when Christians drew and painted, whether portraits of landscapes, they called upon the traditional repertoire of forms and motifs: Christ is portrayed as an idealized young Apollo or as a grave seated philosopher; the saints stand in the prayerful *orans* posture of the emperor; and the figuration of Madonna and Child has a long, and pagan, pedigree.

The classical tradition of painting in both book and fresco persisted for many centuries into the new era, but eventually the Christians began to develop their own artistic vocabulary and their own repertory of images and symbols to express the values and beliefs of the new religious culture. Among the first was Constantine's own contrivance of the Chi-Rho monogram—the combination of the first two Greek letters of *Christos*—as his personal insignia. Likewise *ichthus* ("fish"), both the word (whose letters are an acronym for the Greek of "Jesus Christ, Son of God, Savior") and the symbol, began to appear as a shorthand designation for "Christian." At first the initiative and substance for the new vocabulary of a now public Christian art came from the high imperial tradition of emperor and court. Christ, once shown as a youthful and humble shepherd, now emerged as *Pantocrator*, the Ruler of All, enthroned in majesty above the emperor's own seat in the apses of newly constructed Christian basilicas, and bishops were depicted in the raiment and postures of high imperial officials.

Book art was different, however. Here the art was first and foremost illustration, and what was being illustrated was the narrative, the Biblical one of the Old Testament and the evangelical one of the New. In the rolls of the pre-Christian era, illustrations—many of them diagrams in technical works—were simply introduced, unframed and without background, into the column, just before or after the matter they were intended to illustrate, but with no connections between illustrations. The earliest codices, the Christians' preferred form, followed the same practice, but in time the codex developed its own aesthetic. Illustrations floated to the margins of the text and the tops and bottoms of pages. These more independent pictures were used to illustrate not so much a specific *text* as the *matter* of the narrative, and pictures were now often strung together in a row to form a narrative sequence of their own, as in the synagogue of Dura Europus, which reminds us once again that the early Christian illustrators may well have had Jewish illustrated books—Bible histories, perhaps, rather than Bibles—in mind when they were illustrating their own Old Testaments.

In many cases the illustrations became a parallel text, with increased importance of content, now framed to focus attention, and a greater grandeur in execution, as in the introduction of increasingly rich backgrounds into the scenes. Margins offered both the now liberated artist and the commentator an invitingly empty space on which to unfold their work. Both used it, sometimes singly, one or the other, sometimes in tandem, commentator and illustrator working together. The ascent of the illustration, and the final display of its independence from the text, came to term in the giving over of an entire codex page to illustrations.

Illustrations of Biblical and evangelical narratives generally follow the Scriptural text, whether of a Gospel or the book of Kings, though the choice of event to be illustrated, or the emphasis on one or another figure in it, may well be a matter of underscoring a particular doctrinal or liturgical point—the Eucharistic character of the Last Supper is inevitably underlined, for example—usually in the broad field of salvation history. There is also a certain amount of what might be termed iconographical "chatter" in these apparently narrative illustrations, animal and vegetal signs and symbols delivering their own particular message to the viewer.

Christians were quick to introduce into their illustrated Bibles the same principle that appeared early on in their general understanding of the Old Testament, that events that occurred in the Jewish Scriptural record foreshadowed or typified what would happen, more consequentially, in the New. Favorite themes were Moses raising up the bronze serpent in the wilderness, the foreshadowing of the Crucifixion, and Jonah emerging from the whale, the very type of the Resurrection. Another sort of typing was to juxtapose Ezra, the prototype figure in the shaping of the Old Law, with the shapers of the New, the four evangelists, each with his own iconic symbol and often shown being dictated to by an angel or a dovelike representation of the Holy Spirit. Elaborately framed evangelist portraits—still bearing a marked resemblance to ancient philosophers—soon became commonplace in all illustrated Gospel books, often facing the first page of text, itself decorated with a large illuminated initial letter.

Though the Renaissance later turned it into a tour de force, architectural decoration appeared early in the Christian manuscript tradition. Its most common appearance is a columnar framing device around the Eusebian Canons, the tabular presentation of parallel Gospel passages from the four evangelists that appears early and often as the front matter in Gospel manuscripts.

For as long as Bibles were copied by hand, complete copies of the Scriptures generally restricted their illustrations to miniatures enclosed within initial capital letters, particularly of individual books. Sometimes the author was represented, David or Matthew or Paul, but at others times the matter of books suggested an emblem, like Jonah and the whale. These initial images please the eye but they may also have served, absent running heads on the pages, as a kind of index or table of contents for what was a rather large and complex book. The reader could thumb through the initial miniatures until the appropriate place was found.

In contrast to the relative austerity of the complete Bibles—their initial capitals and border decorations could be quite elaborate—copies of more specialized sections of the Bible, or selections from it, were sometimes a riot of illustration. Psalters or books of Psalms, and the oddly named *Bibles moralisées* and *Biblia Pauperum*, were all richly illustrated, as much picture books as they were Scripture. And down to the fifteenth century the pictures in them were of course hand-drawn and hand-colored, paintings on paper or parchment.

⚭⟋⚭   *Note: The Music without the Words.*

      If the Psalter and the book of Revelation are the two most illustrated books of the Bible in the age before printing and, in the first instance at least, in a manner that had little to do with the text before the reader, two other medieval creations, the *Bible moralisée* and the so-called *Biblia Pauperum* showed that it was possible to dispense with the text and present a version of Scripture that could do without the words of Scripture. *Bible moralisée* or "Bible Lessons" is a modern name for a medieval artifact.

    The Psalms were undoubtedly the Christians' chief appropriation from the Old Testament—they were, among other things, the backbone of the monastic liturgy, the Sacred Office chanted day and night in monasteries across Christendom—and they were often copied and bound as a separate book, a Psalter, either for liturgical use or as private prayer books. Preserved copies of these latter are the most richly illustrated. Book painting was a specialized and costly enterprise and so the best-preserved and most handsome copies of illustrated Psalters were invariably designed and paid for by the rich nobility, and the finished product was so exquisite—and so expensive—that it was not readily discarded like last year's doublet and hose.

    Medieval and later Scriptural illustrations were not intended merely to please the eye by their beauty or to narrate in pictures what the text was saying in words. Illustrations were very often commentaries, and the most common type of Christian commentary on the Old Testament is on display in the illustrated Psalters of the Middle Ages. Christians read the Old Testament in general and the Psalms in particular as a form of prophecy, either explicitly as in the Prophets or the Psalms, or implicitly in the lives of Moses or David, which cast a long shadow forward to the life of Jesus. The Psalter illustrations make the point by juxtaposing events in the life of David, as described in Samuel, Kings, and Chronicles, with their parallels in the life of Jesus as told in the Gospels. At first these were presented without comment, but as the thirteenth century passed into the fourteenth, first citations of Biblical passages appeared and then ever fuller captions accompanied these freestanding illustrations.

    The Psalter illustrations, which thus showed the viewer how the events of the Old Testament foreshadowed those of the New, were by no means tied to the text of the Psalms, which they were simply contextualizing, either materially or typographically. They served rather as an illustrated introduction to the Psalms, and as such they usually appeared grouped together before the text proper. And the two units, scenes from the life of David and the life of Christ, were tied together by what became an ubiquitous picture in medieval Psalters, the Tree of Jesse. The Gospels of Matthew and Luke had already tied Jesus to David (and beyond) by way of genealogies presented early in their Gospels (Matt. 1:2–17; Luke 3:23–38); here the artist reproduced the line of descent, actually ascent, in the form of a tree rooted in the loins of David's father, Jesse, often shown sleeping at the base of the tree, with David's descendants, and so Jesus' ancestors, depicted in miniatures appearing as blossoms on its branches.

The Psalter was a prayer book and eventually it began to look like one rather than just a collection of Scriptural hymns. In addition to the illustrated front matter, various devotional prayers were gradually added to the end, and as the cult of the Virgin grew more widespread and powerful, these chiefly celebrated and venerated Mary. This pious appendix developed in time into a form of office like the monks' own, with Marian prayers to be recited at the appointed liturgical "hours." In the end this appendix, with its own illustrations, broke off under its own weight to constitute a freestanding work, the *Book of the Hours* (of the Virgin Mary), with its own celebrated cycle of illustrations.

The Psalter, with its broad liturgical circulation and obvious typological possibilities, was the most commonly and profusely illustrated text of the Old Testament, while the Apocalypse of John was that of the New Testament that attracted the most artistic interest. This last book of the New Testament had a particular interest in the Middle Ages when chiliastic expectations came and went with suddenness and ferocity. If there was to be an End of the World, the author of the book of Revelation imagined it in a vividness and detail that seems simultaneously to have stimulated the inventiveness of the medieval illustrators and whet the appetites of the faithful. The format appears to have become standardized: two illustrations across the top of the page and the Apocalypse text in two columns beneath.

The vogue for illustrated Apocalypses was on the wane by 1300 but one book unaffected by this apparent loss of interest was the extraordinarily successful commentary on Revelation written by the Spanish monk called

Beatus in 776, when the apocalyptic moment was the still fresh Muslim conquest of Spain, and both text and illustrations were revised by him in 784 and 786. We do not know if Beatus was an artist, but it was he who planned the drawings for what was intended as an illustrated book from the outset, and an important one since Beatus regarded the Apocalypse— he used a North African Latin translation older than the Vulgate—as the key to understanding the rest of Scripture. And illustrated it was; of the thirty-five extant copies of the Beatus Apocalypse, fully twenty-six are illustrated, the oldest surviving being that executed by a certain Maius sometime before 945 at a monastery in the Duero valley in northern Spain.

Printing with Pictures

Two fifteenth-century technical advances changed the face of Bible Illustration and indeed the very making of Bibles. Woodcuts are made by carving away those portions of the face of a wood block not intended for reproduction. The lines and figures of the remaining surface are then coated with ink and pressed onto a permeable surface like cloth or paper. Though known much earlier in China, this kind of block printing made its appearance in Europe sometime about 1400. Printing a single figure or scene, like the Saint Christopher dated to 1423, is far less complex than reproducing an entire page of writing on a single woodblock face. It was nevertheless done, particularly in Germany and the Netherlands, and by 1455 there were in circulation copies of a blockbook edition, figures and text, of the almost forgotten *Biblia Pauperum*.

At about the same time as the northern whittlers were working on their blockbooks, Johann Gutenberg of Mainz used the same technique of pressing an inked block onto a sheet of paper but instead of using a single carved wood block, he fitted cast metal typefaces—which could be recast again and again from the same molds—into a fixed artificial frame. He produced—printed—an entire Bible by this fixed metal type method in 1456. The flexibility and economy of this method of making books, or simply of disseminating information, was immediately apparent. But the early Gutenberg Bible, though it looked remarkably like a manuscript copy, was different in one notable respect. Although they were elegant and clean, when the copies, some of them on paper, some on parchment, emerged from his Mainz press, they were austerely plain, without decoration or illustration. Gutenberg had left places for such, if the purchaser desired. But it was up to the buyer to provide whatever adornment or illustration was required from another contractor.

At first this work of adornment was done mostly by hand, and expensively, by the same artisans who had been painting on manuscripts for centuries. Quickly, however, the new woodblock technology was introduced into the production of printed books, either as single blocks printed as full-page illustrations or as miniature woodcuts fixed in the appropriate place in the same frame that held a page of metal text type. For more than a century, that of the Renaissance and the Reformation, Bibles and other books were illustrated by the woodblock method, which was pioneered in Germany and rapidly spread to the rest of Europe.

The siblings of the medieval painted manuscript illustration were the contemporary wall frescoes or paintings on wood or canvas; one was simply a miniature version of the other. The object of all these forms of painting was, of course, to instruct, but they were also intended to gratify, in this instance the tastes and sensibilities of the rather high-born audience that sponsored and paid for them. Unlike the labor-intensive and artisanal manuscript production, printing was a mass medium, and the new woodcut images that adorned Bibles and other books belonged to the same fifteenth- and early sixteenth-century world of popular tastes, popular beliefs, and popular devotions as the saints' pictures ("holy cards") and playing cards that tumbled out of the new presses in great profusion.

In 1483, the year of Luther's birth, the printer Anton Kroberger produced at Nuremberg a great printed Bible, the *Biblia Germanica*, illustrated with woodcuts designed to be colored by another hand. Though an Albrecht Dürer, who produced a magnificent woodcut-illustrated Apocalypse in 1496–1498, could raise the medium to great heights—his Apocalypse illustrations stand a world away from the crude blockbook edition of the 1450s—the woodcut traded the painted miniature's finesse and elegance for a direct and powerful, if somewhat crude, appeal to the emotions and imagination.

From the outset, Bible illustrations, painted, woodcut, or, later, engraved, portrayed the producer's own religious views as much as they did the text of Scripture. A prime example is the first edition of Luther's German translation of the New Testament, the so-called Septembertestament, which appeared in that month of 1522. The woodcut illustrations have been described as traditional if somewhat haphazard, a judgment that certainly does not apply to the last book of the New Testament. The Apocalypse, we have seen, was the most popular book of the Christian Scripture for illustrators from the middle of the twelfth century onward. This particular one was designed and produced by Lucas Cranach the Elder (1472–1553), whose illustrations are, like the Apocalypse itself, vivid and imaginative, and, when he comes to John's description of the Whore of Babylon (Rev. 17:1–6), he has made Babylon into a tourist postcard of Rome and the brazen lady herself is brazenly and unmistakably wearing the papal tiara. It was an outrageous thing to do, perhaps somewhat too outrageous since, when the translation was revised and reissued in December of that same year, the offending tiara had been quietly removed from the lady's head.

Luther's complete German Bible published in 1534 shows the full effect of the woodcut revolution. Earlier Bibles, generally destined for liturgical or some other form of ecclesiastical use, were decorated but generally had no illustrations beyond the miniatures enclosed within the initial capitals, which served, as noted, as a kind of index for the reader. Luther's Bible, in contrast, Old Testament and New, was filled with them, 184 woodcut illustrations in all, from the splendid title page, also designed by Lucas Cranach, to the end of Revelation. In this Pentateuch the woodcuts are scattered through and illustrate the text, but from the Prophets through the New Testament letters, they are placed only at the beginnings of each book as a kind of introduction. It is only at the Apocalypse that they return to the text, twenty-six of them, many now by Hans Holbein, who stayed somewhat closer to John's text than either Dürer, who was more imaginative, or Cranach, who was more polemical—though it is Cranach's Whore of Babylon who is portrayed, and once again she is wearing her saucy papal headgear.

The Reformation and Images

It might seem odd that in Luther's New Testament there are no pictures illustrating the life of Christ, merely introductory portraits of the evangelists. Luther's program of reform rested firmly on the principle of "Scripture alone" and there may have been some reluctance to introduce traditional forms of pious illustration into the Scripture text. Image veneration was certainly an issue in some Reform circles, among those who read the Second Commandment literally. One such was Andreas Bodenstein von Karlstadt (1480–1541), who, inspired by Luther, began in 1521 to put his own reading of Scripture into practice. It included, boldly and defiantly, the destruction of all sacred images, first in his own Augustinian monastery in Wittenberg and then in city parishes. Karlstadt published the seminal Reformation tract on the subject, *On the Abolition of Images*, in which he argued that the Bible was clear on this point: the veneration of images was a form of idolatry.

Luther was appalled. Karlstadt, who also attacked the idea of Jesus' real presence in the Eucharist, was simply denying sacramentalism, the efficacy of material to work in and on the spirit. The reckless destruction of images in churches and convents was, moreover, one more manifestation of the social disorder that Luther had feared and was already breaking out all over northern Europe in the wake of the more radical Reformers. By 1524 Luther was at war with Karlstadt, with images one of the prominent issues. Karlstadt seemed to yield a bit on the subject, while Luther and his followers were prepared to permit a restrained use of the sacred image, notably that bone of contention, the crucifix, a cross with an effigy of Jesus on it. But Karlstadt found willing ears in other quarters elsewhere. Zwingli in Zurich and Calvin in Geneva both embraced iconoclasm, and statues and holy pictures were smashed, defaced, and burned in the churches of the "puritan" Reform, while the organ and all forms of instrumental music were banned from the worship service.

The issue with the iconoclasts was, as it had been in the Eastern Church, that veneration was being offered to manmade images, which is a form of idolatry. That hardly seemed a problem when such images appeared in the familiar format of Biblical illustration, but here as always, the question was where precisely to draw the line. If Luther, out of an abundance of caution, avoided pictures in his printed Gospels, and others preferred not to have them in their churches, he, and the rest of the Reformers after him, fully embraced representational art to illustrate the rest of his Bible, which was both written and designed for popular use.

The Word Unpictured: Islam and Images

The Islamic tradition, whose core is in the Quran, is buttressed by a great mass of "Prophetic reports" or *hadith* that purport to transmit from eyewitnesses what Muhammad said or did during the course of his lifetime. They reported among much else an unmistakable aversion to images and image making. "Angels do not enter houses," he was heard to say, "where there are either dogs or pictures," and, in a somewhat more philosophical mood, "Those who will receive the most severe punishment on Resurrection Day are those who imitate what God has created." Images, then, or pictures, are not only despicable; they are also blasphemous.

There are no guarantees for the authenticity of such reports, but there can be no doubt that the Muslims of the generation in which such reports were circulating preferred, like the Jews of that same eighth–ninth century, a decorative to a figurative art. Muhammad himself may not have put it that way—there is no indication that he much thought about art—but he would certainly have objected to the idols that tradition tells us ringed the sacred space around the Ka'ba in the days before Islam and that he was said to have destroyed. The pre-Islamic Arabs worshiped powers in the guise of things; Islam redirected their attention to that One Great Power that was in no thing and yet in all. Like its confessed Biblical prototype, Islam, the "religion of Abraham," commanded submission to an aniconic God. This seems to be the point to the Quran's only reference to images: "All you who believe! Wine and gambling and stone images (*ansab*) and divining arrows are filth, a work of Satan: avoid them that you may find happiness" (5:90).

As we have already seen, the worship of a God without effigy, though it may point suggestively in that direction, does not necessarily lead to an art that bans all figures, or even merely human figures, an art that decorates rather than illustrates. Muhammad destroyed the idols in Mecca's *haram* but he reportedly spared a portrait—an icon?—of Mary and the child Jesus that had somehow found its way into the Ka'ba. Muslims, like the Jews, seemed perplexed on the matter and, like the Jews, and more recently like the Christians, groped their way through it to a solution that, unlike the Second Commandment, was never chiseled in stone. Two of the earliest decorated Muslim monuments, the late seventh-century Dome of the Rock on the Temple Mount in Jerusalem and the former Church of John the Baptist rebuilt as the cathedral mosque of Damascus, feature nonfigurative or at least inanimate decoration: intertwined leaves, jewels, and crowns in the Dome, something similar plus broad architectural, but uninhabited, landscapes in the mosque. But the same Umayyad rulers also built for themselves villas and baths on the edge of the Syrian steppe where rulers in fresco sit and gaze benevolently as cartoon scenes of everyday life unfold before them on the opposite wall or at scantily clad dancing girls who cavort on the pillars between.

Is this the difference between sacred and profane art or simply Muslims trying to puzzle out where the line between idolatry and artistry lies? The coinage of the era suggests the latter. At first the Muslims simply counterstamped the coins of their non-Muslim predecessors. Then, when they began to produce their own coinage, they engraved on them their own caliphs' figures in much the same garb and much the same posture as the shahs' and *autokratores*' they were replacing. But in the end they opted for coins without figures and decorated instead with verses of the Quran. They continued to adorn their walls with human figures, but, like their Umayyad caliphs, chiefly in the privileged or private resorts of the secular society, in the grandiose public rooms of palaces, in the restricted women's quarters (*harim*) in the homes of the wealthy, and in the what-happens-here-stays-here sanctuary of the bath or *hammam*.

Drawing in the Book

The mints spoke louder than the palaces or baths, however: what soon became the standard aniconic Muslim coinage made clear to all that the emblem of Islam was not an effigy nor even a symbol of God, nor of Muhammad, the Envoy of God, nor even a figure of the Prophet's successors, the caliphs, but the Words of God. Quranic passages are lifted up on high in gold inside the Dome of the Rock and eventually appear, engraved, inlaid, painted, or worked in mosaic, on the walls and ceilings of mosques, schools, and palaces across the Abode of Islam. Shortly we shall cast a glance at this "migrated" Scripture, but first the integral text of the Quran must be considered in the form in which it was conceived almost from the outset, as a book; indeed, as The Book.

As we have already seen, God's revelations to Muhammad are self-identified as "The Recitation" (*al-Qur'an*) and then, only somewhat later in the series of revelations, as "The Book" (*al-Kitab*). This latter expression appears to refer not to the bound artifact, which would have been beyond the capabilities of Muhammad or his contemporaries to produce, but to the notion of a book revelation, to what we call "Scripture." What you are hearing from the Prophet's lips is *Scripture*, the Quran announces, with as little embarrassment or even awareness of the paradox as we ourselves have in repeating it. It is not impossible that Muhammad had seen, or was at least aware of, the actual artifact revered by the Jews and Christians, and would have imagined the "Mother of the Book" of which the Quran spoke (3:7) as a written text.

At some point the Quran became just such a written artifact, a book in the ordinary, physical sense, transcribed by pen and ink on vellum or papyrus. By the time it did, Muslims lived in the midst of other Peoples of the Book who not only had their own carefully wrought Scripture but were also heirs and custodians of a secular bookish tradition from a Greco-Roman, Iranian, and Indian past. The Muslims, we know, envied the books of their subjects and from the mid-eighth century had them translated for their instruction and pleasure. Many of the translated manuscripts were illustrated—the Greek scientific manuscripts, translations of Dioscorides and Galen, are the best known—and the Muslims not only translated the text; they also copied the illustrations. Our examples are all from the twelfth century or later, long after the actual translations—indeed, there are no Arabic manuscripts with illustrations preserved before that date—but the style and manner of the pictures is so redolent of classical models that we must assume a continuous tradition of illustration.

Among those figured texts circulating in the Muslim milieu were the Syrian Christians' illustrated Scriptures, like the highly adorned and skillfully lettered Rabbula Gospels of 586 CE. Bibles of any sort were neither copied nor translated by the Muslims, who regarded all such texts of their fellow monotheists as hopelessly corrupted and which were, in any event, superseded by the Quran. And when it came to the Quran, Muslims went their own way. From beginning to end copies of the Quran were, like the Jews' *Sefer Torah*, without illustration of any kind. But where the *Sefer Torah* kept its pages pristine, the copyists of the Quran early on began to decorate the text. Some of the earliest preserved manuscripts from the eighth century have already put the sura headings in decorative frames with twisted geometric and vegetal patterns and with a leaf-shaped pattern extending into the margin on one side. This feature, the rectangular framed and colored sura head, with an attached palmette extending into the margin, remained the chief element on Quranic manuscript decoration throughout the manuscript age. It is here too, in an area at least partially exempt from the strictures that inhibit the decoration of the text, where the calligrapher has his greatest scope. If there is anything like illumination within a Quran manuscript, it occurs in the sura headings.

The first extraneous items to appear in a Quranic manuscript—extraneous, that is, to the text itself—are probably the simple strokes initially used to separate the verses of a sura. These began to appear in color and then yielded to a colored rosette that is obviously as ornamental as it is functional. The Quran was a liturgical text from the beginning, and if verse distinctions were a matter of the natural rhythm and rhyme scheme of the original, the early division of the text into units of five or ten verses, where a prostration might be required, reflects a developing recitative practice rather than any internal textual principle. Here again the division is marked off by some type of ornamental figure, sometimes a rosette or a stylized letter *ha* signifying "five," or, for the tenth-verse division, a gold roundel in the text or even in the margin.

These intratextual markers and even their extension as roundels into the margins give little scope to an artist already restricted to geometric and vegetal shapes and patterning. But another, much larger stage eventually opened. Ancient books had dedication pages, often with a portrait of the patron, and Christian Bibles had a good deal of front matter, like the Eusebian Canons, which usually featured figured decoration. The Quran required neither but it soon acquired front pages, with or without a devotional text, though not with *the* text, and, of course, without figurative art. Such pages at the beginning, and sometimes at the end, of copies of the Quran—and of other Muslim books as well—are called carpet pages because of their resemblance to the intricate and usually dense designs on Eastern carpets.

If the mature versions of these front and end pages look like carpets, their early prototypes look more like sura frames, horizontal boxes framing not a title or a text but a geometric design and with a rosette or palmette extending into the margin. A century later the box was vertical, though with the palmette still extending into the side margin. The pages keep that orientation, and the palmette, and simply grow more complex in their geometry and design, and more distinct in their styles so that they, like the script hands that produced the text, can be discerned as "Eastern"—from the Middle East—or "Western"—from Spain or Morocco.

Are these decorative elements anything more than ornament? Quranic illumination has been described as "mainly an art of geometric ornament, [with] vegetal patterns as secondary motifs." Do these figures and patterns, released into their own space from the confinement of the text page, have any symbolic content? Despite the overwhelmingly powerful sense that the meaning of the Quran rests exclusively in its very words, in short, in the text itself, it has been argued that Quranic decoration, now separated from the inhibiting presence of the textual God-speech, does add another level of meaning, if not to the Quran, then to the reader's copy. The enlarged and liberated rosettes and roundels have been thought to represent the sun and its rays and the various intertwined vegetal motifs to suggest trees. Indeed, the highly stylized disks that began life as modest rosettes were called by the Muslims *shamsa*, a variant of *shams*, "sun."

Chapter 9

Giving Voice to the Word

᠗᠙᠙

Revelation begins with a voice, whether from Sinai or on a mountain outside Mecca. The voice is heard, remembered, repeated, and finally recorded in writing. The voice becomes a text, the text becomes a document. But in the end, the Revelation comes full circle and is once again given voice by the very creatures to whom they were first addressed. The words that God once spoke to humankind are now unceasingly repeated back to Him by His creatures as their prayer.

When Jesus was instructing his disciples how to pray, he composed "on his own authority," as his contemporaries remarked of him in astonishment, a new prayer enshrined in Christian practice as the "Our Father." The practice of composing prayer was not unknown to them, but Jews, Muslims, and Christians, like many other religious communities, tend to pray to God in some version of His own words, in short, by reciting Scripture back to its Author. But not exclusively: the liturgies and rituals of the monotheists also included their own petitions, praises, and supplications.

What such recitative exercises had in common was that they were, like the various performance rituals that accompanied them, both public and social; personal, private, and silent prayer did not play a major role in them until popularized by the Protestant Reformation. The passage from formal and social to private and personal in prayer also marked the descent down the vocal scale from singing to chanting, to recitation, to reading, and, finally, to words uttered only in the heart.

Talking Back to God

Jewish ritual began with a powerful sense of the presence of God as set out in the Torah. God dwelt with the Israelites, visibly as a cloud by day or as a pillar of fire in the night sky as they crossed the wilderness of Sinai on their way to the Promised Land. He was enthroned as well atop the Ark of the Covenant, and when that throne-shrine was placed within the Jerusalem Temple, the Temple became God's fixed dwelling. All the great Jewish sacrificial rituals unfolded, as did the Greeks' and Romans', on the high altar that stood before the habitation of their God.

The Torah is detailed in its instructions on what must be the form of the worship of God but it is remarkably—to our ears—silent on what should be said or sung during those ritual sacrifices. Did silence reign in the Jerusalem Temple? Did only the cries of the slaughtered beasts echo through the courts of the Lord and rise up to the heavens?

The rabbis, those somewhat unreliable antiquarians, did not think so. They opined that Moses himself had introduced the reading of his own Pentateuch into the rituals, and that Ezra established the practice of reading the Law continuously and cyclically. Ezra seems a not implausible guess, and in any event, it is almost inconceivable that there was no prayer with Jewish sacrifice, particularly in the light of what followed, namely, a synagogue liturgy that was in effect a concert version of an operatic Temple ritual: all words and no action, and the words almost all of them Scripture.

Christianity reverted to the opera form, so to speak, words and ritual acts together, sacrifice and Scripture almost as one. But we can nonetheless discern the seam lines where the Scripture prayer-derived part of the synagogue service was joined to Eucharistic sacrifice in the Christian liturgy. There is a pause in the Christian Mass, as the Latins call the Eucharistic liturgy, a sort of soft elision where the cleric lector closes the Scripture on his lectern and turns to the altar to assume the role of priest.

But before he addresses the altar, the Christian cleric is a lector, a reciter of Scripture much in the Jewish style, though somewhat more sacralized, as we shall see, and the recitation of Scripture is an essential part of the central liturgies of both the Jews and the Christians. But not of the Muslims. Muslim piety is as profoundly Scriptural, and it seems safe to say that the Muslim, at least in a Muslim society, hears more Scripture than the Jew and certainly than the Christian. The recitation and hearing of the Quran is recommended always and everywhere in the Prophetic traditions. And yet only one short sura of the Quran is integrated into the *salat*, the Muslim canonical prayer. The memorization of the Quran may very well have occurred because the text was being used liturgically. If so, it was quickly replaced by prayers that, though they represent an unmistakably Quranic spirituality, are not the Quran. The Muslim liturgy is, in short, manmade.

Reading through the Torah

We learn from the law book called the Mishnah that by 200 CE there was a regular cyclic reading of the Torah in synagogues, and that in the centuries that followed down to the completion of the Babylonian Talmud in 600 CE, the rabbis who then controlled the religious life of the Jewish communities across the Middle East took pains to regulate the style, manner, and circumstances of that reading. We can look backward from that point only with great difficulty, back to the Temple times or even the post-Exilic era when both the Temple and synagogue were functioning as places of religious resort.

A strict construction might suggest that public Torah reading, like much else in Jewish life, was introduced in the post-70s era to compensate for the loss of the Temple and its sacred rituals. Prayer thus assumes much of the ritual burden of sacrifice in this odd new era in Jewish life. But it is nonetheless almost impossible to imagine Temple without Torah. For as long as the Temple stood, the priests who were its masters were also the wardens and interpreters of the Torah, which was bade be read by the *kohens*, no doubt in the person of their scribes, and to Israelite kings and laymen alike (Deut. 17:18–19; 31:10–13).

In post-Temple times, because of the scrupulousness of the rabbis, we are clear on the details of the practice and liturgical cast that surrounded the public reading of the Torah. It was a *lectio continua*, a formal and continuous reading of the text of the Pentateuch, universally on the Sabbath, and in some circumstances on Monday and Thursday as well. The Law was divided into fifty-four portions (*parashahs* or *sidrahs*) so that its reading might be spread over a year of Sabbaths, to conclude with the Festival of Simhat Torah, only to begin immediately once again. There was a three-year cycle current for a time in Palestine, but the Babylonian sages' single-year cycle eventually prevailed in all quarters.

Sections of the Prophets (*haftarahs*) were read as well—the New Testament Acts of the Apostles already refers (13:15) to "the Law and the Prophets" being read in the synagogue—not, however, as a *lectio continua* but selectively, as appropriate for the Torah portion mandated for that Sabbath. The Writings too appear in the synagogue service, but they are used chiefly for commemorative purposes rather than for liturgical prayer; the Scroll of Esther, for example, is read on Purim, and that of Lamentations on the Ninth of Ab, the anniversary of so many Jewish misfortunes.

✎✎   *Note: Tenebrae.*

The Lamentations of Jeremiah reappear in Christian service in the special liturgy for Wednesday, Thursday, and Friday of Passion week, when they are intoned, while the candles in the church are slowly extinguished, to commemorate the sufferings and death of Jesus.

These are merely the mechanics of the Jewish Scripture recitation; it is the ritual aspects that stamp it as liturgical. The reading must be done from a *Sefer Torah*, the rigidly controlled, pristine hand-copied Pentateuch scroll that is carried aloft, bedizened and with great ceremony, from its Ark-niche shrine in the synagogue. It is placed on the *bima* (Gk. *bema*), the ever more ornate platform that serves as both a lectern and a pulpit and is the most important architectural element in the body of the synagogue.

Any adult male Israelite may be summoned up to read the Sabbath portion, but the increasingly widespread Hebrew illiteracy and the growing demands of the cantillation made inevitable the appearance of professional reciters to perform this important sacred office. The act was highly ritualized: the Scripture was cantillated rather than merely read; the etiquette prescribed to the readers was carefully detailed; and it required the presence of ten adult males to validate the service. But it was more than a liturgy: the Torah recitation was intended to be instructive as well. To guarantee this latter it was originally mandated that the Hebrew Torah reading be accompanied by a careful line-by-line translation—in three-line segments for the Prophetic haftarahs—into Aramaic, the lingua franca of the day. Didactic too rather than liturgical was the attachment of a homily to the reading: the congregation was to be instructed from the same bima on the significance of what they had just heard first in God's own salutary words and then in their own tongue.

The recitation of Scripture lay, then, at the heart of the synagogue service that was and is the chief form of Jewish worship from the destruction of the Temple to the present. The "performance" of Scripture, the Torah, and somewhat less formally, and solemnly, the Prophets, was preceded by the Scriptural prayer called the *Shema* from its opening words, "Hear, O Lord," and a series of blessings called simply *tefillah*, "the prayer." After Scripture came the homily followed by the prayer called the *Kaddish*.

And the Scripture was, as the rabbis are already telling us in the Mishnah, chanted, not simply read aloud. As with Scripture reading generally, we cannot tell how far back the tradition of Scriptural cantillation goes, but it seems a fair guess that for as long as Scripture was "performed" in public that performance was rhythmical, if not necessarily melodic, a kind of plainchant with a slight melodic cadence to mark the end of sense or rhythmical unit. The chant raised the ceremonial level of the act—the words were intoned rather than simply sounded—and the articulation of a phrasing and minor melodic punctuation were applied *ad sensum*, not *ad melodiam*.

The scribal rabbis controlled the chanted Scripture in two different ways. The masoretic text was glossed with written cantillation directions, even though the recitation of the Torah, like the later recitation of the Quran, was an art best learned by imitation. Here, as often, writing was a back-up guidance, the last rather than the first resort. But those same scribes also created the specialized collections the Christians called lectionaries, an assembly of Scripture texts often accompanied by prayers and hymns suitable for the times and seasons as well as Scriptural collections and compilations required by local practices or customs.

The Scripture in Church

The Christians' own liturgy began in that interval in late Second Temple times when both Temple and synagogue were functioning as places of worship for Jews, the Temple principally, of course, and the synagogue we guess as a prayer and study place. The synagogue was a scribal and lay establishment rather than a priestly one, but since priests and scribes had a share in the wardening of the Torah, it seems more than likely that Scripture was a central feature in both places. Jesus and his immediate disciples after him, Jewish to the core, though of both the Hellenized and the non-

Hellenized varieties, worshiped—and preached—in both places. In what the worship of the earliest members of the Jesus movement consisted it is difficult to say, though certainly the commemorative reenactment of Jesus' last Eucharistic supper had a privileged place in it. And already in Paul's generation, that very first generation of post-Jesus Christians, it was understood, as the Letter to the Hebrews makes clear, that the Eucharist involved a sacrificial act: the table at which the Apostles had supped was an altar and he who stood at its head was a priest, not a *kohen* of the line of Aaron but a new, specifically Christian *sacerdos* of the order of Melchizedek (Heb. 4:14–5:14).

The Acts of the Apostles shows the Jesus movement spreading through the synagogues of Palestine and then of the entire Mediterranean Diaspora. The priestly Eucharist could have no place there—it was for a long time celebrated in houses, like the Jewish Passover in post-Temple times— nor could anything the Christians were coming to regard as Scripture. The "Good News" of the Jesus story could be told of course in the context of the synagogue homily, as Jesus himself had once done at Nazareth (Luke 4:14–30). At some point—perhaps toward the middle of the second century—this cohabitation ceased and the followers of Jesus the Messiah were expelled, or withdrew, from the synagogues. When, a century and a half later, at the end of the last Roman persecutions that had forced them underground, the Christians were able to build their own houses of worship, they built not "places of assembly" for Jewish-type prayer but temples for their Eucharistic sacrifice.

The Christian "church," though similar to the synagogue in name— *ekklesia* expresses the same assembly notion as "synagogue"—and architectural form (the Roman imperial basilica), is in function and furniture a miniature simulacrum of the Jerusalem Temple, where an all-male clergy—habitual female ritual impurity had no place in the sanctuary— presided at a sacrificial altar located within the taboo sanctuary area. There are neither altars nor altar rails, rood screens or *ikonostaseis* in a synagogue or a mosque to mark the tabooed domain of a priesthood. But the Christians nevertheless carried the synagogue with them: when we are given our first detailed account of a Christian worship service in the mid-second century, it is unmistakably a composite of a synagogue service, with the Scripture at its center, and the reenactment, on an altar, by a priest, of the Eucharistic Last Supper.

By the time the first literary descriptions of the Christian liturgy were being written, what was being read in the Christians' assemblies on "the day of the Sun" was not only the Old Testament but what Christians had come to regard as their own "New Testament," chiefly the Gospels and the letters of Paul. "The memoirs of the Apostles or the writings of the Prophets for as long as time permits," says Justin Martyr writing of the Christian ekklesia about 150 CE. Earlier still, Paul had commended that his own letters be read "to all the brethren" (1 Thess. 5:27), and if that setting is still not quite liturgical, a later reference in Colossians (4:16) is more suggestive of the fact that the Pauline letters were being read in some kind of assembly (*ekklesia*).

But the Christians did not recite the Bible as the Jews did, for principally liturgical purposes. Their purpose was more argumentative, more exegetic, and, though the setting was clearly liturgical, more didactic than in Jewish synagogue protocol. Hence the Christian emphasis on the Prophets rather than the Torah since it was out of the text of the Prophets that the case for Jesus as Messiah was principally drawn. So too the Christians had no need of a quasi-sacramental cyclical reading of either the Old Testament or the New. Though there is at least a suggestion that the Christians may originally have followed the Jewish practice of a lectio continua, quite early the occurrence of Scripture texts in the Christian service had become selective, circumstantial and occasional. The occasions were the great festival days of the rapidly developing liturgical year, not merely the Christians' "high holy days" of the still lunar Easter week and Pentecost in its Jewish wake, but the very un-Jewish solar Christmas fixed on December 25, and eventually too the commemoration of Jesus, his mother, and his saints on every day of the year. The New Testament texts were chosen and tied to these liturgical feasts and the Old Testament selections then tied exegetically to the New.

The eventual neglect of the lectio continua is not the only indication that the Christians regarded the liturgical role of Scripture differently from the Jews. In Christian services the texts were read in Greek (and eventually in Latin), the New Testament in some version of the original, the Old Testament in its Septuagint translation, and though this latter might have been the practice in some Diaspora synagogues, the rabbis' emphasis on the (increasingly unintelligible) Hebrew original remained powerful and effective. Nor was the Christian text of the Bible an integral one. As we have already seen, one of the original purposes of the codex notebooks favored by the Christians may have been to give easy access to collections of Prophetic texts (in Greek) that were pertinent to the case for Jesus' Messiahship. The Christians had no need for a *Sefer Torah* for their essentially confessional use of Jewish Scripture: excerpts would readily serve the purpose.

So Scripture, its public reading if not its recitation, was from the beginning an essential part of Christian communal worship and as time passed, when and what was read became further determined by congregational use. Nobody had to tell the Christians that their own writings were as much "Scripture" as the Jewish Bible, but as these writings became fixed in liturgical practice, it became important for the congregations to determine what should be read, in short, to fix the *canon* of this New Testament. Marcion, as we have seen, tried to fix his New Testament on doctrinal grounds. The churches had their own views on doctrine, but their Scriptural choices may well have been made in the liturgical context of the readings permitted in their services.

Christian usage shaped, church by church, the books read in the liturgy. As far as Scripture was concerned, what was required were New Testament texts, chiefly the Gospels and the letters of Paul, distributed across the calendar of the liturgical year, the annual cycle of the Church's feast days and saints' memorial days, and the Old Testament texts that foreshadowed those events in the New. The book that met this need was the lectionary, which first appears in partial form in the fifth and sixth centuries and then as complete texts arranged day by day for the liturgical year in the seventh.

The practice of using a lectionary for the liturgy was more pronounced in the Eastern than in the Western Church. In the Latin West a complete copy of the Gospels and the Pauline letters was read with marginal markings to indicate on which day the various passages should be read. In the East the Gospels at least were copied as lectionaries or reading texts where the Gospels were broken up and distributed across the liturgical calendar. The texts that pertained to the feast days of the saints (and Christmas) on the solar calendar were collected in a volume called the *Menologion*, while the Scripture readings for the Church's great lunar feasts (Easter, Pentecost, and the days depending on them) were found in the *Synaxary.*

As the use of Scripture in the liturgy grew more formal, so too did it become more ceremonial, particularly in the Eastern Church where the *eu-*

angelion took on some of the external trappings—the production of its text was not subject to the close supervision exercised by the rabbis—as the *Sefer Torah* used in the synagogue. In the synagogue-derived section of the Christian liturgy, the part significantly called in the Eastern Church the Liturgy of the Word, a sacralized copy of the Gospels, its exterior ornately adorned, is carried aloft in procession amid prayers by the officiating cleric through the congregation, which venerates it, and into the sanctuary through the Holy Doors in the center of the iconostasis, the tall screen that separates the sanctuary from the rest of the church. The entire event is called the "Little Entrance" and is a long-standing feature of Eastern liturgies. It is not impossible that Muhammad knew or heard of such ritual exaltations of the Book by Jews and Christians and so quite properly came to regard them as People of the Book.

At the center of the synagogue-derived Liturgy of the Word, which the Westerners more prosaically called the Mass of the Catechumens since those under instruction for baptism (*katechesis*) were permitted to attend, occurred a public reading of Scripture. And it was as little informal as what was occurring in synagogues. Like his Jewish counterpart, the Christian lector—usually the officiating priest, though "lector" was one of the minor grades or offices leading to the priesthood—stationed himself at the *bema*, otherwise called an *ambo*, a Latinized foreshortening of the Greek *anabainein*, "to go up." Like the synagogue *bima*, this could double as both a pulpit from which a homily was later delivered and a lectern from which the Scripture was read. Or rather, recited since all signs point to the fact that from the beginning the Scripture was not "read," as we understand that term, but rather cantillated or chanted in a manner somewhere between speaking and singing, a rhythmo-melodic rendering of the text, generally on a single note, with a brief melodic flourish at the end of each unit and a pause as dictated by the syntax and meaning of the text. The chant added solemnity to the text, to be sure, but it also, by its pauses and phrasing, clarified the passage for the listener.

The reader had, of course, himself to understand the text, and so it was perhaps inevitable, as happened with the Hebrew cantillation next door, that by the fourth century the Christians had official readers of Scripture for liturgical purposes. And equally inevitably, there would be books to make the task easier. Scripture began to be copied in some instances, not according to the ancient method of stichometry, a standard number of syllables to the line, but by the method called *per cola et commata,* which took up more space and so was more expensive. The text was copied according to larger and smaller sense units, a technique that could sensibly guide the reader, and his audience, through a text that was otherwise just a series of letters without spaces, punctuation, capitalization, or indentation, all the typographical means by which we begin to grasp the meaning of a text at sight.

Praying the Quran

The Quran, and the Muslim tradition in its wake, knows two kinds of prayer. The first is the private and personal "calling" (*du'a*) upon God, which was also the prayer of pre-Islamic Mecca, and whose efficacy, if directed to the One True God, is guaranteed by the Quran: "I am near," God says, "I answer the Call of the caller when he calls upon Me" (2:186). But of far greater importance to the Quran and to Muhammad was the establishment of the liturgical prayer (*salat*; 2:130; 50:39; 52:48, etc.) that is obligatory for every Muslim and is one of the identifying markers of the community. Number and timing were still somewhat undetermined in the Quran (17:30; 21:80), perhaps in hesitation between two models, the Jewish one of three prayer times each day and the Christian monastic practice of almost an *oratio continua* through night and day (see Quran 17:81).

The difference between the Quran's private prayer and its liturgical version was not merely formal but circumstantial. In Mecca, during the first twelve years of Muhammad's public preaching of Islam, the practice of the new religion, at least in its external cultus, would often have been dangerous and so the full institution of the salat had probably to await the Peace of Medina (622–632 CE). We do not know how Muhammad thought of the canonical salat though it seems safe to conclude that the earliest Muslims followed his example. A pre-Islamic word for a place of worship is *masjid,* "a prostration place," and so there may have been a commonplace practice behind the series of *rak'a*s or "bowings" into which the salat was later analyzed: two at the dawn prayer, four each at the noon and mid-afternoon prayers, three at sunset, and four again in the early evening. Each "bowing" may in turn be broken down into a set of postures, seven in all, each accompanied by its appropriate hushed-tone recitation. The postures are all drawn from the universal human repertoire of subservience and petition in the face of the divinity, but neither they nor the other ele-

ments that interested Muslim jurisprudents, like the direction of prayer—
originally toward Jerusalem, but later, early in the Medina period, redirected toward the Ka'ba at Mecca—or the purifications that must precede
it, need concern us here. Rather it is the voicings that accompanied those
"bowings" that draw us back to Scripture.

Each rak'a opens with the recitation of the *Fatiha* or "Opening," the first
sura in the Quran and one that has the unmistakable sound of a prayer. A
series of ejaculations exalting and praising God follows. But there is in
practice a space between the first two rak'as, and it is permissible, even
praiseworthy, to insert the hushed recitation—all of the salat is performed
sotto voce—of a sura in them: sura 32 after the first rak'a of the Friday
noon prayer, for example, or sura 76 after the second rak'a of that same
prayer, and the recitation should be "distinct, prompt, and without interruption." There is another tradition that suras 62 and 63, or suras 87 and
88, may be inserted between those same rak'as at the Friday congregational prayer.

Further traditions, most of them going back to the Prophet's own practice, embellish the salat—for surely that is what is being done—by insert-
ing between the first and second rak'as of the daily prayers, suras 108 and
112 or 109 and 112 during the sunset prayer, for instance. But it is also recommended that suras of the Quran be recited simply as a private devotion
outside the salat. The recitation of sura 118 is especially recommended for
Fridays, and particularly for Friday night. The famous Throne Verse
(2:255) is an efficacious prayer at all times and in all places, and particularly upon retiring, together with suras 112, 113, and 114. Suras 113 and
114 should also be said at the completion of every day and verses 190–200
of sura 3 upon retiring.

Muslims are obliged, after a ritual cleansing, to perform these
Scripture-oriented prayers daily at the five stipulated times, though the
Quran, as we have seen, does not fix either the times or indeed the places
where prayer might be made. In the end it was felt that any decent place
might do for individual prayer. Jews too might pray where they would
once the Temple was destroyed, but the synagogue already existed as a
convenient place not merely to pray, which was an individual require-
ment, but for Torah recitation, which was a community obligation. The
Quran prescribes only the individual's salat but a community obligation
began to develop at Medina, not of a communal recitation of the Quran

but of a kind of community assembly. The assembly place (*jamiʿ*) was no less than the courtyard of Muhammad's house at Medina, which thus became the first mosque.

Indeed, the mosque does not seem to have been "instituted" at all but simply to have grown into its function, from being no more than the courtyard of Muhammad's residence at Medina and the natural place for Muslims, who at first were not very many, to gather. Then, in the course of the ten years' growth of the Islamic enterprise and the gradual institutionalization of the practices that were now considered "Islamic," the place of customary resort became the place of regular assembly. And whether in imitation of Jewish Sabbath eve preparations or not, Muhammad's courtyard became part of the Friday salat after which the Prophet delivered a homily to the assembled community of Muslims.

Under the circumstances these Friday addresses by the Prophet were more likely hortatory than exegetical, or perhaps more like "orders of the day" than what we might think of as a sermon, an identification underlined by Muhammad's and other early preachers' practice of leaning on a sword or a bow while speaking. This was the origin of the Muslims' Friday sermon (*khutba*), Muhammad's weekly instruction and exhortation to a community (*umma*) that was almost constantly engaged in military operations. And as we learn from the mouths of his successors, this Friday address is liberally braided with passages taken from the Quran, this in accord, we are told, with the Prophet's own example.

The Scripture as Libretto

We have just seen that the reading of "Scripture" was very little like our reading of a book, which is a silent, internal affair and was first famously noted with astonishment by Augustine of Ambrose, the bishop of Milan between 374 and 397 CE. Augustine had reason to be surprised at the silently reading Ambrose: even private reading was done at least semivoiced well into the age of printing. Scripture recited at a mosque, a church, or a synagogue is not a private affair but a public performance, and so it does not surprise us that it was done aloud and, on occasion, very loud. But once again, it was more than a public reading: the text, whether from usage or prescription, was intoned with prolongations and retards alien to merely reading aloud, with vocal underscoring and melodic, hexameter-like thrusts at the ends of long phrases. In a liturgical context, Scripture was chanted rather than read, and to the great enlightenment of even the literate among the listeners, when they had the Words of God translated from an endless procession of letters across a page into intelligible units of sense.

The rhythm of the chanted and embellished Scripture came from the text itself, from what was being read rather than from any aesthetic impulse. The process of such sense-derived rhythm has been called "logogenic," as opposed to "pathogenic," whereby the rhythm seeks to achieve its own effect. Here the rhythm is a servant of the sense. But it was sometimes unruly and aggressively creative. All rhythm aspires perhaps to the condition of music, and indeed some Scripture seems to issue an open invitation to ascend to that state, for cantillation to rise to song, a passage that in its polyphonic end would reduce Scripture to libretto.

The Cantorial Scripture

Chanting the Hebrew text of the Bible in the weekly Sabbath services must soon have been beyond the capabilities of most Jews. In rabbinic times the text experts took great pains that the recitation be done correctly, and the masoretic text is nothing less than a scored copy of Scripture. It was not the one that lay before the reader, to be sure—that was the unmarked *Sefer Torah*—but the heavily annotated one from which that reader prepared his performance. Those fifth- and sixth-century notations were not innovations, the beginnings of a system of recitation instruction for Scripture, but merely its first fixing in writing. Manuscript from Qumran and fragments of the Septuagint from elsewhere show that there were already manuscript directions—spaces marking pauses, for example—and that some sort of tradition of Scriptural recitation was probably in place even earlier than the second century BCE when we first detect its manuscript traces.

And what of the congregant who was expected to perform the Scriptural recital according to the scribal and later rabbinic expectation? Undoubtedly he was the one who emerged in the seventh and eighth centuries as the *hazzan* or cantor, though that latter term owes more to nineteenth-century virtuoso German choirmasters than to an early medieval hazzan struggling through Leviticus! As with many other high offices, this one began as a synagogue official of undistinguished and indeterminate status and ended as the resident community master of this

Scripture recitation. And something more as well. The first specialized use of *hazzan* in the ninth century CE is a not uncharacteristic performative one, and in the context critical of the introduction of non-Scriptural hymns (*piyyut*s) into the synagogue liturgy and their rendering by hazzan. Indeed, in the sequel, the hazzan is often criticized for being too much the musician and too little the pious performer of Scripture. Little wonder since these once chaste chanters of Scripture, or so the rabbis hoped, lived from the fourth century onward in the shadow of first Byzantine and then Arab-Muslim musical grandeur. The offending piyyuts too had precedent. Choirs of Levites had sung David's piyyuts in the Temple. But they had become Scripture; the contemporary songs of Baghdad had not.

The piyyuts, whatever their importance for the cantorial art, take us beyond Scripture. More pertinent to the performance of Jewish Scripture is the notion of *nussah*, the accepted or traditional way(s) of reciting Scripture. There had necessarily to be more than one such sense. Jewish communities from the eighth century on existed on two sides of a great cultural divide, that principally between Latin Christendom and Middle Eastern and North African Islam, which created the subcultures of Ashkenazi Jewry in the first and Sephardic in the latter. Performance in accordance with the nussah, and not only of Scripture but of the *nussah hatefillah*, the traditional chants for the prayers of the synagogue service, was the responsibility of the hazzan, and though they were all identically the Words of God, they sounded quite differently in Cairo and Trier.

The Divine Office

It was once thought, and it is still tempting to think, that the Christian practice of the liturgical recitation of the Psalms, which can be discerned occasionally in the early Church and becomes fully attested in the fourth and fifth centuries, stems directly from Jewish practice. But the Jewish sources do not much encourage this. Though the Psalms were undoubtedly sung in the Temple on certain occasions—they seem occasional in nature—there is no trace of their recitation in synagogue practice until that same fifth Christian century. But there is no need for a synagogue connection. Christianity had its own confrontation with First Temple times and practices directly through the Bible, and taking over the practice of chanting the Psalms liturgically may well have been in conscious imitation of Davidic precedent.

The Psalms were being recited by Christians in some undefined liturgical setting perhaps as early as the third century CE, to which were gradually added from the fourth century onward the Christians' own petitions, and still later, when Benedict of Nursia (480–543) made the Psalms the basis of the monastic liturgy, they were surrounded by a whole complex of prayers and readings. The recited Psalms were apparently from the outset more melodic than the rest of the recited Scripture. They began after all as hymns, and their independence from the Eucharistic liturgy allowed them to develop further in that direction. And as happened among the Jews, the introduction of new levels of musical sophistication into psalmody particularly affected the performer, who begins to appear not simply as a *lector*, as was found in the first part of the Eucharistic liturgy, but as a *psaltes*, who was first noted in the fourth century. As always, the appearance of this particularly profane Muse in the sanctuary predictably made some churchmen uneasy.

If there were Jewish antecedents, Christian practice soon took a notable turn of its own. The Acts of the Apostles shows Jesus' earliest followers praying at various times of the day and night (10:3, 9; 16:25), perhaps in rhythm with observance in the still-standing Jerusalem Temple. But such practices must have been reduced or completely disappeared when the Temple was destroyed and Christianity became progressively remote from its Jewish roots. Then, at some point, Christians seem to have rediscovered if not their Jewish roots, then at least their Biblical ones. Perhaps it was those Christian "Fathers of the Desert," the largely illiterate Egyptians who in the late fourth century fled to the wildernesses beyond the Nile and began to test the limits of human endurance with long vigils and constant prayer. The Scripture was the meat and drink of these athletes of God, and Scripture recited from memory rather than read from the page. We cannot say if it was they who "discovered" the Psalms for the Church, but they certainly dwelled on them, first privately when the life was largely solitary, and then in assembly when the monks began living in communities. The abbot Pachomius (d. ca. 346 CE), who was one of the first to attempt to describe that emerging way of life, put enormous emphasis on the memorization and repetition of Scripture and particularly of the Psalms. John Cassian (d. 435), who introduced the monastic ideal to the West, maintained that meditation on Scripture was an essential act of the monk's life.

We stand here at the dawn of Christian monasticism that was instrumental in shaping the life of the Church. What was at first irregular and unregulated eventually became institutionalized; the customary behavior of the community's founding holy man as a model for a way of life eventually hardened into "the rule" that governed the life of the monks down to the smallest detail, even their worship. The nightly vigils and incessant prayer became the "Divine Office," the carefully scripted community performance of the Psalms that was the hallmark of the monastic life and of clerical life generally.

The Benedictine way or "order" is the earliest Western manifestation of the regulated form of an ascetical community life, regulated from within by the presence of the "Rule," and from without by a progressively more centralized and powerful papacy that took all Western ecclesiastical institutions under its supervision. The monastic manner of life was chiefly characterized by the collective—"in choir"—recitation of the Psalms and supplementary material throughout the day and night according to the norms found in the Breviary, the book form of the Divine Office, as it came to be called, or, more recently, the Liturgy of the Hours.

Though the Western version of the monastic life was more regulated by the Great Church, the Eastern forms, which took their most common form from the Rule attributed to Saint Basil the Great (329–379), followed directly in the tradition of the Desert Fathers and emphasized the repetition of Scripture and of the Psalms in particular. West and East, the book of Psalms, the Psalter, became the most frequently copied Scriptural text and the most often illustrated. The Western Breviary added all the supplementary material that had grown up in the monastic tradition of the West and was distributed piecemeal across the daily recitation of the Psalms over the liturgical year.

In its Western version, beginning at Matins (2:30 A.M.) and ending at Compline (6 P.M.), the 150 Old Testament Psalms were distributed over eight "hours" spread across the twenty-four of each day so that the whole of the Psalter was completed in a week. The Psalms were fixed by Scripture, but the growing body of material that surrounded them—specially composed prayers, extracts from the early Fathers of the Church, or lives of saints—was chosen and arranged in accordance with the commemorative and festival days of the liturgical year.

The spiritual counterpart of the monastic performative *officium divinum* was the *lectio divina*, the thoughtful reflection on the recited text that lay at the heart of monastic culture and is one of the earmarks of Western spirituality. Monastic piety was nothing more or less than Scriptural piety from its Egyptian origins onward. And the Divine Office continued to be sung in choir by the new twelfth-century mendicant orders of Franciscans and Dominicans who galvanized the life of the Church in the High Middle Ages.

The Art of Qira

The Quran, as has already been noted more than once, began its life as a "recitation." It remains significantly so today even with the spread of textual literacy and the phenomenon of printing, which was, however, a very late introduction in the Muslim world. We have seen too how the written text was a later and imperfect descendant of the original recitation as it came forth from the mouth of Muhammad and was repeated both by? and from memory by his followers.

The Quran as a fixed document—if not yet as a fixed text—came into being as part of the process of memorization and liturgical repetition that began and proceeded under the Prophet's own direction. Muhammad must have repeated his recitations until his followers had them by heart. We cannot be absolutely certain in these matters, but since it was doubtless he who counseled and directed the liturgical recitation of the Quran, it was likely Muhammad too who composed (and edited?) the suras for that purpose; he may even have arranged them in their present order. There can be little doubt that the Quran we possess is some sort of revelation lectionary, a collection of the lifetime of messages sent down to Muhammad and here arranged for liturgical recitation.

The Muslim tradition would be uneasy with "lectionary," which smacks of human arrangement, just as it is with the notion of arrangement generally as applied to the Quran—even though it is universally admitted that the present "arrangement" of the suras was not the order in which they were revealed. But if it is a recitation, the Quran comes to us without its original masorah or even the more modest Byzantine recitational notations called "neumes," which indicate in Hebrew and in Christian manuscripts of Scripture the *modes* of its recitation.

Muhammad's original recitation of God's Word was obviously in some form of cantillation, that is, in a style more rhythmically enhanced than that of everyday speech. That is the minimalist position. But there are grounds for thinking that not only the rhythm was heightened but that other aspects of the recitation, the rhyme surely, but perhaps the tonal quality as well, had moved far enough in the direction of music to be again defined, if not as song—we have little idea what the contemporary Arabs regarded as "song"—then at least as poetry. The Muslim literary tradition, with its interest in the Quran as a "Book," has concentrated its attention on the rhetoric of the written text and has little to say about the recitational tradition, the *qira*. It does speak early on of *qurra* (sing. *qari*) or "Quranic reciters," who are clearly a specialized subdivision of the *rawis*, the rhapsodes who shaped and transmitted the contemporary Arabic war poems and love poetry.

We are on firmer ground here than with the speciously detailed tradition regarding the written Quran since we are now looking at texts and techniques that have parallels in many oral traditions, including the Arabs' own. The rawi, whether in the native Arabic version or in his Hebrew sofer incarnation, was a skilled professional with considerable creative freedom, both in the actual performance of an already traditional piece and in the touching up of a "song" between performances. Did the qari, the Quranic reciter-transmitter, enjoy the same freedom? The Muslim tradition has granted eternal immutability not only to the Heavenly Book but even to its "Recitation" by Muhammad, and, with even less regard for the nature of such recitations, to the human copy of that latter.

The actual history of the Quran, as of the Bible, strongly suggests otherwise. It took the highly literate scribes of rabbinic Judaism until the eighth or ninth century to fix the text of the Bible, and then only by reducing it firmly to writing and accompanying it with an elaborate prescriptive apparatus. The Uthmanic recension, if it occurred, hardly fits that bill. There are grounds for thinking that it did not exist in the first place. But if it did, what it produced was then unvoweled consonantal text, and in a script so imperfect that it could indicate only the broadest lines of meaning. Perhaps that was all the early qurra needed, a basic prompt text, and the rest they filled in on the basis of their own performance scale and traditional memory.

That seems to have been the condition of the Quran both before and after the alleged Uthmanic attempt at producing a *textus receptus*. Uthman's decision to proceed with his program was supposedly prompted by differences among the qurra on the *qira'at*, the specific recitation values to give to the consonantal text.

Note: Qira.

The Arabic *qira* (pl. *qira'at*), "recitation" or "the act of recitation," de-rives from the same verbal root as Quran and can mean three different though obviously related things. It can signify the very act of Quran recitation; a specific reading of a word in the text, or what is referred to in text criticism as a "variant"; and finally, any one of a number of sys-tems of reading the Quran.

If the Uthmanic enterprise straightened out the consonantal difficulties to some degree—the seventh-century script was so crude that even some of the consonants cannot be distinguished one from another—the differ-ences in recitation went on. Local traditions began to emerge in what were becoming Arab urban centers: Mecca and Medina in Arabia, growing and often restless; Damascus in Syria, which the Arab conquerors had taken over and were making their own religiously and linguistically; and the Arab frontier towns of Basra and Kufa in Iraq. The qurra there all had the Uthmanic mushaf before them but they continued to read it differently, based in part on their claimed expertise in Arabic—Arabic grammar was beginning to flourish in some of those places—and the text could now surrender some of its uncertainties (or be emended?) in the light of that new understanding. And finally, in cases of continued doubt one could al-ways rely on the local tradition: "This is how so-and-so, who had studied with so-and-so, recited it."

What we next hear of may be an eirenic gesture of reconciliation or else an act of desperation. In any event, there was an ongoing problem with how the Quran should be read, its qira. The number of ways of doing this had multiplied greatly in the interval between Uthman's mid-seventh-century attempt at fixing a consonantal text and 934, when the Quranic scholar Ibn Mujahid (d. 936) decided on his own authority that there were only seven accepted systems of vocalizing the Quran and then quite un-usually convinced the caliph to enforce his decision as a matter of state policy; recusant qurra were publicly scourged. But such gates are not easily closed in a still profoundly oral society, and this one was soon pried open to permit a number of subvariants of the anointed Seven. And, as might be expected, there were traditions intended to dispel the notion that the acceptance of the seven readings was either a tenth-century innovation or a concession to irreconcilable diversity. According to one, God had recited the Quran to Muhammad in one qira, and when the Prophet asked for more, He gave him six additional ways of reciting the revelation. Another had Muhammad in a classic bargaining exchange with God, continually asking for one additional manner of recitation to make it easier for his community to recite the Quran. So God finally gave him, one by one, all seven of the canonical qira'at.

The effect of this personal-political fiat on the part of Ibn Mujahid was to create not one Quranic masorah but seven acceptable masoretic options, each of which could be laid out on the consonantal text because by then, and only by then, the frustrated Arabic scribes had developed or, more likely, had borrowed from the Syrian Christians not only a system of dots to distinguish the ambiguously written consonants but a range of other diacritical marks to indicate which vowels were to be enunciated with each consonant. This diacritical code, which had already been slowly working its way into the manuscript tradition, was the genuine Uthmanic moment, the closest to a textus receptus that the Muslim world would possess until 1924, when King Fu'ad's Egyptian commission chose, as much on political as on scholarly grounds, the canonical subvariant called "Hafs, from Asim" as the basis of the printed edition of the Quran, which is the one in general use today. *Solvitur imprimendo.*

What the untutored "reader" of the Quran did or does in private recitation may be left to the imagination and to the judgment of God; what concerns us here is the public and professional recitation of the Quran, not in the subdued *vox reducta* of the salat, but fully voiced in a public venue, as was done from the time when Muhammad first taught the Recitation to his followers, though perhaps not in precisely the same "prophetic" manner as he himself had first publicly proclaimed it. And he taught them the salat, certainly at Medina if not at Mecca. The two acts of worshiping God, Quranic recitation and the canonical salat, are obviously different, as has already been remarked: the lectio continua of the Quran is delivered in the cantillation mode; the salat is semivoiced prayer in which only sura 1 is prescribed, while other short selections are only recommended.

The more important liturgical use of the Quran, its lectio continua, takes place in the setting akin to the Jewish practice of reciting the Torah. But here too, as in many other comparisons between otherwise similar Jewish and Muslim practices, the Muslim usage is shaped by the fact that

Islam, like Christianity, was the state, or rather, the imperial, religion of the places where it was practiced and hence not only publicly proclaimed but lavishly supported, whereas the Jewish liturgy, and Jewish life generally, operated within imposed political and social restraints. Thus, if the reading of the Torah was necessarily restricted to the synagogue, the cyclical recitation of the Quran could be, and is, performed in a variety of public venues, acoustic and electronic.

One set of issues surrounding the recitation of the Quran was settled by Ibn Mujahid's tenth-century choice of the seven permissible systems of vocalizing or voweling the text, but it by no means addressed the manner of cantillation, the systems of pauses, adagios, retards, and tonal effects that accompanied the words of the text. Here too there were local and even individual traditions—the qurra, after all, were not the only rhapsodes in the Arab cultural tradition—with the stamp of an anonymous performer on them. Time and circumstance would probably have accomplished what Ibn Mujahid did at a single (caliphal) stroke, just as time and circumstance eventually narrowed down his canonical Seven to a basic Two, "Hafs, from Asim" and "Warah, from Nafi." But with the style of cantillation, the etiquette of qira, there was not a preemptive foreclosure of the Ibn Mujahid type, perhaps because the style of recitation did not affect the meaning of the Quran as directly as its vocalization.

We have moved here from the voicing of the text to the manner or style of its performance, and the issue, as almost always in revealed religion, is that of authenticity, as becomes plain in the very naming of the phenomenon. What has been called here by the simply descriptive name of *qira* is also known by its two certified Quranic names: *tilawa*, which in the Book seems to mean no more than simply "recitation" (2:44, 121; 28:53), and *tartil*, which characterizes the recitation, perhaps "an orderly and well-spaced recitation," the way God in fact transmitted it to Muhammad (25:32) and the way the Prophet was bade repeat it to his listeners (73:4). There is also the post-Quranic, and perhaps more forthcoming, *tajwid*, "embellishment." The first two claim authenticity on the basis of Quranic precedent; *tajwid*, in contrast, puts its cards directly on the table. The manner of recitation adds to the Quran embellishment or beautification, a claim saved from utter blasphemy by a hasty retreat to text and tartil: "Recite the Quran with *tartil*," the Book commands (74:4), and so Quranic recitation, whatever it is called, is nothing more than an attempt to replicate the original embellishment attached by God Himself to the transmission of His Words. For the Muslim, neither the text nor the performance of the Quran has evolved: both text and tajwid are from God.

If we step away from the theology, we can readily recognize that tajwid is far more than mere embellishment. As in the case of both the Torah and Christian psalmody, cantillation solemnizes and at the same time clarifies a text that is, absent modern aids to understanding like punctuation and capitalization, always more intelligible in its oral than in its written form. And that effect is achieved by observing the rules of tajwid as they have been handed down. Tajwid is a performance study and, like all such, is best and most effectively learned by imitation rather than by instruction. There have been manuals on the subject of Quranic recitation—the earliest to have written down the rules was thought to be Musa ibn Ubayd, the exact contemporary of Ibn Mujahid in the vauntingly literate tenth century—but from the beginning to the present, tajwid is learned not so much by reading as by listening and doing. Nor is there any need of a written text to practice on: the first step in learning tajwid is to memorize the Quran. The ideal qari is also a *hafiz*, someone who has committed the entire Quran to memory.

As already remarked, the formal recitation of the Quran occurs in two different contexts. The first is as an act of personal devotion, perhaps the supreme act of noncanonical devotion; the other is in public performance. The act of personal devotion is by no means a casual affair, and there is considerable discussion regarding the comportment or adab of an individual undertaking to recite the Quran: his posture and manner as well as the speed of the recitation. A late medieval authority offers the information that the record for Quran recitation was eight times through the full text in a twenty-four-hour period, but the common opinion frowned on such posturing and counseled avoiding a speed that was extravagantly fast or excruciatingly slow. Silently or aloud? The majority of experts seem to have preferred an audible recitation to a silent one, but the hadith report the Prophet himself warning against vainglorious recitation of the Book, much as Jesus had against the ostentatious prayers of the Pharisees (Matt. 23:14).

Reciting the Quran is a highly valued spiritual act taught at the very earliest stages of a traditional Muslim education. But hearing the Book recited was likewise meritorious, and there developed early among Muslims the practice of public recitations that became, with the growth of a professional class of reciters, the qurra, a performance in a theatrical or concert sense. But the performance was expected to fit the circumstances. Where the setting was principally didactic, the preferred style was *murattal*, orderly or measured, with an emphasis on clarity of enunciations and steadiness of pace, a presentation that was earlier called logogenic in the context of Christian plainchant. The other style of Quranic recitation might similarly be termed pathogenic, where the object is affect, the Arabic style called *mujawwad* or embellished.

It is in the mujawwad style that chant's aspiration toward music most strongly manifests itself. That natural aspiration was confronted in Islam by a powerful resistance to music in a sacred context. Music is associated with poetry, and though Islam's ascetics and mystics, all those collected under the rubric of Sufi, have accepted both music and poetry into their "séances," what is called a *sama* or "audition," and use both for the expression of their highly individualistic piety, neither has much impressed the traditionalists: music, like poetry, is far too "creative" for the theologians' tastes, and both music and poetry smack too much of the pre-Islamic pagan past of the Arabs to be allowed contact with the Quran.

Manuscripts of the Quran are not as pristine as the *Sefer Torah*; though they are never illustrated, they bear a full vocalization in the text as well as markers that show the divisions into recitation portions, which incidentally served as memory portions as well. The most common division is into thirty sections. Each section (*juz*) is further subdivided into two parts, and then each again into four quarters so that the Quran may be distributed in a number of different ways to suit the occasion. All these divisions are identified by emblems of varying sizes and shapes. In addition, there may be notations to guide the proper tajwid, showing pauses, prolongations, and so forth. Finally, the text may also indicate, by a marginal "s," a *sajda*, one of the fourteen places that custom dictates (so Quran 84:21) a prostration should be made by the reciter and his listeners.

Scripture, then, does not generally occur on an unmarked page. The *Sefer Torah*, the sacramental Law used in liturgical recitation in the synagogue, has a privileged void around its consonantal signs, but all other Scriptures are marked in one fashion or another to ensure proper recitation of the text, which is the primary Scriptural act. The Words of God require in the first place accuracy, which, since they were delivered orally, means that they be sounded and vocalized correctly. This is no problem for a Hebrew or Arabic speaker who hears, memorizes, and repeats. But when it later becomes a question of a written text, the two Semitic writing systems used for Hebrew and Arabic do not indicate which vowels, if any, are to accompany the transcribed consonants, and so methods had to be worked out, chiefly in connection with Scripture, one imagines, since there a mistake is not an error but a moral transgression. And so the vowel sounds came to be noted in the text by a symbol above or below its consonants.

But more than accuracy is at stake with Scripture; there is also the matter of understanding. The one who listens to the Word—and this is the way the revelation was first transmitted—must also understand it. And so the text must be pronounced clearly and intelligently, and intelligibility, as we have seen, depends on knowing the correct phrasing and correct emphases. Again, one listens and remembers and repeats. But once again written transmission presents its own problems. They are solved by another set of signs and spaces, what we call capitalization, punctuation, and indentation, which in one form or another are introduced into the text of the Bible, the New Testament, and the Quran.

Finally, there is what may be called the elevated performance of the text, where not only clarity is sought in the recitation of the Scripture but also a certain, though at times grudgingly admitted, aesthetic appeal. And here too the written text must convey the coded information that memory possesses by audition. And so we find the manuscripts filled with still another set of signs, from the Christian Psalters' outright musical notations or neumes to the Quran's more reluctant symbolic confession, not certainly to music, but to a heightened emotional affect achieved by prolongation and elevation of syllables.

Three Books, Side by Side

༄༺༄

Scripture is a byword in the religions of the world. Though the English word owes its prevalence to Christianity, the notion of something written or, more specifically, a book stands as both background and foundation for many faith communities. In the case of the Jews, Christians, and Muslims, the connection is clear and essential. The Creator God, it is held, has spoken directly with His creatures. Those words of His have been remembered, recorded, and enshrined in a Book, to which the word Scripture, "The Writing," preeminently applies.

If we look more closely, however, we can discern interesting and profound differences in the Scriptures of the three communities. Jews and Christians, for example, called their Scripture "the Bible," a word whose origin, the Greek *ta biblia*, "the books," points to both an artifact or a document, and, indeed, since it is plural, a collection of such. Muslims refer to their Scripture as *al-Qur'an*, "The Recitation," and though Muslims also understand their Scripture as a book, the primary emphasis is on its performance, in the first instance by the Prophet Muhammad and thereafter by millions of Muslims who either recite the text or attend to its recitation.

Christians are in the habit of referring to both the Jewish Scriptures and their own as "the Bible," by which they mean a Scripture in two parts, Old and New Testament. Though it originally enhanced Christian claims to authenticity, the assimilation of two Scriptures into a single "Bible" also conceals an enormous difference between them. Both communities of believers affirm that their Scripture is from God, the same God, we have just seen, as do the Muslims. But each of the three Scriptures represents a different mode of divine communication. The Hebrew Bible does indeed record God's words (and His acts); in fact, from Moses' ascent of Sinai in

Exodus down to the end of Deuteronomy, the Biblical text is chiefly composed of God's words, as the Creator, who also has a good deal to say in Genesis, lays down the Law for His creatures.

If we stand back from the Pentateuch and look at the Jewish Bible more broadly, we note that God's words are embedded in a complex set of narratives, reported by a third-person "author," as in the books from Joshua down through Kings, or in the more intimate "second-person" voice of a prophet—an Isaiah, a Jeremiah, an Ezekiel—who announces, if not God's very words, then assuredly God's message. There are also in the Biblical collection hymns to God (the Psalms) and a number of books of wisdom, advice, poetry, or just moral story, in one of which, Esther, God is not mentioned at all.

Both the Jewish Bible and the Quran may be rapidly but accurately characterized as "God's message," even though the former is more elaborately framed in narrative. The New Testament is quite different, however. In the same rapid fashion it may be described as "about God's message." As we have already observed, God's message turned out to be Jesus himself, as expressed in his life, death, and teachings, and the New Testament describes them all and explores their significance. All three—Bible, Quran, New Testament—are "scripture" in the sense that they come before the believers in the form of a written document; they are "Scripture," however—God's capitalized Word—in quite different senses, and most particularly the New Testament, which is professedly the work of human authors writing about the Word of God, even though, like Muhammad, Moses, and the Israelite prophets, the evangelists worked under some sort of divine, and so inerrant, inspiration.

As Scripture, the Quran is more patently pronouncement and less obviously story than the sacred books of the other two monotheist communities, and editorially there have been additional layers of intervention in the Scriptures of the Jews and Christians. God's immediate message in the Bible and Jesus' teachings in the Gospels have been embedded in a surrounding frame story. The giving of the Law on Sinai occurs in what is a pause in the Israelites' trek from Egypt to the Promised Land; Jesus' teachings have been inserted, not always realistically and sometimes intrusively, in the Gospels' story of his life. The creation of the frame and the insertion of God's immediate revelation into it were both the work of human author-editors: all the books of the Bible and the New Testament have in fact their assigned authors, mortals to whom either the book itself or the later tradition ascribed an authorial role. True, Moses and the evangelists were thought to be divinely guided in their work, but it was work nonetheless: the Pentateuch and the Gospels were wrought in a sense that the Quran never was. Muhammad is never credited as the "author" of the Quran; its words and its style, its form and its content, are all God's.

A second layer of intervention absent in the Quran is what might be called "Act Two" of the Bible and the New Testament. Whoever assembled the Bible and the Christian sensibilities that stand behind the New Testament were interested not only in the terms of the Covenant, Original or Revised, but in its implementation as well. The Biblical Covenant is reported in the chapters in Genesis that deal with Abraham, whose career frames the accord. What has already been called its "small print," God's elaborate codicil to the Covenant, is inserted in a freeze-frame at Sinai and spreads in its details to the end of Deuteronomy and of the Pentateuch. But the Bible moves on from there, just as the New Testament does beyond the four Gospels. If God is in the details, then salvation is in the sequel.

On one hypothesis, the Bible's original form reflected that same perspective of contract-plus-implementation in the anonymous "Deuteronomistic historian's" packaging of the book of Deuteronomy with Joshua, Judges, and Kings as the first "Bible," as some claim: what God demanded and how Israel did (or did not!) comply, and this, of course, for the benefit of the struggling Israelites of the seventh century who under King Josiah were attempting to reestablish covenantal Judaism in Israel (2 Kings 23:1–25). The New Testament strategy is identical. The Gospel accounts of Jesus' life, death, and resurrection are immediately followed by the Acts of the Apostles, which describes the unfolding of the New Covenant in the community of the believers.

The Quran is quite other. It is the immediate report of God's message. It has been packaged and reparceled, certainly, but has been neither framed nor enfolded in an author's explanatory narrative. The Quran does occur in Muhammad's lifetime, but not in the literary context of Muhammad's life; indeed, Muhammad's life is so deeply concealed behind and beneath the Quran that it is impossible to extract even its outline. It fell to a later generation of Muslims to collect the memories of the Prophet's life and to spread the Quran's suras across them as best they could. The "Second Act" of Islam was written not by God but by Muslim historians.

If the Quran has a Biblical parallel, it is most likely the Biblical books of Isaiah or Ezekiel, though here too we get scraps of explanatory narrative, while the very literary Jeremiah is altogether too eager to tell his own story (1:4–10) and already has a scribe sitting at his textual elbow (36:1–8). The Quran in fact most resembles what modern New Testament scholars have called—appropriately for our purposes—Q, what is supposed to have been an early collection of Jesus' "sayings" (*logia*) that both Matthew and Luke had before them, together with a copy of Mark, when they composed their Gospels, or even the "Gospel of Thomas," another collection of Jesus' logia from fourth-century Egypt.

At base, the Muslim view of their Book is radically different from those of the Jews and the Christians. For the Jews, revelation opened and closed with the Bible: it was both the first and the last divine communication with humankind. The Christians' New Testament is not, properly speaking, a successor to the Bible or its replacement: the Bible as the "Old Testament" continues to be regarded by Christians as in some sense a definitive revelation. The New Testament is rather like a codicil to the Bible, various texts regarding a change in the Covenant. It is not a new voice from Sinai; it is a description and clarification of the Jesus event and the election of a new Chosen People, not precisely "revealed" in the sense the Torah had been revealed to Moses or God had spoken to Jeremiah, but all of it set down under the inspiration of the very Biblical Holy Spirit.

The Quran's perspective is also quite other. It looks back across and recognizes a number of revelations to humankind mediated through a series of prophets—the later Muslim tradition generously numbered them at 360,000—that stretches from Adam (2:37) and Noah (23:27), through the often mentioned Abraham and Moses, to David (38:34) and Solomon (4:163), on to John the Baptist (19:12) and Jesus. It includes, somewhat surprisingly perhaps, the local Arabian prophets Hud (7:65–72) and Salih (7:73–79), unlikely monotheists both and unknown to either the Jews or the Christians. And the line of prophetic revelation ends in Muhammad, the "Seal of the Prophets." And, God generously adds, "We make no distinction among them" (2:285). These earlier revelations led in some instances to prophetic "writings" (*suhuf*, "leaves"). Abraham is credited with such (87:19), though not much is made of it, and David is recognized as the author of "Psalms" (*Zabur*; 4:163). But the foundation of the prophetic experience is that God had spoken to all the prophets just as He was now speaking to Muhammad (38:70; 43:43; 72:1, etc.).

The centerpieces of the Quran's view of the Revealed Books are the Torah (*Tawrat*) and the Gospel (*Injil*), always in the singular, the first "sent down"—the Quran's usual word for revelation from God's perspective—to Moses and the second to Jesus. There is, however, no suggestion that one Book replaced the other. Where supersession does occur is in the notion of the Chosen People. Abraham's "leaves" may have been the founding document of the "submitters" (to the One True God)—in Arabic, *muslimun*—but this is our inference; the Quran does not spell out the social consequences of Abraham's "Book." It is quite another matter with the Torah and the Gospel, however. In these instances the prophet and his Book led directly to the formation of a community (*umma*), the Torah to that of the *Banu Isra'il*, the "Children of Israel"—the Quran reserves the word "Jew" (*yahud*) for their more stiff-necked descendants at Medina—and the Gospel to that of the Christians. It was this latter community that succeeded the Jewish one in God's favor, just as the newest "submitters," the more authentically Abrahamic Muslims, the spiritual offspring of Muhammad and the Quran, have now replaced both the Christians and the Jews as the Chosen People of God.

Replaced but not eliminated. Just as the Quran has not formally replaced the Torah and the Gospel—the copies of those Books now in the possession of the Jews and Christians have, however, been irretrievably tainted by tampering (*tahrif*)—the Muslims, though they are now God's chosen, have accepted the other two monotheists as authentic worshipers of the One True God, albeit now deformed with various forms of unbelief. These stand somewhere between the true Muslims on one hand and the polytheists (*mushrikun*) and the unbelievers (*kafirun*) on the other.

In the Quran, the Tawrat or Torah—and this in the narrow sense of the Pentateuch since the "Prophets" and the "Writings" play no part in the Quran—is no longer a *Heilsgeschichte* because it has been stripped of its significant narrative thread: the "acts of God" have now been reduced to moral exempla chiefly because the Torah protagonists, the Banu Isra'il, have been thrust into the background. A clear proof that this is so is the Quranic introduction of new prophetic exempla where the (chiefly silent) role of the Children of Israel is played by other, non-Biblical groups like the Ad and the Thamud (7:65–79, etc.).

Nor are the Gospels treated as textual documents in the Quran. The word in fact is used only in the singular there (*Injil*), and its sole field of reference is that of a "Book" that was "sent down" to Jesus much as the

Torah was to Moses (3:3) and the Quran was to Muhammad. This is consonant with the Quran's view of Jesus as a prophet (3:48–51, etc.), and just as Moses, Jesus, and Muhammad are functional parallels as prophets, so too the book given to each served as "Scripture" for the communities that heeded those prophets. Where the Quran does recognize the textuality of both Torah and Gospel is in its contention that the Prophet had been mentioned in both. When a slightly later generation of Muslims were told there were no such allusions to Muhammad—they were still a very long way from inspecting an integral text of either Scripture—they retorted with the charge, which may in fact have been Muhammad's own, that both had been tampered with by the Jews and Christians respectively, something that has rendered the present versions of these once authentic revelations at best useless and at worst dangerously misleading for Muslim readers.

There is no canonical sequel to the Quran. The Medina suras of the Quran are still immediate revelations of God's words, not a book of Joshua or an Acts of the Apostles. And when the Muslims finally did come to write their "Acts of the Apostles" in the form of the history of the caliphs or successors of the Prophet, they did not include it in the canon of Scripture.

Finally, as we have seen, of the three sets of Scriptures, only the Quran enjoys a self-conferred canonicity. Unlike the Bible and the New Testament, both of which underwent a long (and largely invisible) process to achieve a status that was, in the end, conferred by the community of believers, the Quran anoints itself as both Revelation and Scripture.

Glossary

࿐

Adab (**Ar.**): A manner of behaving, an etiquette; style, culture, education.

Allah (< **Ar.** *al-ilah* > *allah*): "The God"; the high god of Mecca, whose cult was widespread among the pre-Islamic Arabs and who is identified with the Yahweh of the Bible.

Apocalypse (**Gk.** *apokalypsis,* "**unveiling**"): As a literary genre, the unveiling or revelation of the events of the End-Time; the name of the last book in the New Testament.

Apocrypha (< **Gk.**): Sequestered or set aside; works excluded from the canon of Scripture.

Apostle (< **Gk.** *apostolos,* "**one sent**"): One of Jesus' chosen circle of twelve; also (< **Ar.** *rasul,* "one sent") applied to Muhammad.

Aya (**Ar.**): "Sign," often of a miraculous nature; thence a verse of the Quran.

Bimah (**Hb.** < **Gk.** *bema*): The raised platform that served as both lectern and pulpit in the synagogue.

Breviary: A book in which the Psalms, plus a growing body of supplementary prayers and readings, were distributed, for monastic chant or clerical reading, across every day of the liturgical year.

Canon (**Gk.** *kanon,* **a standard or measure**): The list of those works accepted as Scripture; see Apocrypha; "The Canons," a tabular method of comparing parallel texts in the four Gospels contrived by the Greek Church historian and Biblical scholar Eusebius of Caesarea (ca. 260–340) and prefaced to many Christian manuscripts of the Bible.

Codex (**Lt.**): A book; writing material (parchment, papyrus, and, finally, paper) bound at one edge (left for Greek, Latin, and the European vernaculars; right for Hebrew, Arabic, and Semitic scripts) and protected front and back with covers.

Dead Sea Scrolls: The Jewish sectarian library, probably of the group called Essenes, discovered in 1947 at Qumran (q.v.) in Israel. The manuscripts in Hebrew and Aramaic were devoted to the Bible and its exegesis—they are our oldest preserved Biblical manuscripts—and to the group's own sectarian (and messianic) concerns.

Divine Office: The cleric and monastic-prescribed recitation or cantillation of a body of prayers, chiefly the Psalms, spaced at intervals ("the hours") over a twenty-four-hour day.

Ekklesia (**Gk.**): Assembly; congregation; church.

Euangelion (**Gk.** > **Lt.** *Evangelium*): Good news; gospel.

Eucharist (Gk. *eucharistia*): "Thanksgiving"; the ritual reenactment of Jesus' final meal with his Apostles (q.v.) before his arrest and execution; the central act of Christian worship.

Gentiles (< Gk. *ethne*; Lt. *nationes, gentes*): Jewish term for non-Jews; the *goyyim* (Hb.).

Hadith (< Ar.): "A report," here specifically a report professing to record, on eyewitness testimony, a saying or deed of Muhammad.

Haftarah (Hb.): The selection from the Prophets to be read after the Sabbath Torah portion; see *Parashah*.

Hajj (Ar.): Pilgrimage; the pre-Islamic complex of rituals performed in Mecca and then "purified" by Muhammad and integrated into Islam as an Abrahamic rite; every Muslim is obligated to perform the *hajj* at least once in a lifetime.

Haram (< Ar.): Taboo or prohibited, a characterization of people, places, and things; "The Haram" is the simple designation of the taboo or sanctuary zone in the center of Mecca, and the Noble Sanctuary (*al-Haram al-Sharif*) of that atop the Temple Mount in Jerusalem.

Hazzan (Hb.): Cantor; a synagogue official promoted in the early medieval era to chant responsibilities (both oversight and performance) with the introduction of non-Scriptural hymns (*piyyuts*) into the service; eventually, in more modern times, the music director of the synagogue.

Hexapla (< Gk.): "Sixfold"; the Christian scholar Origen's (ca. 185–254) six-columned comparative version of the Bible displaying, across the page, the original Hebrew and a variety of translations.

Injil (Ar. < Gk. *euangelion*): Gospel; the Quranic term for Christian Scripture.

Islam (< Ar.): "Submission," that is, acknowledgment, by confession and act, of the One True God; see Muslim.

Ka'ba (< Ar.): "The Cube"; a cubelike building located in the midst of Mecca and believed be the "House of the God (Allah)"; a focus of Muslim devotion and of the hajj ritual.

Kerygma (< Gk.): Pronouncement, preaching, identified by intent, manner, or content.

Ketib (Hb.): "The written," that is, the base consonantal text of the Hebrew Scripture; see *Qere*.

Khutba (Ar.): Address, sermon; particularly the sermon at the Muslims' Friday congregational prayer.

Kohen (Hb.): priest; in Judaism, males descended from Aaron and designated as the unique officers of Jewish sacrificial worship.

Koine (Gk.): "Common," i.e., the common Greek written and spoken around the Mediterranean in late antiquity.

Lectionary: Something to be read; a collection in book form of Scripture texts, often accompanied by prayers and hymns, suitable for the liturgical times and seasons.

Liturgy (< Gk.): Formal, and generally social, worship of God through prayer and ritual.

Masorah (Hb.): "Tradition," the traditional way of transmitting a text; hence, the masoretic text, the Hebrew text of the Bible standardized by the scribal editors (*masoretes*) of the seventh–ninth centuries CE.

Minbar (Ar.): The lofty pulpit in the mosque.

Mishnah: Transcription and the topical arrangement into six "orders" of legal discussions among Palestinian rabbis of the preceding three centuries; the reduction to writing ca. 200 and under the auspices of Rabbi Judah ha-Nasi ("The Prince") of the growing body of oral law; see Talmud.

Mushaf (Ar.): Written leaves (*suhuf* q.v.) collected into a single work between covers; a book.

Muslim (< Ar.): "One who has submitted"; a monotheist; a Muslim, a member of the community of Islam.

Nussah (Hb.): "Copying"; like the Ar. *qira* (q.v.), it refers to the traditional or accepted way of chanting Scripture, though "traditional" may refer to many regional or local variants in practice. Its observance is the responsibility of the cantor or *hazzan* (q.v.)

Occasions of Revelation: The circumstances surrounding the revelations in the Quran; the literary genre devoted to the collection of such.

Parashah (Hb.): A portion of the Torah, one of fifty-four to cover an annual cycle of Sabbath readings in the synagogue. That is the Sephardic usage; the Ashkenazis call such a *sidrah* and reserve *parashah* for the smaller Torah portions read on festivals or one of the subsections of the Sabbath reading.

Parousia (Gk.): "Presence"; Jesus' return at the End-Time; the Second Coming.

Pentateuch (Gk.): "Five pieces"; the first five books of the Bible; the Torah.

Polyglot Complutense: The six-volume multilanguage edition (Hebrew, Greek, Latin, Aramaic) of the Bible prepared at the university of Alcalá under the direction of Cardinal Jiménez de Cisneros (1436–1517) and published between 1514 and 1517.

Psalter: A book constituted of the Biblical Psalms, usually for liturgical purposes.

Qari (pl. *qurra*; Ar.): Reciter; a Quranic reciter.

Qere (Hb.): "The recited"; the Hebrew text of Scripture as recited; that is, the consonantal text (see *Ketib*) with signs or symbols indicating how it is to be vocalized.

Qira (Ar.): "Recitation"; a system or style of recitation of the Quran (see *Nussah*) or the particular pronunciation of a single word of the text.

Qumran: The site, at the northwest corner of the Dead Sea, where a Jewish sectarian library was discovered in 1947 concealed in cave; see Dead Sea Scrolls.

Quraysh: The paramount tribe of Mecca who from the first opposed Muhammad until their capitulation in 630 CE.

Rak'a (Ar.): "Bowing," and more particularly, a short series of postures and prayers that constitute one unit of the Muslim's liturgical prayer or *salat* (q.v.).

Rawi (Ar.): Reciter, rhapsode.

Salat (Ar.): Prayer, and more particularly, the liturgical prayer that every Muslim is required to perform at five designated times every day.

Sefer (Hb.): Something written; a book; *Sefer Torah*: the ceremonial prompt copy of the Torah kept in the synagogue for liturgical purposes.

Semite, Semitic: A language family and, somewhat less certainly, an ethnic or racial family denominated by its supposed descent from Shem, the son of Noah. The Hebrews, Arameans, and Arabs may or may not be descendants of a single ancestor, but what is far more assured is that Hebrew, Aramaic, and Arabic are, semantically and structurally, closely related members of the same "Semitic" linguistic family.

Septuagint (< Gk.): "Seventy"; the Greek translations of the Sacred Books of the Jews done in Egypt from the third century BCE onward. According to a widely circulating (but legendary) story, the translation was done, with miraculously certified accuracy, by seventy (or seventy-two) Jewish scholars imported from Palestine by the pharaoh Ptolemy II Philadelphus (r. 285–246). It was in broad use among the Greek-speaking Jews and then the Christians.

Sidrah **(Hb.):** See *Parashah.*

Simhat Torah **(Hb.):** "Rejoicing of the Torah," the feast day celebrating the completion of the annual cycle of Sabbath readings of the Torah.

Sofer **(Hb.):** Scribe; scribal editor.

Suhuf **(Ar.):** Sheets, leaves; something written upon; a "book."

Sunna **(Ar.):** "Custom," and particularly the "custom" or "customary behavior of the Prophet" as reported in the *hadith* (q.v.) and normative for Muslim behavior and belief.

Sura (< Ar.): One of the 114 units or chapters into which the Quran is divided.

Tajwid **(Ar.):** "Embellishment," with particular reference to recitation of the Quran.

Talmud: The body of commentary on the Mishnah (q.v.) either by the scholars of Palestine ca. 500 CE (the "Jerusalem" or "Palestinian Talmud") or of Iraq ca. 600 CE (the "Babylonian Talmud").

Tanak: Acronym of the Hebrew words for the three divisions of the Bible: *Torah* (Law), *Nebi'im* (Prophets), and *Ketubim* (Writings); a Jewish designation for the Bible.

Targum (< Hb.): A translation; specifically an Aramaic translation-paraphrase of a book of the Hebrew Scripture.

Tartil **(Ar.):** Orderly and well-paced recitation of the Quran.

Tawrat **(Ar.):** Torah; the Quranic term for the Jewish Scripture.

Tilawa **(Ar.):** "Recitation," particularly of the Quran.

Ulama **(Ar.):** "The learned," that is, those learned in the science of jurisprudence; Muslim lawyers.

Umma **(Ar.):** Community; the community of Muslims that constitute Islamic society.

Volumen **(Lt.):** "Roll," specifically, a roll of writing material (papyrus or parchment) joined end to end to form a long (up to thirty ft.) strip of writing surface, attached at either end to rollers that permit horizontal scrolling.

Vulgate (< Lt.): "Widely circulating," "in common usage"; the Latin replacement translation of the Bible made, at papal request, by the Latin scholar, theologian, and ascetic Jerome (ca. 340–420).

List of Illustrations

∂⑥∂

Plate 9. *Lindisfarne Gospels.* Eadfrith, Bishop of Lindisfarne, scribe; Aldred, glossator. *Incipit* page introducing St. Jerome's letter to Pope Damasus: text, with decorated initial "N." Northumbria; early eighth century. British Library, Cotton MS. Nero D.IV, f.211.

Plate 10. Silos Apocalypse. Beatus of Liébana, commentator; Dominicus, scribe; Nunnio, scribe. Illustrator: Petrus. The woman clothed with the sun; the seven-headed dragon attacked with spears by St. Michael and his angels. [Double opening.] Northern Spain; c. 1100. British Library, Add. MS. 11695, ff.147v–148.

Plate 11. Page from the Gutenberg Bible, with Erfurt illumination, and a heading added by hand in red ink. A letter "F" has been supplied in green and maroon highlighted with gold pen-work within the body of the letter, extending further down the inner margin and merging with a full border of flowers and scrolling foliage with birds perching on leaves. Mainz; c. 1455. British Library, C. 9. d. 3.

Plate 12. *The Bedford Hours,* containing a calendar of festivals. Old Testament miniature: the exit from the Ark and the drunkenness of Noah. The Bedford Master and his studio. Paris; c. 1423. British Library, Add. MS. 18850.

Plate 13. Calligraphic specimen of Hadith, attributed to the scribe Shaykh Hamdullah. Ottoman Turkey; eighteenth century. British Library, Or.11925. f.13.

Plate 14. Pages from an elaborately decorated Qur'an. This is one of the few that survived the Christian reconquest of southern Spain. Volume 39 of a Qur'an in sixty parts, copied on vellum in Maghribi script. Probably Granada; thirteenth century. British Library, Or. 12523C ff.14v–15.

Plate 15. A hajj pilgrimage certificate. Mecca; fifteenth century. British Library, Add. MS. 27566.

Plate 16. An elaborately decorated text page from Sultan Baybars' Qur'an. Calligraphy by Muhammad ibn al-Wahid, illumination by Muhammad ibn Mubadir and Aydughdi ibn ʿAbd Allah al-Badri, Cairo; 1304. British Library, Add. MS. 22406, ff.2v–3.

Index

⤳⑥⤳